AUTOGENIC THERAPY

WOLFGANG LUTHE, M.D., EDITOR

Volume II

MEDICAL APPLICATIONS

By WOLFGANG LUTHE, M.D.

*Dr. med. (Hamburg), L.M.C.C. (Ottawa),
Scientific Director, Oskar Vogt Institute,
Kyushu University, Fukuoka; (visiting)
Professor of Psychophysiologic Therapy,
Medical Faculty, Kyushu University, Japan.
Formerly Assistant Professor of Psychophysiology,
University of Montreal; College of Physicians and
Surgeons, Province of Quebec, Montreal, Canada.*

and JOHANNES H. SCHULTZ, M.D.

*Dr. med. (Göttingen), Dr. h. c. (Tübingen),
Professor of Neuro-Psychiatry, Berlin,
West Germany.*

GRUNE & STRATTON/New York and London

AUTOGENIC THERAPY
WOLFGANG LUTHE, M.D., *Editor*

Vol. I. Autogenic Methods
J. H. SCHULTZ AND W. LUTHE

Vol. II. Medical Applications
W. LUTHE AND J. H. SCHULTZ

Vol. III. Applications in Psychotherapy
W. LUTHE AND J. H. SCHULTZ

Vol. IV. Research and Theory
W. LUTHE

Vol. V. Dynamics of Autogenic Neutralization
W. LUTHE

Vol. VI. Treatment with Autogenic Neutralization
W. LUTHE

Volume IV contains the central Bibliography for all six volumes. Volumes V and VI contain additional bibliographic information.

Vol. II: Copyright © 1969
Grune & Stratton, Inc.
381 Park Avenue South
New York, N. Y. 10016

Library of Congress Catalog Card No. 70-76888
Printed in U.S.A.
G-B

Contents

VOLUME II: MEDICAL APPLICATIONS

PART II. APPENDIX

VOLUME I: AUTOGENIC METHODS

PART I.   METHODS OF AUTOGENIC STANDARD THERAPY

VOLUME III: APPLICATIONS IN PSYCHOTHERAPY

PART I.   CLINICAL APPLICATION

VOLUME IV: RESEARCH AND THEORY

PART I.   PSYCHOPHYSIOLOGIC CHANGES

VOLUME V: DYNAMICS OF AUTOGENIC NEUTRALIZATION

VOLUME VI: TREATMENT WITH AUTOGENIC NEUTRALIZATION

PART I.   FORMS AND MANAGEMENT OF RESISTANCE

Foreword to Volume II

The various chapters of this volume focus on the clinically oriented application of autogenic therapy. The reader may be surprised at the diversity of medical disorders to which autogenic training has been applied as an adjunctive approach, or as the mainstay of treatment. The fact that autogenic approaches have found such a wide range of therapeutic application has frequently elicited disbelief and emotionally colored criticism from those with only superficial or even no experience or knowledge about the psychophysiologic nature and the therapeutic potentialities of autogenic methods. However, more recently, as clinically and experimentally oriented research advanced along various physiologic and pathophysiologic dimensions, the voices of prejudiced and unenlightened critics became fainter. At the same time, an ever increasing number of colleagues appears to realize that there is hardly any other therapeutic approach which can claim a similar range of therapeutic usefulness.

Usually overlooked is the fact that autogenic methods have been applied mainly in the treatment of a variety of medical conditions, and much less frequently in the area of psychiatric disorders. This may be largely a reflection of the clinically desirable self-regulatory readjustment of various physiologic functions (e.g., circulatory, respiratory, gastrointestinal, metabolic) which tends to ensue as *case-adapted* autogenic methods are practiced regularly.

It will be obvious from the following chapters that our knowledge about the therapeutic dynamics of autogenic methods is advanced in certain areas, still relatively limited in others. It is hoped that this volume will stimulate positively oriented criticism and promote additional systematic research.

In order to facilitate research work in specific clinical areas, a list of relevant references has been added at the end of clinical sections, and in many instances also at the ends of chapters. The reference numbers of publications which contain information considered to be of particular interest, appear in *italics*.

Information resulting from research carried out during the last decade has added precision to the clinical application of autogenic methods in many respects. For example, it has become obvious that a patient's history requires more detailed consideration in order to understand the clinical significance of various modalities of autogenic discharges. This is considered to be particularly important in problems of differential diagnosis, a trainee's resistance against autogenic therapy, and relevant matters of therapeutic management. In this connection, the critical reader is invited to consult also relevant sections of the other five volumes of this series, in which he will find indispensable complementary information about specific aspects of a technical, clinical, experimental or theoretical nature.

The text of this volume is divided into two parts. Part I encompasses fourteen sections in which the application and therapeutic management of specific medical disorders are discussed. In Part II, the "Appendix," the reader finds a glossary of technical terms frequently used in the field of autogenic therapy, the index of authors and the subject index. The references for numbers 1-2450 are to be found in the central bibliography at the end of Volume IV. An extended "Table of Contents," permitting a quick orientation to the organization of Volumes I, III, IV, V and VI, forms part of the conventional front matter of this volume.

Published and unpublished case material included in this volume was contributed by: H. Altmann (Case 32), H. Binder (Cases 4, 45), W. Causse (Case 64), I. Demscak-Kelen (Case 3), U. Diesing (Case 53), R. Durand de Bousingen (Cases 52, 55), G. Fisher-Hoppenworth (Cases 36-39), K. D. Hoppe (Case 42), H. Kenter (Cases 12, 18), D. Klare (Case 35), H. Kleinsorge and G. Klumbies (Cases 11, 29, 43, 44), G. Klumbies (Case 30), W. Kurth (Case 51), J. A. Laberke (Case 78), W. Luthe (Cases 1, 7, 8, 9, 13, 23, 31, 33, 40, 41, 48, 49, 54, 57, 60, 73, 75, 76), D. Müller-Hegemann (Cases 15, 24), F. Pensel (Case 5), P. Polzien (Case 61), H. J. Prill (Case 62), F. Ruck (Case 21), W. Rudolph (Case 6), M. Sapir (Cases 17, 25, 56), J. H. Schultz (Cases 16, 20, 26, 27, 28, 34, 47, 50, 58, 59, 63, 65, 77), H. W. Schumacher (Case 14), J. Seabra-Dinis (Cases 10, 66, 67, 68, 70, 71), H. Strotzka (Case 22), K. Thomas (Case 72), J. N. Wagner (Case 69), H. Wendt (Case 2), K. Wolter (Case 46).

Any suggestions, criticism and information which would help us to improve future editions of "Medical Applications" are always very much appreciated.

W. Luthe
Montreal
July 1969

J. H. Schultz
West Berlin
May 1969

PART I. APPLICATION

1. Clinical Application

Autogenic training has been applied to patients suffering from a variety of psychosomatic disturbances, a number of mental and behavior disorders, certain organ diseases and the psychophysiologic effects resulting from mental and bodily stress in general.

The method can be applied individually or in groups of adolescents and adults of all ages. Since, by its nature, the approach requires the reliable collaboration of the patient, its application is difficult or impossible in cases with severe mental deficiencies or certain mental disorders. Difficulties are also frequent in children below the age of ten, in teenagers, and in other persons lacking either seriousness of intention or average intelligence.

The average clinical therapy centers around the standard exercises and additional specific approaches designed to meet the therapeutic requirements of the individual case. Autogenic training at the meditative level may be applied as what has been called "Nirvana therapy" in clinically hopeless cases (e.g., cancer) or in monotonous and desperate situations as they may occur during warfare or under other particular circumstances. The meditative exercises have been also found to be of particular value in depth-dimensional psychotherapy. In general, it has been observed that the effects of the more physiologically oriented standard exercises are reinforced by the meditative training, although the meditative exercises are not introduced to the average patient.

The effectiveness of the patient's technique of passive concentration, and the progress of the therapy, is reflected by the patient's training symptoms and by physiologic and psychologic tests. Measurements of skin temperature, pneumograms, frequency of respiration, and heart-rate and blood-pressure readings are valuable controls when taken repeatedly and under quasi-experimental conditions (for procedure, see, for example, Fig. 23, p. 118). Since there are persons who respond with paradoxic reactions, for example, rise in blood pressure and increase in heart rate, it is advisable to control these factors repeatedly before and during the course of therapy.

For the reliable control of psychologic changes, the behavior and subjective remarks of the trainee and the impression of the therapist and other persons may be supplemented by psychologic tests which can be applied repeatedly (e.g., Drawing Completion Test).

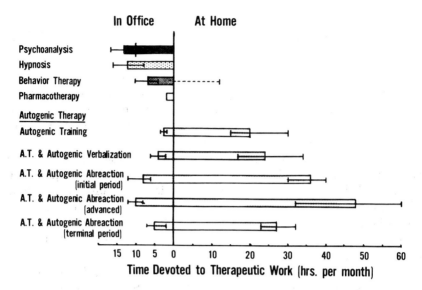

FIG. 1. Schematic presentation of time (hours per month) devoted to therapeutic homework in various forms of treatment: psychoanalysis, hypnotherapy,
behavior therapy, pharmacotherapy and various combinations of autogenic
.h ərapy. While psychoanalysis and hypnotherapy are limited to office treatment, autogenic therapy emphasizes the patient's active participation in his
treatment by promoting independence from the therapist and intensive therapeutic work at home.

Since autogenic therapy operates in a highly differentiated and delicate
field of neural mechanisms, it must be emphasized that the clinical application of the method should be carried out by physicians who have
learned the technique themselves under the guidance of an experienced
colleague.

Of particular clinical and therapeutic interest are occasionally occurring disturbing modalities of autogenic discharges (e.g., crying spells,
anxiety, headaches, pain, motor discharges, nausea). Such subjectively
disturbing, however, harmless and therapeutically even desirable processes of brain-directed discharges may be mistakenly considered as symptoms indicating a deterioration of a given clinical condition. In order to
avoid relevant erroneous impressions and conclusions, it is important
that the patient fully understands the beneficial nature of brain-directed
autogenic discharges, and assumes a postively oriented permissive and
accepting attitude whenever his brain desires to engage in such processes of unloading. Patients who do not understand the beneficial
nature of such training phenomena and who block or antagonize the

needs of their brain, are known to encounter training difficulties and tend to develop increasing resistance against autogenic therapy.

However, since it would be a serious clinical error to consider all training symptoms as innocuous, medically favorable autogenic discharges (see Case 10/I, p. 35; Case 17/I, p. 63; Case 28/I p. 116; Case 4, p. 23; Case 24, p. 74; Case 40, p. 108; Case 41, p. 112), a careful differential diagnostic evaluation is required in many instances. Reassuring clinical examinations are a diagnostically and therapeutically important factor in the management of patients to whom autogenic therapy is applied. In order to facilitate the differential diagnostic evaluation of autogenic discharges, and in order to avoid incorrect conclusions or unnecessary clinical examinations, a therapist must be familiar with relevant details of the patient's history (e.g., minor and major accidents, traumatizing clinical procedures, educational variables, fainting spells, diseases), the physiological and psychophysiological implications of the patient's actual medical condition (e.g., gastro-intestinal disorders, heart disorders, diabetes mellitus, hypothyroidism), his actual situation (e.g., emotional stress, professional activity, sexual deprivation), and the clinical significance of various modalities of autogenic discharges.

In the past autogenic approaches have been more frequently applied in the treatment of medically oriented disorders than in the treatment of psychodynamic disturbances (e.g., severe neurotic disorders, phobic reactions, personality disorders, psychotic disorders). More recently, however, case-adapted combinations of autogenic approaches are used more and more frequently in the field of psychodynamic disorders. It is in this connection that the emphasis on the patient's active participation in his treatment, his relative independence, and his therapeutically oriented homework are appreciated as clinically and therapeutically desirable factors (see Fig. 1).

2. Disorders of the Gastrointestinal Tract

Constitutional and psychic factors, together with stress-producing situations, have long been recognized as playing a potent role in the pathogenesis of various disorders of the gastrointestinal tract. Although it has not been proved whether each of these factors is causative or merely contributory, it is agreed that the autonomic system with its coordinating mechanisms in the diencephalic area serves as central mediator of the pathogenic variables. The central role of autonomic regulation in the development of gastrointestinal disturbances, and the increasing body of evidence that autogenic training effects a relieving of stress and a normalizing of autonomic regulation, has greatly furthered the application of autogenic therapy in this field of medicine.

In the clinical literature published during the past forty years there are many reports that various chronic disorders of the gastrointestinal tract (e.g., constipation) have been markedly improved and/or cured with the help of autogenic exercises after conventional approaches had failed repeatedly. So far, autogenic therapy has been found effective in the treatment of patients suffering mostly from chronic disorders like constipation, psychoreactive diarrhea, gastritis, peptic ulcer, ulcerative colitis, deviations of gastric secretion,[1072] irritable colon; and functional disorders of the gallbladder and bile ducts. Other disorders like benign migratory glossitis (geographic tongue),[645,2065] achalasia (cardiospasm), anorexia and nausea and vomiting, as well as hemorrhoids, have been also approached effectively.

The effects of the standard exercises on the gastrointestinal tract require further elucidation by experimental studies. It is nonetheless common experience that there often occurs a spontaneous increase in intestinal rumbling and splashing during passive concentration on heaviness in the limbs. These symptoms indicate that the neuromuscular elements of the gastrointestinal tract respond without being focussed upon by organ-specific formulae. Furthermore, it has frequently been observed that a number of gastrointestinal disorders spontaneously disappear or noticeably improve under the influence of heaviness and warmth exercises.[493,1086]

One of the most important aspects of autogenic therapy is the prophylactic effect of regular training. Patients suffering from gastrointestinal disorders, and particularly cases with peptic ulcer and ulcerative colitis, should practice a carefully selected sequence of case-adapted autogenic exercises over periods of 12 to 18 months and longer. Regular control of these patients and group discussions once or twice per month are necessary in order to keep the patients doing the exercises and thus to cut down the relapse quota.

Only in recent years have a few experimentally interested investigators started to carry out more systematic studies of a limited number of gastrointestinal functions during passive concentration on (a) standard formulae, (b) clinically oriented organ-specific formulae, and (c) so-called experimental formulae (E.F.)[906] which do not appear to be of direct clinical value (see Vol. IV).

Clinically of particular interest are series of systematic radiocinematographic evaluations of patients with and without organic gastrointestinal lesions or relevant functional disorders (see Fig. 2, 4), which have been carried out by M. Sapir, A. Dehouve, F. Reverchon and R. Philibert[1166,1172,2119,2121]. Comparisons of radiologic films taken before and during passive concentration on Standard Formulae revealed radiologically significant differences of certain gastrointestinal functions in corresponding phases of the passage of identical contrast media at various levels of the gastrointestinal canal. Generally, the investigators observed an initial transitory period of a sharp reduction of motor activity of the stomach after the beginning of autogenic exercises. Following this atonic phase, which may last several minutes, a readjustment of motor activity, characteristic for autogenic training, occurs. In comparison with motor patterns observed in the normal state, the gastric contractions appear to be more ample and energetic. The peristaltic pattern is more regular and the transport function enhanced. This usually is associated with better filling effects as indicated by sharper contours, particularly in the antrum (see Fig. 2a and b). Emptying is more complete, and previously disturbed patterns of pyloric activity tend to normalize. Radiologically there are multiple indications that functional improvements (e.g., better filling effects, better transit, more regularity of motor pattern) also involve the duodenal cap and the second and third duodenal portion (see Fig. 2 and 4). Jejunal loops also show significant changes towards improvement of function and efficiency. The pattern of peristaltic waves is much more regular, larger quantities of contrast media pass more rapidly, and in correspondence with this, there is a better, more homogeneous filling effect with sharper contours (see Fig. 2a and 2b). These remarkable changes are largely in correspondence with similar effects resulting from relevant parasympathomimetic medication. Of particular clinical interest is, however, the observation that these changes towards greater efficiency of normal physiologic functions have also been noted in patients with various inflammatory and organic lesions as, for example, peptic ulcer, duodenitis, hiatus hernia and gastrectomies (see Fig. 4, and Vol. IV).

Fig. 2. A 37-year-old female patient who complained about gastric discomfort (anxiety reaction, phobic manifestations). Radiologically: no evidence of organic lesions. Fig. (a) and (b) were taken from corresponding phases (about 9 min. after ingestion of contrast media) or radiocinematographic films.

(a) Without autogenic training: poor filling effect in horizontal portion of stomach (s.), antrum (a.), pylorus (p.), duodenal cap (d.c.) and second duodenal portion (2nd d.p.); lack of clearly defined peristaltic waves (p.w.).

(b) Several days later, during autogenic training; good filling effect with clear contours (s., a., p., d.c., 2nd d.p.), symmetrically arranged pattern of peristaltic waves (p.w.); evidence of efficient transport function. (Courtesy of M. Sapir, A. Dehouve, F. Reverchon and R. Philibert, Paris.[1166, 1172,2119,2121])

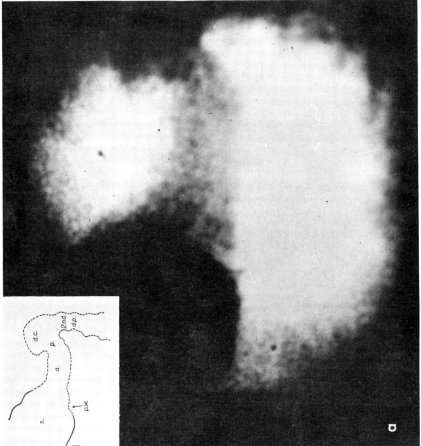

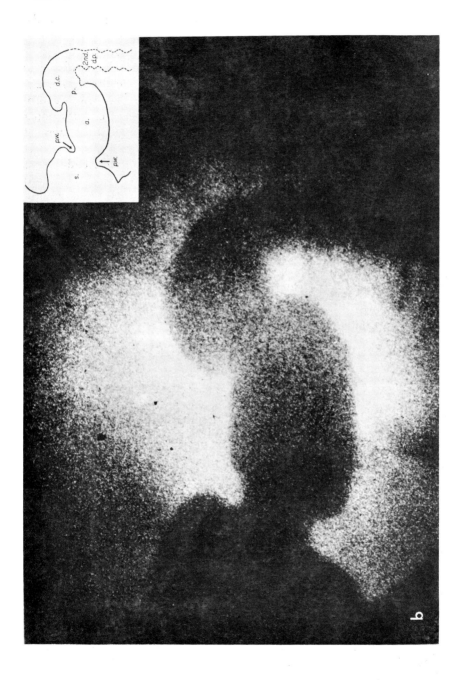

As in other areas of psychophysiologically oriented investigations of the effects of autogenic training it is of particular interest to note that functions of the digestive tract may be heavily influenced by the release of variable intensities of different forms of autogenic discharges (see Table 1). The unpredictibility of the occurrence of such autogenic discharges and their modifying effects (e.g., blocking, reinforcing, disturbing, reducing, paradoxical reactions) on the physiologic functions under investigation imply that a certain degree of variability of the pattern of physiologic reactivity may be regarded as a psychophysiologic manifestation of the effectiveness of autogenic training. The unpredictability of occurrence, the variable degrees of intensities of interfering discharges and the wide variations of different combinations of various types of autogenic discharges also imply that repeated testing of certain gastrointestinal functions (e.g., motility), under almost identical conditions (e.g., x-ray cinematography), may even yield ("unexplained") contradictory results. Furthermore, as indicated by the content of Table 1, there is some evidence supporting the assumption that each standard formula is associated with individually different effects as far as the nature of autogenic discharges is concerned. In this connection, the effects of the Fifth Standard Formula ("My solar plexus is warm") require particular consideration (see Table 1).

Disagreeable modalities of autogenic discharges involving the gastrointestinal tract (e.g., feeling of nausea, vomiting, cramp-like sensations) are of particular clinical interest for the therapeutic management of patients suffering from psychophysiologic autonomic and visceral disorders.

Generally it has been observed that the recurrence of disagreeable autogenic discharges during or after practicing autogenic standard exercises lead patients to believe that their condition is getting worse. Consequently these trainees develop increasing resistance to autogenic training. In such cases, after relevant organic lesions have been ruled out, it is advisable to re-examine the trainee's medical history. In many of these trainees with disagreeable gastrointestinal discharges (e.g., nausea, cramp-like sensations) associated neuronal material was found (based on data obtained during autogenic abreaction) to be related to certain accidents, traumatisms and other situations in which voluntary or involuntary blocking of reactive vomiting (e.g., cranial trauma, fractures, shock) appeared to have occurred (see Case 1). Other modalities of disagreeable autogenic discharges (e.g., pain, burning, pressure), which are usually described as being localized in topographically more specific areas of the abdominal region, are frequently related to accidents (e.g., car crash), certain pre- and postoperative phenomena (e.g., cholecys-

TABLE 1. *Autogenic Discharges Related to the Digestive Tract*
(*reported by unselected psychosomatic and neurotic patients*)

	Standard Formulae					
Autogenic Discharges	I Per Cent	II Per Cent	III Per Cent	IV Per Cent	V Per Cent	VI Per Cent
Gustatory sensations	3.0	1.0	—	—	2.2	—
Salivation: increased	17.0	9.4	10.2	4.5	17.4	2.4
Salivation: decreased	4.0	1.0	8.2	1.5	4.3	4.8
Pain and disagreeable sensations in throat	8.0	10.4	6.1	3.0	4.3	2.4
Swallowing	4.0	4.7	6.1	6.1	6.5	7.9
Feeling of nausea	13.0	13.5	14.3	6.1	6.5	4.8
Vomiting	2.0	2.0	—	—	1.2	—
Feeling of heaviness in stomach area	—	3.1	—	1.5	2.2	4.8
Feeling of warmth in stomach area	1.0	2.1	2.0	4.5	13.0	7.1
Circulatory sensations in stomach area	2.0	—	6.1	1.5	2.2	—
Feeling of tension in stomach area	1.0	3.1	2.0	6.1	—	4.8
Borborygmus	33.0	25.0	10.0	10.6	28.3	16.7
Cramp-like sensation in abdominal area	4.0	5.2	—	6.1	4.3	—
Pressure-like sensation in abdominal area	8.0	6.1	4.1	4.5	6.5	—
Pain and disagreeable sensations in abdominal area	20.0	12.5	8.2	9.1	13.0	4.8
Total (of percentages)	120.0	99.1	77.3	65.1	121.9	58.7
Number of patients	100	96	49	66	46	48
Age of patients (M)	32.62	32.64	30.96	30.73	31.37	30.41
S.D.	9.54	9.53	8.79	8.67	9.56	8.51
Duration of training periods in weeks (M)	7.92	8.96	2.47	5.33	3.04	3.05
S.D.	3.64	4.14	1.18	4.28	2.84	1.93

tectomy, appendectomy, hernias), and othe relevant traumatisms (e.g., blow in the abdomen, hockey or ski accidents). When organic pathology has been excluded and careful evaluation of the trainee's history has indicated a strong probability that the disturbing discharges are related to specific incidents of the past, a patient-adapted discussion is often decisive in overcoming the patient's resistance and mobilizing his motivation to continue practicing autogenic training. As the patient succeeds in maintaining a passive tolerating attitude whenever such brain-selected and brain-controlled discharges are released, such bothersome training phenomena tend to decrease progressively or disappear completely (see Table 1, p. 9). When feelings of nausea and the urge to vomit is noted frequently during the standard exercises, it is helpful to encourage the trainee to permit vomiting. After sufficient vomiting has occurred, the disturbing abdominal symptoms tend to subside. There are, however, a number of cases, where the beneficial effects usually resulting from a regular practice of autogenic standard exercises remain limited or unsatisfactory (see Case 1).

Case 1: A 35-year-old housewife (anxiety reaction, multiple phobias and psychophysiologic reactions; migraine-type headaches, peripheral circulatory disorder, lingua geographica) who at the age of 24 suffered multiple cuts, internal injuries, multiple fractures of the pelvis and loss of consciousness when her car was hit by a train.

While the patient progressed slowly through the standard exercises, she experienced on many occasions disagreeable autogenic discharges which involved the digestive tract and also showed topographic relations with her accident-related injuries. Several examples taken from the patient's training protocols are given below:

Dec. 6, 1967   1. During the First Standard Exercise:
                         (a) comfortable, calm, pain in my stomach, nausea, ice cold feet, pain in left arm, pain in my back.
                         (b) tension in trunk, left arm twitching, swallowing repeatedly, all kinds of disagreeable sensations, uncomfortable, respiration nervous, heartbeat very fast.

Jan. 11, 1968   2. After adding the Second Standard Exercise:
                         (a) cold shivers between shoulder blades, disagreeable sensations and impression that my head is lower than my feet and feeling like vomiting, muscles contracting in both thighs.
                         (b) impression of trembling and dizziness, nervous twitching on left forehead, nervous, heart twitching, dizzy, pain in my abdomen.

Jan. 17, 1968   3. After adding the Third Standard Exercise:
                         (a) sharp pain in my head, on my left forehead, left hand jerking, nervous spasms and sharp pain in my stomach.
                         (b) anxiety and feeling like vomiting, dizziness, unable to continue.

Jan. 31, 1968   4. After adding the Fourth Standard Exercise:
                         (a) sharp pain in heart, respiration fine, relaxation good, feeling of numbness in right hand, chills.

(b) a lot of noise in stomach, legs twitching, tense, distracted, chills.

(c) feel like vomiting, pain in back, headache, "I am fed up."

Mar. 20, 1968   5. After adding the Fifth Standard Exercise:

(a) calm, noise in abdomen, pain, contractions and strange chills in abdomen, nausea, dizziness, fingertips numb.

(b) sharp pain in right hip, sharp pain in left hip, pain in left arm and hand, nausea, chills, increasing pain in legs, calm.

Mar. 23, 1968   (a) fluttering eyelids, pain in left buttock, pain in right leg, left shoulder and back itchy, very comfortable and calm, considerable difficulty terminating.

(b) very nervous, eyelids fluttering, anxiety, difficulty in breathing properly, noise in abdomen, frontal headache.[2065]

In such cases, when after several months of autogenic training (and exclusion of organic pathology) no satisfactory improvements are noted, it is advisable to evaluate the practical possibility of adding methods of autogenic neutralization to the treatment program.

An increase of various modalities of sensory and motor discharges in the lower abdominal region has been also observed in trainees with imposed or voluntarily assumed forms of sexual abstinence,[899,2065] and others who practiced autogenic standard exercises during periods of absolute or relative sexual deprivation.

The subjectively disagreeable and disturbing nature of certain discharges (e.g., cramp-like sensations, pressure, pain) usually call for a careful and reassuring differential diagnostic evaluation.

It is in this connection that it is helpful to remember that clinical studies[2065] indicated that abdominal complaints and relevant functional disorders also tend to occur more frequently in patients with a history of prolonged periods of absolute or relative sexual deprivation. Another complicating variable, frequently encountered in this group of patients, is related to the non-acceptance of autogenic discharges involving the genital organs and topographically connected structures in the lower ventral and dorsal regions. As a consequence, this category of patients is prone to develop resistance against autogenic training for what they believe to be moral reasons. In such instances it is important to explain that spontaneously occurring autogenic discharges are, like dreams or nocturnal pollutions, a natural phenomenon of self-regulatory mechanisms.

TABLE 2. *Sensory and Motor Discharges during the First Standard Exercise in Psychosomatic Patients with and without Heterosexual Deprivation (lower abdomen and lower back)**

Autogenic Discharges	With Heterosexual Deprivation N = 60 (age: M = 29.3; AT./weeks: M = 7.9)		Without Heterosexual Deprivation N = 60 (Age: M = 35.6; AT./weeks: M = 6.6)	
	Discharge Score	Number of patients with discharges	Discharge Score	Number of patients with discharges
A. *Sensory*				
1. Lower abdomen	54	24	11	8
2. Lower back	14	9	2	1
B. *Motor*				
1. Lower abdomen	27	16	9	4
2. Lower back	9	9	0	0

* Discharges involving the genito-anal area, the thighs and the buttocks are not included.

Particularly disagreeable autogenic discharges involving the abdominal region and the lower back have been also encountered in trainees with a history of (a) an abortion carried out under unfavorable circumstances (e.g., without anesthesia), or (b) a traumatic delivery. In these cases abdominally oriented sensory and motor discharges are frequently associated with anxiety, depressive feelings, need for crying and resistance against autogenic exercises. Increased motor discharges and labor-like phenomena have been also observed in female trainees with a strong unfulfilled wish for motherhood (e.g., sterility).

Only in relatively rare cases did material obtained during autogenic abreactions provide sufficient evidence which could be viewed as supporting the hypothesis that autogenic discharges involving the gastrointestinal tract or the abdominal area are related to traumatic experiences involving early relations between mother and child (e.g., deprivation of food, irregular feeding).

DISORDERS OF DEGLUTITION

The application of autogenic standard exercises and Special Formulae in the treatment of psychophysiologically oriented disorders of deglutition is recommended after participation of other diseases (e.g., malignancy, esophagitis, benign tumors, diverticula, neuromuscular lesions, myasthenia gravis, scleroderma) have been diagnosed or are excluded. Hysterical dysphagia,[410,1582] globus hystericus,[490,1182] singultus,[274,275,490,645,658,1775] aerophagia,[645,1107,1758] spasms of the esophagus,[161,302,360,410,602,658,1528,1979] functional regurgitation[360,604] and cardiospastic conditions[410,658,659,1182] are reported to respond favorably to autogenic approaches. Most patients note considerable improvement, or even spontaneous and permanent disappearance of the functional disturbance, during advanced phases of autogenic standard training.

Case 2: A 41-year-old female patient who had suffered from singultus for about seven years learned to stop the disorder by applying autogenic standard exercises.[1775]

Case 3: A 12-year-old girl (I. Q. Wechsler: 85, developmental dysgraphia, spasmodic hiccough, emotional instability) came for treatment of singultus, which had started three months earlier. The patient's mother was considered to be suffering from marked anxiety, and her father seemed not to care much for his family. Her achievement in school was poor, and the spasmodic hiccough was interfering severely with the patient's class work. Sedative and antispasmodic medication had yielded no results.

Autogenic standard exercises in combination with supportive medication (calcium, Mellaril, Librium) was started. The patient's collaboration was very satisfactory, and after three therapist-controlled sessions, the singultus had disappeared. However, supervised treatment with autogenic training was continued for about six weeks. Parallel to this, reeducational training focussing on the dysgraphia was applied, and satisfactory progress was noted. A control after six months indicated that the patient's improvement persisted.[274,275]

In cases in which there is little or no satisfactory improvement after the patient has practiced the standard series for at least three months, the application of additional organ-specific exercises is indicated. The first step is a local reinforcement of the standard exercises by passive concentration on heaviness and warmth in the topographic area of the organ-specific disturbance. In addition to this, formulae of still more specific nature may bring about the desired result. In a case of functional dysphagia, Siemenroth,[1582] for example, successfully applied "My throat is wide,"* in combination with the intentional formula, "Swallowing doesn't matter" ("Swallowing doesn't affect me").†

In patients suffering from cardiospasms or spasms of the esophagus, passive concentration on "waves of downward-flowing warmth" has been reported as having a particularly relieving effect.[161,1377] The patient's mental contact during this specific phase of passive concentration is usually enhanced by his taking small quantities of hot milk, tea or alcohol, which act as a liquid tracer, before starting the exercise.

---

* "Mein Schlund ist weit."
† "Das Schlucken is unwichtig."

According to radiocinematographic studies carried out by M. Sapir, A. Dehouve and F. Reverchon,[1166,1172,2119,2121] the normalizing effects of autogenic standard exercises on motor functions of the esophagogastric portion of the intestinal tract are also observable in trainees with hiatus hernia (see Vol. IV).

GASTRITIS

The application of autogenic training in the clinical treatment of different forms of chronic nonspecific gastritis (atrophic, superficial, hypertrophic) has been found of particular value in four respects: (a) the gradual harmonization of the neurotic patient's psychoreactive pattern, (b) the reduction of hyperirritability of the autonomic system, (c) the elimination or reduction of periodic aggravation, and (d) as a prophylactic measure against relapses and/or progressive organic destruction.[1997] In this sense, Laberke[759] found that the method was effective in 70 per cent of 210 cases.

Usually, the standard exercises are introduced to the patient during the second week of hospitalization. Preference should be given to the horizontal training posture. Daily control of the training symptoms and individual introduction of each new formula is desirable. In addition to this, group discussions between patients suffering from gastritis and allied disorders should be held twice a week.[658] During an initial period of two to four weeks, symptomatic treatment should run parallel with the training until the complaints subside under the influence of regular exercises. Usually, four sets of exercises are performed each day: in the morning before getting up, before and at the end of a rest period at noon, and at night before going to sleep.

Since there is hyperirritability of the vasomotor system in many patients suffering from gastrointestinal disorders, reduced warmth-exercises starting out with passive concentration on warmth in the feet (see Case 15/I, p. 45) are frequently indicated (see p. 43). The fourth standard exercise ("It breathes me") tends to have a particularly agreeable and relieving effect in gastritis patients and therefore should be emphasized during each set of exercises.

The Fifth Standard Exercise ("My solar plexus is warm") should not be used in *acute gastritis,* since an additional increase of blood flow (see Vol. IV) into the already hyperemic mucosa and a drastic increase of gastric motility (see Vol. IV) is contraindicated. Likewise, in cases with *chronic atrophic gastritis* a careful clinical assessment is necessary *before* passive concentration on abdominal warmth is used. Since chronic atrophic gastritis may be associated with superimposed acute inflammation, with gastric ulcer or carcinoma, it is preferable not to use the Fifth

Standard Formula. Passive concentration on "My solar plexus is warm" may, however, be helpful in patients with *simple gastric atrophy* which is not associated with an inflammatory process but often seen in cases of pernicious anemia. These clinical considerations imply that the Fifth Standard Exercise is left out in most cases, and that the Sixth Standard Formula ("My forehead is cool") follows directly after the Fourth Standard Exercise.

Referring to the radiocinematographic studies carried out by M. Sapir, A. Dehouve and F. Reverchon,[1166,1172,2119,2121] it must be emphasized that the solar plexus exercise is not indispensable, and that very favorable changes towards normalization (see p. 7, 21, 26) do already occur during passive concentration on heaviness in the limbs. For example, in certain alcoholics, Y. Kohno[2030] observed significant improvements within 2-6 weeks when the practice of autogenic training was limited to the formulae of the First and Second Standard Exercises.

The use of autogenic training in hemorrhagic patients is contraindicated[1086] unless they are hospitalized and under steady medical control. Likewise, clinical supervision is indicated in patients with advanced forms of hypertrophic gastritis.[1086] In these cases it is considered necessary to exclude the possibility of lymphoma or other neoplasms before treatment with autogenic training is started. However, in cases with diagnosed abdominal malignant disease autogenic training, with the exception of abdominally oriented warmth formulae, may be very helpful as an adjunct to other conventional forms of treatment. N. Henning, P. Polzien and S. Polzien[493] observed disappearance of intestinal spasms in a sarcomatous patient during the practice of heaviness exercises.

Although a number of clinical and experimental observations (see Fig. 3) indicated that autogenic training influences gastric secretion,[161,639,1039,1086,1377,2003] more systematic research is required in order to determine the specific effects of each standard formula and relevant organ-specific approaches. Since the Fifth Standard Formula ("My solar pleux is warm") and the more general approach ("My abdomen is warm")[1086] are both associated with reactive gastric hypermotility (see Vol. IV), and since there is some evidence that "abdominal warmth" produces an increase in acidity of the gastric juice,[1086] and an increase of blood flow in the stomach wall,[546,906,1008,2096] the Fifth Standard Formula should not be used in cases of hyperacidity, in patients suffering from inflammatory gastric disorders or, for example, peptic ulcer, carcinoma of the stomach and portal hypertension.

Information about the effects of autogenic training on simple forms of achlorhydria and other forms associated with chronic macrocytic (pernicious) anemia and gastritis is lacking. In this connection it is however helpful to remember that degenerative changes in the nervous system and peripheral nerve degeneration may result in paresthesias and other phenomena (e.g., stiffness in limbs, hypotonia, euphoria) which have a resemblance to relevant modalities of autogenic discharges.

J. H. Schultz[1433,1528] reported successful application of autogenic approaches in a 60-year-old patient suffering from gastric succorrhea. In this case, J. H. Schultz combined the regular practice of autogenic standard exercises with passive concentration on the texture and dryness of blotting paper, which in this instance served as a substitute for a verbally structured formula aiming at a reduction of the excessive gastric secretion. In order to maintain a vivid imagination of "absorbent dryness," it was suggested that the patient pass his fingers slowly over the texture of blotting paper everytime before he started practicing autogenic exercises. Clinical control tests verified that the excessive secretion had normalized within 10 days.

J. H. Schultz's successful use of a topographically (e.g., stomach) and functionally (e.g., decrease of secretion) oriented Intentional Image (e.g., dryness of blotting paper) for clinical purposes agrees favorably with experimental studies carried out by Y. Ishida.[552,553,2003] While investigating the effects of autogenic standard exercises on gastrointestinal motility (see Vol. IV) and gastric secretion (see Fig. 3, p. 19), Y. Ishida also applied passive concentration on Experimental Formulae (e.g., "My stomach slows down") and functionally oriented Intentional Images (e.g., an enraging situation in the trainee's office). Using such approaches, Y. Ishida found that the pattern of gastric secretion corresponded well with the functional direction of the thematic content of different Intentional Images (see Fig. 3, p. 19).

DYSPEPSIA

In the absence of demonstrable organic disease, two forms of indigestion may be distinguished: (a) reactive dyspepsia, and (b) what has been called "nervous dyspepsia." Experienced trainees who occasionally suffered from reactive dyspepsia (e.g., after overeating, ingestion of food with high fat content, eating too rapidly, poorly prepared food, excessive consumption of alcohol,[2030] heavy smoking, ingestion of large quantities of gas-forming vegetables, orally taken medication) with feelings of fullness, nausea, epigastric discomfort, belching and perhaps vomiting, have noted that the practice of autogenic standard exercises appears to be very helpful in overcoming and shortening such periods of reactive indigestion.[484,853,994,2030,2065] For example, P. Lowys, A. Bégoin, J. Bégoin, M. Laures and J. Roux reported that in patients suffering from pulmonary tuberculosis, chemotherapy (e.g., isoniazid, streptomycin, aminosalicylic acid) became more tolerable with significant reduction of dyspeptic and other toxic symptoms, when these patients practiced autogenic standard exercises regularly.[853] Similarly W. Luthe[2065] observed that gastric irritability, abdominal discomfort, nausea and reactive anorexia in patients taking orally administered antibiotics tend to be reduced or to subside completely (in addition to dietary measures) when autogenic exercises are practiced more frequently for prolonged periods (e.g., 20-30 min. per set). According to H. J. Prill[1101] significantly less satisfactory results have been observed in pregnant trainees who suffered from nausea, heartburns, belching, abdominal discomfort and other symptoms of indigestion.

When non-organic vague dyspeptic symptoms without constant relationships either to time or food (e.g., diffuse discomfort across the abdomen, cramp-like sensations, capricious or impaired appetite, nausea, fullness and pressure in abdomen, private folkloric diet, "weak stomach") and presence of anxiety, irritability, insomnia, weakness or a feeling of tension indicate "nervous dyspepsia," autogenic standard exercises are reported to be very helpful.[2,141,156,197,302,360,484,529,602,612,646,647,648,730,994, 1003,1111,1182,1528,2003] Particularly rewarding results have been reported when autogenic standard exercises were applied to children (after age 8) and adolescents complaining about (non-organic) abdominal discomfort, spasms, nausea and anorexia.[53,274,275,305,312,526,604,956] Equally encouraging improvements were obtained in cases suffering from anxiety-related psychogenic vomiting.[53,305,360,490,604,612,658,2003]

A particular problem involving differential diagnosis and case-adapted management of autogenic therapy concerns patients with a history of moderate to severe accidents (e.g., fractures, car crash, fall on the head) and certain other traumatic situations (e.g., swallowing water while about to drown). W. Luthe observed 32 patients with a history of one or more accidents or traumas, who, during treatment with autogenic standard exercises, experienced during transitory phases various phenomena of dyspepsia (e.g., abdominal discomfort, pressure sensations across the upper abdomen, nausea, vomiting). These autogenic discharges were found (as verified by material obtained during autogenic abreactions) to be related to specific accidents, traumatizing situations and medical procedures carried out under unfavorable circumstances (e.g., difficult deliveries, abortions without or with insufficient anesthesia, bone marrow puncture). When the trainee's history indicates relevant traumatic episodes, and feelings of nausea with urge to vomit persist for longer than a week, it is advisable to explain to the trainee, that similar to crying, it would be relieving to permit actual vomiting during or after autogenic exercises. Since such episodes of vomiting tend to occur repeatedly at variable intervals which are difficult to predict, the trainee should be encouraged to be well prepared at all times (e.g., pail with some water, towels) when he is practicing autogenic training. Voluntary blocking of vomiting tends to increase various symptoms of dyspepsia and may also result in frontal headaches or attacks of migraine. However, when actual vomiting is permitted whenever there is a need to do so, the associated symptoms of dyspepsia tend to disappear rapidly.[2065] It is in this connection that the research carried out by Y. Shimoda et al. (Tottori University, Japan) is of particular clinical and theoretical interest.*

PEPTIC ULCER

In the treatment of patients suffering from peptic ulcers in the lower end of the esophagus, the stomach or the duodenum, a combination of the usual medical procedures (e.g., diet, rest, antacids, anticholinergic drugs, environmental manipulations) with autogenic training (excluding the Fifth Standard Formula) has been recommended by various authors.[198,201,302,410, 421,493,526,553,574,669,670,750,757,758,759,761,766,768,771,906,994,1057,1072,1086,1111,1137,1163, 1166,1171,1172,1182,1427,1433,1528,1566,1622,1997,2003,2030,2047,2153,2155,2161,2308]

Clinical observers generally agree that the first four and the sixth autogenic standard exercises appear particularly helpful as a non-specific adjunctive approach aiming at normalization of stress-induced alterations of vasomotor, motor, and secretory functions (see Fig. 3) of the gastrointestinal tract. It is assumed that the depression or normalization of gastric secretion during autogenic training (abdominal warmth excluded) (see Fig. 3) is one of the essential elements which participate in promoting the healing of peptic ulcers.[553,906,1086]

However, it must be noted that the treatment response in peptic ulcer is variable.[81,198,574,639,669,670,758,760] Failures of improvement,[81] unsatisfactory responses[574] and very encouraging observations have been reported. For example, a statistical investigation by H. Kleinsorge[639] (no detailed data published) failed to prove that autogenic training promotes recovery from gastric ulcers. Contrasting with this are reports by J. A. Laberke,[758, 760,761] and others[198,201,526,750,1057,1137,1171,1566] who observed cases in which gastric ulcer did not respond to conventional clinical approaches, but in which penetrating niches disappeared permanently under the influence of

---

* Shimoda, Y., Yoshino, Y., Namba, M., Tanaka, K., Ashida, Y., Fukuda, M. and Shindo, S.: Varieties of six and fourteen per second positive spikes and their clinical characteristics. *Yonago Acta Medica*, 1964, 8, 1, 59-68.—Yoshino, Y.: A study on abdominal epilepsy and so-called cardiospasm. *Yonago Acta Medica*, 1963, 7, 2, 69-87.—Tanaka, K., Shimoda, Y. and Yoshino, Y.: A case of dysrhythmic migraine with six and fourteen per second positive spike pattern. *Yonago Acta Medica*, 1965, 9, 2, 88-93.

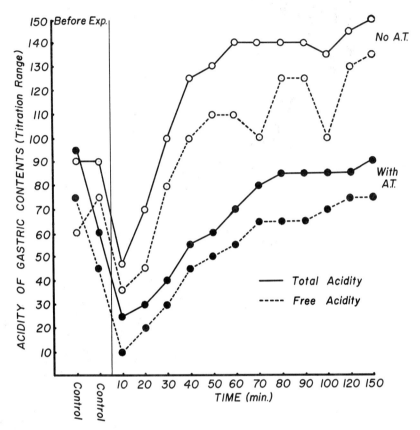

FIG. 3. Changes of gastric acidity in a 23-year-old male student (duodenal ulcer, tuberculosis).

"No A.T.": Pattern of gastric secretion representative for several control analyses carried out before learning autogenic training.

"With A.T.": Pattern of gastric secretion after four weeks of practicing autogenic standard exercises regularly. During this evaluation the patient started autogenic training at the vertical demarcation line. Note the significantly slower increase of free acidity (lower) and total acidity (upper), and the generally lower level of gastric acid secretion during autogenic training. (Courtesy of Y. Ishida, Tokyo.[553,906])

autogenic training. In peptic ulcer patients the inconsistency of treatment responses to autogenic training has been viewed as being related to variables of psychodynamic nature. While A. Jores[574] pointed out that desirable changes in the ulcer patient's personality dynamics cannot be brought about by autogenic training, others[81,198,201,302,750,758,760,761,1057,1171,]

FIG. 4. A 50-year-old male patient (anxiety reaction, obsessive manifestations) with gastrectomy (recurrent peptic ulcers) performed 15 years earlier. In spite of this surgical intervention he continued to suffer from various gastric complaints (e.g., spasms, pressure, "nervous stomach," fatigue). After learning autogenic training, without changes of the neurotic personality dynamics, his gastric complaints disappeared, he gained 14 lb., and the radiologic control showed significant changes:

(a) Without autogenic training: poorly and irregularly filled, contracted rather static jejunal loops (j.l.) with evidence of inefficient peristaltic activity. The radiocinematographic survey revealed rapid filling of the gastric stump (g.st.) and poor filling of the anastomotic section (an.) of the efferent jejunal loop (j.l.) with reduced peristaltic activity.

(b) Several weeks later, with autogenic training: the same jejunal loop (j.l.) with good filling, good distension and containing a large amount of contrast medium, peristaltic waves (p.w.) are well defined and more regular and energetic. Radiocinematographic evaluation showed a slower filling of the gastric stump (g.st.), improved timing with better spacing of the passage through the anastomotic opening (a.n.), and after the characteristic period of transitory atony, enhanced widening of the anastomotic opening. (Courtesy of M. Sapir, A. Dehouve, F. Reverchon and R. Philibert, Paris.[1166], [1172,2119,2121])

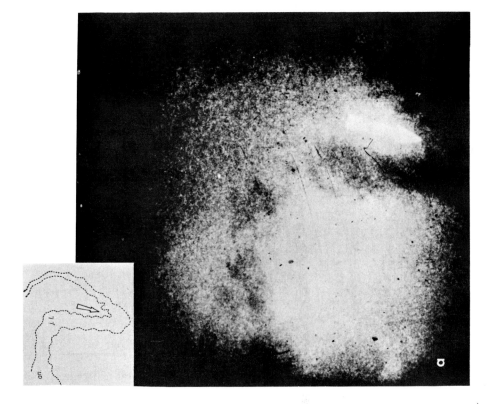

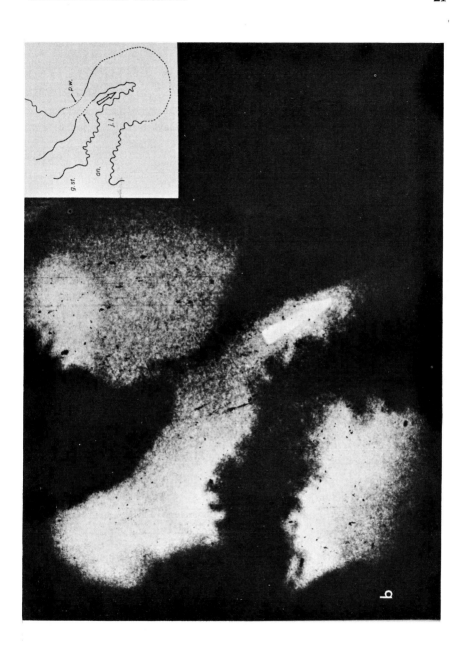

[1427,1528] emphasize the clinically favorable psychodynamic changes which are reflected by changes of attitude, better adjusted behavior patterns and reduction of unfavorable reactivity to emotional stress.[460] Although these psychodynamic changes do not necessarily imply a change of personality (see Fig. 4), they are considered of particular clinical value, since they are viewed as participating in bringing about a significant decrease in the number of relapses in ulcer patients who continued to practice autogenic training after leaving the hospital.[760]

Depending on the author's perspectives, the inconsistency of therapeutic responsiveness has been ascribed to constitutional or typologic differences, to differences of participating psychodynamic disorders,[198, 201,574] and to variables which are considered to be closely related to the manner in which autogenic training is applied.[1171] In patients with peptic ulcers it is recommended that therapeutic elements be emphasized which mobilize and support the trainee's motivation to practice standard exercises regularly over prolonged periods of time (e.g., 12-18 months). Group-training[639,1182] (e.g., abdominal group), individually adapted supportive and problem-focussed discussions at regular intervals (e.g., 2-4 hr. per week in the beginning, 1 hr. every 2 wk. later) and periodic control of the patient's therapeutic homework after discharge from the hospital, are considered valuable factors in the therapeutic management of adolescent and adult patients. A similar though simpler approach has been used with children.[526,1137] Furthermore it has been noted that peptic ulcer patients tend to do better when the learning of autogenic standard exercise follows a slow, detailed, very gradually progressing pattern.[1171]

Practice of the Fifth Standard Formula ("My solar plexus is warm") is contraindicated in all cases suffering from peptic ulcer (see p. 14, 18). Until further clinical research on the effects of autogenic training on gastrointestinal bleeding and other variables (e.g., acidity) is available, autogenic training should not be applied to patients with a history of gastrointestinal haemorrhage.[1086] Acute episodes of ulceration and the presence of occult blood in the stool are also contraindications for autogenic training, unless the patient is hospitalized and under vigilant medical control. The use of the Fifth Standard Formula ("My solar plexus is warm") is contraindicated in patients with peptic ulcer. Experimental findings have indicated that passive concentration on warmth in the abdominal area produces hypermotility of peristalsis, significant increase of blood flow in the gastric mucosa and augmentation of acidity in the gastric juice (see Vol. IV). These changes are unfavorable for peptic ulcer (see Case 4).

Case 4: A male, adult patient who participated in group-training under supervision by H. Binder[141] had no particular difficulties while he was progressing through the first four standard exercises. After adding "My solar plexus is warm" he noticed epigastric pain when he practiced autogenic training. A radiological examination carried out at this point revealed a gastric ulcer.[141]

Case 5: A 29-year-old electrician (duodenal ulcer, mild gastritis, moderate duodenitis). Autogenic Standard Exercises were applied in combination with other conventional approaches. Coming twice a week for control sessions, the patient learned autogenic training without difficulties. His complaints subsided. A radiological control after six weeks verified that the duodenal ulcer had disappeared. The patient kept practicing standard exercises regularly. No further gastrointestinal lesions occurred during a five-year period of observation. It is felt that the regular practice of autogenic training contributed (a) to the healing process of the lesion observed initially, and (b) that the probability of recurrence of similar pathologic lesions was favorably influenced by autogenic exercises.[1057]

BILIARY DISORDERS

After the nature of biliary tract disease has been identified and clinically satisfactory treatment programs have been instituted, autogenic standard exercises may be added to reduce or to help to eliminate unfavorable functional components and to promote the patient's recovery.[493,574,639,646,647,648,662,768,994,1091,1163,1171,1182] In this sense autogenic standard training, with emphasis on the Fifth Standard Exercise ("My solar plexus is warm") has been reported to be of particular value in patients suffering from biliary dyskinesia with or without cholecystectomy.[646,647,648,662,768,1171,1182] Relevant clinical observations indicated that the mechanics of bile flow improve as muscular spasms and pain (e.g., due to abnormal pressure relations) in the biliary region subside. Likewise, spasms of the sphincter Oddi have responded to autogenic training.[1163,1171] Improvements such as reduction or elimination of spasms and pain in patients with relatively mild forms of cholelithiasis[1163] have been noted. Patients suffering from biliary colics observed that attacks appear to be milder and of shorter duration when autogenic exercises are started as soon as prodromal symptoms develop.[994]

ULCERATIVE COLITIS

With hospitalized patients the autogenic standard series has been used in combination with symptomatic therapy, analytic approaches and hypnotherapy.[261,263a,1131,1625] Apart from the normalizing effects on intestinal functions (see preceding sections) the autogenic approach has been credited with facilitating and promoting analytically oriented psychotherapy. The mutual reinforcement of hypnotherapeutic and autogenic effects are viewed as potent factors in speeding up recovery from the disease.[200,410,574,768,771,1528,1946,1948,1967,2047] The largest group of patients (N = 32) suffering from a chronic, non-specific, inflammatory and ulcerative disease of the colon and treated with autogenic training has been reported by G. Schaeffer.[1183] Clinically 9 cases were mild, 10 moderate and 13 judged as severe. In 23 patients occasional rest-hypnoses were added to conventional clinical support and treatment with autogenic training. With control periods ranging from 12 months to 12 years, G. Schaeffer reported no improvement in 3 patients, significant improvement in 6 cases and 23 as clinically cured. Medication was used sparsely and in most cases not at all. In summarizing his clinical observations, G. Schaeffer concludes that autogenic training (a) stabilizes and normalizes disturbances of relevant autonomic functions better than any other known method; (b) reduces progressively the frequency of relapses; (c) shortens and diminishes the degree of severity of relapses; and (d) eliminates the necessity of medication in most cases or reduces required medication in others. G. Schaeffer emphasizes that the regular daily practice of possibly prolonged standard exercises over many months or years is an essential factor in the successful treatment of chronic ulcerative colitis.[1183]

Very encouraging results, corresponding with those reported by G. Schaeffer, have been also obtained by A. J. Burger,[198] F. Curtius and H. G. Rohrmoser,[261,263a] H. Enke,[355] H. Kleinsorge and G. Klumbies,[645,658, 659,662] U. Spiegelberg,[2153] E. Valdivielso[2178] and J. N. Wagner.[1758] Equally encouraging are clinical results obtained with children who learned to practice autogenic standard training.[53,526,1137]

Technically, H. Kleinsorge and G. Klumbies[662] preferred to use "My abdomen is warm" instead of "My solar plexus is warm." This topographically more general approach was adopted on clinical grounds. Whether this approach is in favorable correspondence with clinico-pathologic requirements and relevant experimental studies (see Vol. IV), carried out by P. Polzien et al.,[1086] and by Y. Ikemi et al.,[546,906,1008,2096] remains to be investigated. The polygraphic investigations verified that passive concentration on "My lower abdomen is warm" is, as far as the lower parts of the intestinal tract are concerned, more effective than passive concentration on the topographically limited (upper abdomen) standard formula "My solar plexus is warm." However, considering the increase of blood flow in the mucosa of the colon and the regional activation of motility (see Vol. IV) it appears questionable if the organ-specific formula "My lower abdomen is warm" should be applied to patients with

ULCERATIVE COLITIS (♀,7yrs.)

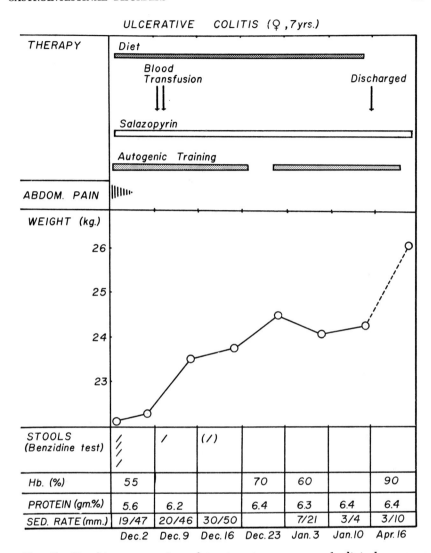

FIG. 5. Graphic presentation of treatment program and clinical progress of a hospitalized 7-year-old girl suffering from ulcerative colitis. (Courtesy of L. Hohenauer, University of Vienna, Austria.[526])

ulcerative colitis. However, in case passive concentration on warmth in the lower abdomen is applied (see p. 14, 24, 27), a careful control of a possible increase of haemorrhagic effects is mandatory. Passive concentration on this formula ("My lower abdomen is warm") must be stopped whenever there is evidence of clinically undesirable effects.[1086]

IRRITABLE COLON

This relatively common disorder of the large bowel, with its characteristic pattern of constipation, abdominal discomfort (*syn.*: mucous colitis, spastic constipation, spastic colon, spastic colitis) and occasional bouts of diarrheal manifestations ("nervous diarrhea") is frequently associated with other complaints (e.g., headache, insomnia, tiredness, indigestion, anorexia) the functional nature of which are known to respond well to autogenic training.[602,658,1163,1171,1183,1433,2003]

Autogenic training has been effective in the readjustment of conditions characterized by chronic constipation (see p. 27ff) with passage of hard, dry stools covered with mucus, and also in patients who suffer from attacks of functionally determined forms of diarrhea with or without the typical watery stools in the morning.[200,302,360,410,525,602,604,658,768,994,1163,1171,1182,1433,1566,2153,2155]

As the regular practice of autogenic training progresses through the Standard Series of formulae, improvements may be already noted after about three weeks of autogenic training (see Case 6). Alternating conditions of constipation and diarrhea tend to occur less frequently, and in cases of chronic (functional) diarrhea, a significant decrease in the frequency of bowel movements and more solid feces (see Case 6) may be noted.[1148,1377] Likewise it has been reported that flatulence and relevant complaints (e.g., abdominal distension, gastric fullness, abdominal cramps, attempts at belching, excessive passage of flatus) tend to subside as the practice of autogenic standard exercises is carried out regularly.[645,658,994,1163,1171,1182] Referring to such improvements, H. Kleinsorge[645] hypothesized that the clinical amelioration of cases suffering from an excessive accumulation of gas in the stomach or intestine, is largely due to a better absorption into the blood stream made possible by an increase of blood flow in the gastric and intestinal mucosa (see Vol. IV). Guided by clinical observations, H. Kleinsorge emphasized the effectiveness of the Fifth Standard Exercise in cases with flatulence.[645]

Case 6: A 42-year-old banker had for the past 20 years suffered periodically from muco-watery diarrhea, restlessness, sleeplessness, and headaches. The patient had consulted numerous physicians and specialists (invariable diagnosis: mucous colitis). Relevant pharmaceutical products were of merely temporary or no help.

In 1954, superficial psychiatric evaluation of the patient's personality revealed lack of self-confidence, inner insecurity, inhibition of self-expression, shyness, compulsive trends, pedantic handling of business and private affairs, lack of initiative and fear of responsibility. The onset of diarrhea, restlessness, sleep disturbances and headaches were found to be closely related to his work and particularly to business situations which demanded initiative and decisive action from the patient.

After three weeks of autogenic training (group sessions), the diarrhea ceased and did not start again (nine months' control). The frequency and intensity of headaches, restlessness and sleep disturbances were also reduced significantly.[1148]

After involvement of other pathologic factors have been excluded and the functional nature of the colonic disorder is evident, autogenic standard exercises with emphasis on "My lower abdomen is warm" appears to be the method of choice.[906,1008] However, regular control of these patients is necessary and autogenic training must be stopped as soon as clinically undesirable effects (e.g., abdominal pain, haemorrhagic manifestations), as for example, reported by P. Polzien, N. Henning, L. Demling, H. Kinzlmeier and S. Polzien;[1086] S. Maeda, Y. Sasaki and A. Yasumatsu;[2079] Y. Ikemi[541] and Y. Sasaki,[2122] are noted.

In cases where irritable colon is associated with allergy to foods, a combination of autogenic standard exercises with a six-step systematic desensitization procedure as elaborated by Y. Ikemi, S. Nakagawa, T. Kusano and M. Sugita[547] is recommended (see p. 30, 31). Other case-adapted combinations of autogenic approaches vary with the clinical exigencies of those disorders (e.g., haemorrhoids, back pain, insomnia) which are frequently associated with irritable colon.

CONSTIPATION

The treatment of patients suffering from difficult or infrequent evacuation of feces (inactive colon, colon stasis, "lazy" colon, atonic constipation; "dyschezia," "imaginery" constipation, colonic constipation, constipation associated with irritable colon or food allergy) is known to be one of the main fields of autogenic therapy.[132,141,241,302,360,410,493,525,574,602,604, 645,658,662,756,757,758,759,760,761,829,939,994,1093,1101,1148,1167,1171,1182,1200,1377,1433,1477, 1528,1562,1590,1699,1824,2024,2122,2192]

The effectiveness of autogenic standard exercises in bringing about progressive or "sudden unexplained" normalization of bowel movements in patients with chronic forms of non-organic constipation, was initially discovered in trainees who practiced autogenic training for other reasons (e.g., asthma).[574,761,829,1200,1377,1433,1528] Generally it has been observed that, at the end of the first month and during the second month of regular standard training, most patients note a gradual or complete disappearance of abdominal discomfort, headache, indigestion, and other symptoms like belching and meteorism. As these symptoms fade away, the patient's feeling of well-being increases. Better sleep and a favorable adjustment in appetite and body weight are usually reported. In less severe cases, various indications of a normalization of deranged colonic function are already noted after two to three weeks of autogenic training. Patients often report an urgent need to defecate and the occurrence of normal evacuation right after a set of exercises.

These and similar clinical observations stimulated N. Henning, P. Polzien and S. Polzien[493] to test the hypothesis that passive concentration on heaviness in the extremities is sufficient in itself to cure habitual constipation. Sixteen out-patients, 23 to 60 years of age, of above-average intelligence and suffering from habitual constipation for two years and longer, were selected for heaviness training. The use of laxatives was restricted to urgent situations. Of this group, four patients rejected the autogenic approach and insisted on prescriptions for laxatives. In two other cases there was no success at all. In another case the disorder returned after the patient discontinued the exercises. However, this patient had had normal evacuations for a period of six months. Nine patients were cured (control periods: 5–24 months). Six of these patients noted the onset of normal evacuation after two to three weeks of regular heaviness training, two after five weeks, and another one after nine months of passive concentration on heaviness in the limbs.

Although the heaviness and warmth exercises exert a normalizing effect on the functions of the colon, emphasis should be placed on practicing the entire standard series. Certain patients responded to the therapy only after longer periods of regular training with emphasis on prolonged phases of passive concentration on "My solar plexus is warm."

More recent investigations carried out by Y. Ikemi et al.[546,906,1008] (see Vol. IV) and Y. Ohno[2096] demonstrated particularly favorable effects on the lower parts of the digestive tract during passive concentration on "My lower abdomen is warm." Stimulated by these experimental findings, W. Luthe[2065] applied this formula to six chronically constipated patients who had not noted any improvement after several months of regular practice of autogenic standard exercises. In all six cases, satisfactory results, with elimination of laxatives, were noted within 1-12 days (see Case: 7, 8, 9).

Case 7: A 23-year-old secretary (anxiety reaction, moderate depression, overweight, chronic constipation for many years) who had practiced standard exercises for six months without improvement of her constipation, started a pattern of normal bowel movements within three days after "My lower abdomen is warm" was added to the standard series of autogenic formulas (control: 10 weeks).[896]

Case 8: A 24-year-old female student (anxiety reaction, mild depressive reaction, sexual deprivation, multiple psychophysiologic reactions, chronic constipation), five months autogenic standard training, experienced a normal bowel movement within 24 hours after she had started to use "My lower abdomen is warm." With some transitory relapses, progressive normalization with elimination of laxatives occurred within 4 weeks (control 11 weeks).[896]

Case 9: A 60-year-old patient (multiple sclerosis, chronic anxiety reaction, multiple phobias, moderate depression, chronic constipation) was able to eliminate laxatives within one week after "My lower abdomen is warm" was added to the standard exercises (control: 8 weeks).[896]

These observations indicate that the topographically more specific nature of "My lower abdomen is warm," is of particular clinical value in chronically constipated patients who do not improve while practicing autogenic standard exercises.

When there is evidence that there is unusual distensibility of the rectum, associated absence of any desire to defecate (dyschezia) or a chronic disregard to follow the urge to defecate, it is advisable that the practice of autogenic standard exercises be combined with (a) relatively prolonged phases of passive concentration on "My lower abdomen is warm," and (b) a case-adapted Intentional Formula which supports a program of re-education of bowel habits by aiming at time-regulation of evacuation (e.g., "After getting up in the morning I have a good bowel movement").[141,645,658,662,994]

Significantly less favorable results have been noted in patients suffering from constipation during pregnancy. In a group of 40 pregnant patients, H. J. Prill[1101] observed 26 failures, some improvement in 9, and normalization in only 5 cases. The low rate of satisfactory response is viewed as being related to a change of unknown physiologic variables as related to pregnancy. Until further research is available, the additional use of the organ-specific formula "My lower abdomen is warm" is considered as being contraindicated during pregnancy.

So far, there is no information about the effects of autogenic training in patients with acquired megacolon or Hirschsprung's disease. When constipation is associated with hypothyroid conditions, it may be expected that autogenic standard training may also exert favorable readjustment influences on certain thyroid functions (see Chap. 5).[890] However, this possibility should not be overestimated and conventional forms of treatment (e.g., dietary, thyroid medication) and periodic testing of thyroid functions are necessary while autogenic training is applied for the readjustment of chronic constipation.

In patients with so-called "imaginary" constipation, when excessive bowel-consciousness (e.g., overconcern about frequency, consistency, color of stools, abusive use of laxatives, enemas) dominates the situation, a different approach is indicated. Apart from re-educational explanations, elimination of enemas and laxatives, it is helpful to add a case-adapted neutralizing Intentional Formula to the standard series at the earliest convenience (e.g., "Bowel movement automatic, color and consistency do not matter"). The use of this approach implies that a careful differential diagnostic evaluation has been carried out before autogenic standard exercises and the Intentional Formula are applied (e.g., irritable colon).

FOOD ALLERGY

In this area of psychosomatic disorders, the application of different combinations of autogenic approaches varies largely with the peculiarities of each patient's psychodynamic constellation, and the psychophysiologic nature of gastrointestinal and systemic reactivity.

In patients who for many years were convinced that they suffered from allergic reactions after ingestion of certain foods (e.g., chocolate, onions, meat, oysters, mustard, cucumbers, bananas), and that these substances are responsible for subsequent abdominal discomfort, nausea, bloating, belching, pressure sensations across the upper abdomen, migraine, insomnia, nightmares and other complaints, it frequently has been observed that their pseudo-allergy disappeared as they progressed through the series of standard exercises.[658,896] Their apprehension and dietary precautions tend to fade away, and almost by accident they realize that the dreaded (pseudo-) allergic consequences did not occur after they forgot not to eat the food which was believed to be offending. Early recognition of the phobic nature of such pseudo-allergic dynamics is essential.

When, after several months of autogenic standard training, there is no evidence of dietary readjustment, and the phobic aversion continues to be entertained, it is advisable to add a case-adapted neutralizing Intentional Formula (e.g., "Diet does not matter, my system is healthy and digests automatically").

In other instances, when allergic reactions are supported by medically acceptable evidence (e.g., eosinophilia, circulatory reactions, urticaria, pruritus, skin tests), the therapeutic management varies with the intensity of the allergic reaction. In mild cases (skin reaction below 5 mm. diameter) the regular practice of autogenic standard exercises may yield satisfactory results in most cases. More differentiated approaches have been applied in moderate and severe cases. It is in this respect that studies carried out by Y. Ikemi, S. Nakagawa, T. Kusano and M. Sugita[547] are of particular clinical interest.

In a group of 83 female high school students who developed various gastrointestinal symptoms after eating certain foods, only 17 girls (21 per cent) manifested noticeable gastrointestinal disturbances, when the offending substances were ingested in disguised form. As far as decisive participation of psychologic variables are concerned, this result is of particular interest, since all girls had skin reactions varying between below 5 mm. and above 21 mm. diameter (66: between 6 and 10 mm.; 2: more than 21 mm.).

Autogenic standard training was applied to 13 girls who had noticed gastrointestinal complaints. This then was combined with discussions and persuasive explanations of mind-body relations in connection with their gastrointestinal symptoms ("interpretation"). With this combined approach 10 girls (skin reactions: 6-10 mm.) improved satisfactorily, and were able to eat the (undisguised) "noxious" food without experiencing any gastrointestinal discomfort. The remaining 3 patients (skin reaction: 6-10 mm.) who did not improve were treated with a more differentiated step-by-step procedure aiming at progressive desensitization by imaginary and actual confrontation with the noxious stimuli (specific foods) during autogenic training. When a patient was far enough advanced with the standard exercises and was able to achieve a complete relaxation of mind and body by practicing passive concentration on autogenic standard formulae, a confrontation with relevant noxious stimuli of increasing degrees was applied. This desensitizing confrontation method distinguishes six stages:

1. Verbalization of the names of the disagreeable foods (auditory confrontation with verbal stimuli related to noxious agent).
2. Imagining that the disagreeable foods are placed in front of them (imaginary visual and olfactory confrontation).
3. Imagining that they are eating the disagreeable foods (imaginary visual, olfactory and gustatory confrontation).
4. Actual eating of agreeable food (actual confrontation with reality factors related to noxious agent).
5. Actual eating of agreeable food under the impression that they are disagreeable (actual confrontation with non-noxious reality factors related to noxious agent plus imaginary confrontation with noxious agent).
6. Actual eating of the disagreeable food under the impression that they are disagreeable (actual confrontation with noxious reality factor plus verbal reinforcement of noxious nature of noxious agent).

In the course of this procedure, which was applied during autogenic exercises, the patient was instructed to raise the left hand if she became apprehensive. When this happened at a certain level of stimulus confrontation, the confrontation procedure was interrupted and a period of passive concentration on autogenic formulae was interjected. This was repeated until the patient did not indicate further occurrence of adverse reactions to the noxious stimulus. Only then did the authors proceed to the next category of stimulus confrontation. When the patient's negative reactivity was found to be too strong, she was asked to come for another treatment period after improving her technique in autogenic relaxation. After completion of their 8-day program, all three patients were able to consume undisguised quantities of "offensive" food without experiencing disagreeable reactions (see Table 3). A similar approach was attempted in the two patients who had shown very marked skin reactions (above 21 mm.). However, these two patients showed very strong resistance and the treatment was abandoned.[547]

Anorexia Nervosa

Psychotherapy of patients suffering from primary or secondary anorexia nervosa can be effectively supported by autogenic standard exercises.[112, 242,533,604,861,1072,1178,2153] In primary anorexia nervosa the therapeutic role of autogenic training is regarded as being of particular value in normalizing the disturbed coordination of autonomic functions (e.g., cold extremities, low blood pressure, obstinate constipation, amenorrhea, low PBI, dry skin) and in reducing the patient's (conflict-induced) tension. In secondary anorexia the additional use of intentional formulae may be advisable when the trainee needs effective support to overcome certain disturbing habits or when neutralization of the patient's undue concern with his digestive apparatus is required. The less severe disturbances of appetite which frequently occur as secondary symptoms of other disorders tend to disappear within two to six weeks of standard training. It is a common observation that patients with or without underweight or disturbances of appetite who are practicing autogenic training for other reasons spontaneously report that they have put on weight (see Case 15/I, p. 120).

Obesity

When overweight assumes pathological proportions by exceeding 20 per cent of a given patient's standard weight, and this development is not due to physical disorders (e.g., pituitary, thyroid, hyperinsulism, hyperadrenocorticism), autogenic training may be of valuable help.[410,908, 1499,1528,1683,2155]

Since overeating is known to be promoted by a complexity of factors, as, for example, "nervous tension," anxiety with defensive regression to oral gratification, sexual conflicts, frustrations, disappointments, depressive dynamics, oral impregnation wishes, fellatic phantasies, the unconscious meanings of various foods, a desire to be pregnant, a defense against heterosexual desires, a lack of self-discipline, an unconscious wish

TABLE 3. *Psychologic Desensitization in Combination with Autogenic Training (Abnormal Reaction to Disagreeable Food)*

No.	Name	Age	Disliked food	Sensitivity Test after "Interpretation"	Preparatory period (AT)	Autogenic Exercises						Final Test	Remarks
						Preliminary Tests — "desensitizing confrontations"							
						a Auditory confrontation with verbal stimuli related to noxious agent (noxious food)	b Imaginary situational confrontation I (noxious food placed in front of patient)	c Imaginary situational confrontation II (eating of noxious food)	d Actual confrontation with reality factors related to noxious agent I (eating of agreeable food)	e Actual confrontation with reality factors related to noxious agent II (eating of agreeable food and impression that it is noxious)	f Actual confrontation with reality factor (eating of noxious food and the impression that it is disagreeable)	g Reality confrontation (eating of noxious food)	
1	M. S.	18	Yolk (fried egg)	±	3 days	1 day	1 day	1 day	1 day	1 day	1 day	1 day Able to eat — no disagreeable reactions	No further symptoms
2	M. S.	17	mackerel	+	3 days	Raised hand immediately — AT intensified — 2nd day: raised hand a little — 3rd day: passed	Raised hand — Exercise repeated two times — 2nd day: passed	Raised hand a little — AT intensified — 2nd day: passed	1 day	1 day	1 day	Dislike initially — able to eat after more AT	No further symptoms
3	Y. I.	16	green pepper	±	3 days	Raised hand immediately — AT intensified — 2nd day: passed	Raised hand — Exercise repeated two times — 2nd day: passed	1 day	1 day	1 day	1 day	Did not mind much — able to eat without difficulty after AT	No further symptoms

of self-destruction, a means of controlling one's environment, or a compensation for loneliness, autogenic training cannot be expected to solve all the intricate dynamics of severely neurotic patients.[658] The practice of autogenic exercises is not a substitute for a lack of energy output, nor a method which can take the place of caloric intake.

However, the regular practice of autogenic training reduces anxiety and "nervous tension." Furthermore, a more favorable adjustment of certain metabolic[888,892] and other physiologic functions (e.g., gastrointestinal, circulatory) may be expected. Additional support may be obtained from the case-adapted use of Intentional Formulae aiming at a reduction of caloric intake, the elimination of nibbling or alcohol, and the promotion of an increase of physical activity (e.g., "I do all the little jobs myself and I go window shopping everyday").

Several authors reported good results with "I am satiated" ("Ich bin satt," "Ich bin ruhig, zufrieden und satt").[1499,1728,1980] J. H. Schultz[1499] considered this particular Intentional Formula as being of decisive functional value in helping patients to reduce up to 50 lb. An interesting attempt by J. H. Schultz[1528] to add a complementary organ-specific approach by using passive concentration on "My thyroid is very warm" also produced a considerable loss of weight. However, it is indicated that such drastic endocrine approaches should be carried out very cautiously under clinically well controlled circumstances.

When there is evidence that aggressive dynamics subserve the patient's drive to overeat, autogenic standard exercises may be combined with intensive use of thematically specific autogenic verbalization (e.g., 30 min. q.d.) thus effectively draining off accumulated aggression.[418,895,2065] In psychodynamically more complex situations, particularly when post-traumatic reactions appear to be involved, intensive use of autogenic abreaction may be expected to promote a desirable readjustment of underlying disturbances.[898]

References: 2, 3, 53, 81, 112, 129, 130, 132, 136, 141, 142, 156, 161, 197, 198, 200, 201, 241, 242, 247, 261, 263a, 274, 275, *302*, 305, 312, 335, *360*, 410, 421, 484, 490, *493*, 506, 515, 525, *526*, 529, 533, 541, *546*, *547*, 553, 574, 602, 604, *612*, 639, *645*, 646, 647, 648, 656, *658*, 659, 662, 669, 670, 728, 730, 750, 756, 757, 758, 759, *760*, *761*, 768, 771, 829, 853, 861, 866, 872, 877, 883, 885, *888*, 896, 906, 939, 940, 956, *994*, 1001, 1003, *1008*, 1057, 1072, *1086*, 1091, 1093, *1101*, 1107, 1131, 1137, 1148, *1163*, *1166*, *1171*, *1172*, 1178, 1182, *1183*, 1200, 1377, 1427, 1433, 1477, *1528*, *1537*, *1541*, 1545, 1562, 1566, 1582, 1590, 1622, 1625, 1699, *1758*, 1765, 1775, 1779, 1787, 1824, 1932, 1944, *1946*, *1948*, *1967*, *1979*, 2003, 2024, 2030, 2047, 2051, 2065, 2079, 2096, 2119, 2121, 2122, 2153, 2155, 2161, 2178, 2192, 2216, 2217, 2228, 2256, 2284, 2308, 2421.

3. Disorders of the Cardiovascular System and Vasomotor Disturbances

The application of autogenic training to persons with functional and organic alterations of the heart and vascular system should not be started unless a careful clinical evaluation and satisfactory screening of differential diagnostic implications has been carried out. Organic disease may be masked by a heavy overlay of psychoreactive functional symptoms, and the functional consequences of organic alterations may be unduly aggravated by psychophysiologic interferences resulting from coexisting psychodynamic disorders. In both instances autogenic training may be helpful.

Although surprising results have been observed in patients with marked organic alterations (see following sections), it cannot be expected that autogenic training can reverse progressive pathological processes. It is in this connection that particular caution, periodic supervision and guidance is required when, with the regular practice of autogenic exercises, a gradually developing feeling of well-being tends to make the patient forget his organically determined limits (e.g., coronary sclerosis, myocardial infarction[574,1175,1433,1528]).

The occasional occurrence of unusually strong vasomotor reactions as, for example, a sharp drop[1424,1565,1566] or sudden increase of blood pressure[883] or heart rate[1072] requires periodic control in all patients with relevant disorders.

Most important is, however, a case-specific adaptation of autogenic training. In correspondence with the organically and functionally determined nature and needs of each patient's clinical condition, it is necessary to evaluate the structure of each formula, to determine the pace of progress with each formula, to adapt the sequence of the standard formulae, and to evaluate the applicability and usefulness of organ-specific approaches and Intentional Formulae. Furthermore, it is important to consider that many patients make better progress and have less disturbing side-effects (e.g., strong vasomotor reactions, disagreeable autogenic discharges), when the number and the duration of autogenic exercises is continuously kept in favorable correspondence with the progressively changing conditions of the clinical and the therapeutic situation.

Patients with disorders of the cardiovascular system require the therapist's attentive presence, and his understanding support. It is in this connection that the application of autogenic training opens the door to a continuity of a positively oriented collaboration between the patient and the therapist.

Treatment of patients with cardiovascular disorders with autogenic training is thoroughly misunderstood when it is thought of as "10 minutes of explication of a certain formula, designed to produce relaxation." Therapists who are inclined to forget that a patient's clinical condition may require more than the practice of autogenic exercises, are cordially invited not to use the method.

Case-specific adaptation of autogenic training and successful management of the trainee during the various phases of autogenic standard therapy depends in many instances on a thorough knowledge of a patient's case history, taking into account intervening events (e.g., accidents, mortality, bad news), and evaluation of the clinical significance of relevant modalities of autogenic discharges. Armed with this knowledge, the therapist will find it easier to answer certain problems of differential diagnosis, and he is in a better position to give a positively oriented support to trainees. Resistance against autogenic training because of repeated occurrence of disagreeable modalities of autogenic discharges (e.g., pain in heart area) can be more easily detected and overcome, once the therapist discusses the patient's training protocols regularly (e.g., once a week). Case-specific problem-focussed discussions and explanations which help the patient understand that, for example, brain-controlled discharges do not result from organic disease but are phenomena which help the brain to reduce the disturbing potency of accumulated tension-producing material. It is in this connection that Table 4 and Table 5 provide an orientation concerning the nature and occurrence of those modalities of autogenic discharges which are of particular interest for the practice of autogenic training with patients suffering from disorders of the cardiovascular system.

Studies concerned with the question why certain trainees respond with an activation of disagreeable heart-discharges and why others react in a different manner are only beginning. So far it is only possible to state that there is some evidence indicating that "anxiety-death" dynamics appear to be decisively involved, and that these dynamics are frequently nourished, maintained and amplified by accumulated material involving (a) confrontation and identification with dying or dead relatives or friends, (b) participation in or witnessing of life-threatening accidents, (c) massive destructive impulses towards self and others, and (d) the consequences of negatively oriented religious education with fear of eternal sufferings in hell (see Fig. 6).

TABLE 4. *Normal Training Symptoms and Autogenic Discharges Involving the Heart, the Chest, or the Upper Trunk*

Localization	Heart						Chest						Upper Trunk					
Standard Exercises	I (%)	II (%)	III* (%)	IV (%)	V (%)	VI (%)	I (%)	II (%)	III* (%)	IV (%)	V (%)	VI (%)	I (%)	II (%)	III* (%)	IV (%)	V (%)	VI (%)
Feeling of heaviness	6.0	2.1	6.1	1.5	2.2	2.4	7.0	4.2	8.2	1.5	2.2	4.8	38.0	37.3	28.6	12.1	17.4	14.3
Feeling of warmth	4.0	6.2	10.2	18.2	4.3	9.5	8.0	8.3	8.2	9.1	17.4	14.3	29.0	32.3	26.5	21.2	39.1	30.9
Feeling of burning	—	—	—	—	—	—	1.0	—	—	—	3.0	—	2.0	—	—	—	—	—
Feeling of swelling	—	—	—	—	2.2	—	1.0	1.0	2.0	1.5	4.3	7.1	6.0	3.1	4.1	7.6	6.5	7.1
Feeling of itching	—	—	2.0	—	—	—	3.0	1.0	4.1	4.5	—	—	12.0	10.4	6.1	6.1	4.3	4.8
Feeling of tingling	—	—	—	—	—	—	3.0	3.1	2.0	1.5	2.2	4.8	15.0	9.4	6.1	9.1	8.7	4.8
Feeling of numbness	—	—	—	—	—	—	—	—	2.0	1.5	2.2	2.4	5.0	2.1	4.1	4.5	3.2	4.8
Circulatory sensations (pulsations, etc.)	7.0	4.2	20.4	4.5	10.9	4.8	9.0	6.2	16.3	6.1	8.7	—	20.0	11.4	34.7	15.1	19.6	4.8
Electrical sensations	1.0	—	2.0	—	—	—	2.0	1.0	—	—	—	—	7.0	2.1	4.1	4.5	2.2	—
Feeling of cold and coolness	—	—	2.0	1.5	—	2.4	—	1.0	—	1.5	—	2.4	—	6.2	6.1	3.0	—	—
Feeling of pressure (in or on)	3.0	1.0	18.4	4.8	13.0	4.8	8.0	8.3	22.4	9.1	15.2	14.3	16.0	11.4	28.6	13.6	23.9	16.7
Feeling of tension or tightness	4.0	4.2	2.0	3.0	—	2.4	7.0	6.2	8.2	4.5	4.3	4.8	28.0	21.9	18.9	19.7	10.9	11.9
Feeling of stiffness, inability to move	—	—	—	—	—	—	—	2.1	—	1.5	2.2	—	5.0	7.3	—	3.0	2.2	2.4
Muscular twitches, jerks	4.0	5.7	6.1	1.5	6.5	4.8	10.0	8.3	6.1	4.5	10.9	9.5	36.0	31.2	38.8	21.2	30.4	21.4
Pain, soreness	9.0	6.2	22.4	7.6	8.7	7.1	18.0	5.2	12.2	12.1	10.9	4.8	52.0	37.5	30.6	30.3	32.6	28.6

* Based on a survey of a mixed group of initially 100 psychosomatic and neurotic patients. The number of trainees who on occasion had noted a given "training symptom" during each of the six phases of autogenic standard training, is expressed in per cent. Eighteen patients with cardiac complaints were excluded from practicing the Third Standard Exercise, 5 others discontinued after starting; 18 had no difficulties, and 26 others continued after initial transitory difficulties. See also Table 1, p. 9; Table 5, p. 38; Table 6, p. 61.

Disorders of Cardiac Mechanisms

Connections between higher centers of the brain, parasympathetic (vagal) and sympathetic elements of the autonomic system, and the normal cardiac pacemaker (sinoatrial node), are known to participate together with other variables (e.g., adrenaline, thyroxine, carotid sinus reflex, blood temperature, organic lesions) in rhythm changes of the heart.

TABLE 5. *Modalities of Autogenic Discharges Particularly Disturbing for Patients with Heart Disorders and Psychophysiologic Cardiovascular Reactions**

Disturbing Modalities of Autogenic Discharges	Standard Exercises					
	I (%)	II (%)	III* (%)	IV (%)	V (%)	VI (%)
I. Cardiac:						
1. Heart: rhythm disturbed	5.0	2.1	22.4	6.1	10.9	7.1
2. Heart: marked acceleration	12.0	9.4	24.5	25.7	17.4	14.3
3. Heart: palpitation, pounding	13.0	5.2	18.4	7.6	13.0	9.5
4. Heart: cramp-like sensation	6.0	4.2	10.2	9.1	10.9	2.4
5. Heart: pain in left chest	2.0	3.1	20.4	9.1	—	7.1
II. Respiratory:						
1. Feeling of strangulation or suffocation (throat)	5.0	6.2	14.3	12.1	15.2	16.7
2. Oppressed, difficult respiration	10.0	6.7	14.3	10.6	4.3	4.8
III. Abdominal:						
1. Pain, disagreeable sensations in abdominal area	20.0	12.5	8.2	9.1	13.0	4.8
2. Feeling of nausea	13.0	13.5	14.5	6.1	6.5	4.8
IV. Psychoreactive:						
1. Anxiety, fear (during)	40.0	30.2	34.7	37.9	32.6	26.2
2. Anxiety, fear (after)	16.0	8.3	16.3	15.1	13.0	14.3
3. Depressed (during)	14.0	13.5	10.2	9.1	10.9	7.1
4. Depressed (after)	12.0	6.2	2.0	7.6	2.2	4.8
V. Others:						
1. Disagreeable feelings (not specified)	19.0	10.4	28.6	12.1	8.7	7.1
2. Dizziness	39.0	22.9	18.4	16.7	21.7	4.8
3. Difficulty of concentration	45.0	27.1	20.4	7.6	13.0	7.1
4. Had to stop exercise	21.0	11.4	14.3*	12.1	6.5	9.5

* Based on a survey of a mixed group of initially 100 psychosomatic and neurotic patients. The number of trainees who on occasion had noted a given "training symptom" during each of the six phases of autogenic standard training, is expressed in per cent. Eighteen patients with cardiac complaints were excluded from practicing the Third Standard Exercise, 5 others discontinued after starting; 18 had no difficulties, and 26 others continued after initial transitory difficulties. See also Table 1/I, p. 21; Table 5/I, p. 82; Table 6, p. 61.

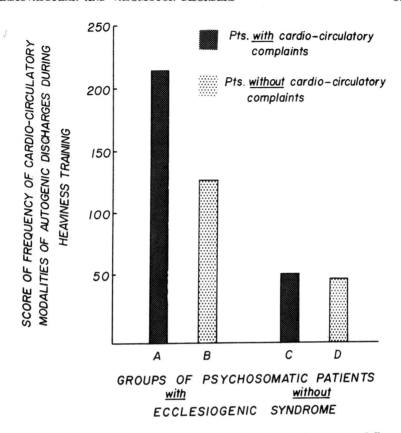

FIG. 6. Cardio-circulatory modalities of autogenic discharges in different groups of psychosomatic patients during corresponding periods of heaviness training.

The groups (A,B,C,D) are matched (sex, age, religion, educational and professional level, N = 15 per group). Groups A and C were found to have cardio-circulatory complaints or symptoms during the initial psychosomatic evaluation. Groups B and D had no relevant cardio-circulatory complaints or symptoms. Groups A and B suffered from psychoneurotic disorders, multiple psychophysiologic reactions and behavior pattern disturbances which (according to material obtained during autogenic abreactions) appeared to be related to, or which were amplified and reinforced by educational influences and other variables of ecclesiogenic nature ("ecclesiogenic syndrome"). Groups C and D also suffered from psychoneurotic disorders, multiple psychophysiologic reactions and relevant behavior pattern disturbances, however, without involvement of negatively oriented variables of ecclesiogenic nature. The difference between groups (A,B) with "ecclesiogenic syndrome" and those (C,D) without, is significant (P<.01). The difference between group A and group B is also significant (P<.01).[977]

Although the participating role of psychophysiologically oriented functions in disorders of cardiac rhythm requires further investigation, it is generally accepted that consideration of psychodynamic variables form an essential part in the clinical evaluation and therapeutic management (e.g., sedation) of patients with various disorders of cardiac mechanism. It is in this connection that treatment programs of certain cases with sinus bradycardia, sinus tachycardia, sinus arrhythmia, as well as ectopic disorders as, for example, auricular or ventricular extrasystoles and paroxysmal tachycardia, have included autogenic standard training (see references p. 68). However, apart from empirically obtained information based on clinical observations, no systematic research on the specific effects of autogenic standard exercises on disturbed patterns of cardiac rhythm have been carried out.

Sinus Bradycardia

The application of autogenic training in cases with *sinus bradycardia*, when the heart rate is less than 60 beats per minute, requires careful evaluation (e.g., raised intracranial pressure, myxedema, infections, jaundice, digitalism, myocardial infarction). After participation of relevant pathogenetic factors have been excluded, a very slow but regular practice of standard exercises is indicated. While W. Luthe[872,877,883,885,890,2065] observed 18 cases who gradually readjusted to normal ranges of heart frequency without any particular training difficulties, J. Seabra-Dinis[1565,1566] reported undesirable effects during the Third Standard Exercise (see Case 10).

Case 10: A male adult patient with bradycardia (62 per min.) practiced the first two standard exercises without experiencing any difficulties. When "Heartbeat calm and regular" was introduced, his heart rate slowed down to 46 and he had to stop the exercises.[1565,1566]

When sinus bradycardia is found in a patient with a history of myocardial infarction or other cardiac abnormalities (see Case: 13, p. 45; Case: 14, p. 49), a very gradual and slow progress through the formulae of the First Standard Exercise (heaviness), and a very slow progress with reduced formulae of the Second Standard Exercise (see Vol. I) is advisable. J. H. Schultz[1424] observed onset of disagreeable sensations of retrosternal pressure and bradycardia during warmth exercises in a patient who suffered a myocardial infarction eight years earlier. A similar, slow and careful approach is required, when trainees with functionally determined disorders of heart rhythm have been taking medication (e.g., quinidine, digitalis) which produces a slowing down of heart rate. In such instances, after cardiologic evaluation has excluded non-functional pathology, a very gradual withdrawal of medication (e.g., digitalis) during slowly progressing heaviness and warmth training with periodic electrocardiographic control, is recommended (see Case: 13, p. 45).

In cases with sinus bradycardia, the use of the Third Standard Formula ("Heartbeat calm and regular") requires case-specific evaluation. In most cases the formula can be used with beneficial effects. However, when a pattern of undesirable reactions (e.g., sharp drop of blood pressure, further decrease of heart rate, disagreeable sensations in chest, anxiety, dizziness, headache) is noted during slow heaviness and warmth training, it is advisable to postpone the heart formula until after the Sixth Standard Formula has been practiced. A careful control of training symptoms,[804] periodic studies of heart rate and blood pressure reactivity (see Fig. 14, p. 73), and occasional electrocardiographic evaluations are indicated.

Sinus Tachycardia

Autogenic Training has been recommended in cases with sinus tachycardia when the electrocardiogram is normal and the increase of rapid (about 100–160 beats per min.) and forceful heart action comes on gradually and tapers off as the cause (e.g., emotion, neurocirculatory asthenia, decrease of vagal tone, stimulation of the sympathetic accelerator nerve) is removed[115,141,149,639,771,872,1182,1537,1541,1952,2047] (see also p. 44). Encouraging observations with progressive normalization of unduly increased heart rates in patients with thyrotoxicosis have been also reported.[602,606,890] However, in all cases with tachycardia a thorough clinical evaluation and exclusion of other pathologic factors (e.g., pericarditis, myocarditis, anemia, infections, hypotension) must be carried out before autogenic training is applied (see Fig. 11, p. 64).

In most instances of uncomplicated sinus tachycardia (e.g., without involvement of anxiety reaction), the standard exercises can be applied without change, and progressive normalization can be expected. In certain cases paradoxical reactions with a further increase of heart rate (see Fig. 7, p. 42) and possible association with a sharp drop of blood pressure may occur (Case 24, 25, p. 74, 75). Considering these possibilities, periodic control of heart rate and blood pressure readings before and after each exercise are suggested. Patients who show patterns of paradoxical reactions during the first two standard exercises require clinical and psychodynamic reevaluation. When disagreeable autogenic discharges involve the cardiac area, it may or may not be preferable to postpone the Third Standard Formula until after "My forehead is cool" has been practiced. In intelligent patients a case-adapted explanation of

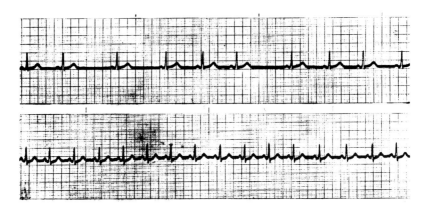

Fig. 7. Electrocardiographic changes after slow step-by-step progress with formulae of the First Standard Exercise in a 24-year-old nurse (anxiety, reaction, multiple phobic reactions, moderate depression, multiple psychophysiologic reactions).

Top: . Before starting autogenic training: sinus arrhythmia with bradycardia (56-60 beats/min.). Bottom: After six weeks of regular practice of heaviness exercises. Note increase of heart rate to 96 and improvement of regularity of rhythm.[872,877,883,885]

autogenic discharge activity may stimulate the tachycardiac trainee to practice "Heartbeat calm and regular" and, while remaining passive, give himself a good chance to make satisfactory progress towards normalization.

Sinus Arrhythmia

Rhythmic variations in the length of the cardiac cycles are frequently associated with sinus bradycardia (see Fig. 7). When there is reliable evidence that the heart rate is increasing with inspiration and decreasing with expiration, and participation of other factors can be excluded, the usual sequence of standard exercises can be applied. In these cases a progressive readjustment within four to twelve weeks of autogenic training has been observed.[771]

Frequently the main cause of sinus arrhythmia appears not to be related to irradiation from the respiratory center but to other variables (e.g., higher centers) which participate in bringing about abnormal reactivity of the medullary cardiac center with relevant variations of vagal tone and associated manifestations of vasomotor instability. Trainees with sinus arrhythmia belonging to this category are prone to show abnormal cardiac and vasomotor reactions (e.g., sharp increase or decrease of heart rate, drop of blood pressure, flushing of face or anterior neck and chest, dizziness) during autogenic training (see Fig. 7). Such abnormal reactivity requires a very slow step-by-step progress with the formulae of the First Standard Exercise, and case-adapted use of reduced warmth formulas (see Vol. I) during warmth training. This training program may extend over three to four months in certain cases. During this period the patient's abnormal reactivity tends to adjust, and additional benefit results from the Third Standard Exercise "Heartbeat calm and regular."[872,877,883,885] However, the use of this formula should be stopped when a pattern of undesirable reactions is noted. In such instances more emphasis is placed on the Fourth Standard Formula ("It breathes me").

Extrasystoles

Patients with premature contractions arising from impulses released by an abnormal focus in the ventricles or atria have responded well to autogenic training.[115,617,620,639,649,662,771,888,994,1182,1923,1952,2042] The application of autogenic standard exercises and the results are largely determined by the nature of the underlying condition and other participating factors (e.g., arteriosclerotic heart disease, tea, coffee, alcohol, anxiety, emotional tension, fatigue, dyspepsia, rheumatic carditis, hypertension, digitalis, hyperthyroidism, myocardial ischemia). Only after a careful clinical, cardiologic and psychophysiologic evaluation, can it be decided if autogenic training may be used as an adjunct in combination with other conventional forms of treatment, alone without medication, or not at all.

Since the annoying symptoms (e.g., choking sensations, "something very disagreeable, like a bang in my chest," irritation by skipped heart beats) are usually anxiety-promoting and tension-producing for certain patients (see Case 18, p. 66), case-adapted practice of autogenic exercises is usually indicated and very helpful in breaking up an unfavorable stress-oriented vicious circle (e.g., extrasystoles–apprehension–anxiety–increase of tension–more extrasystoles). Of a group of 18 patients with extrasystoles (11 functional, 4 with organic components and valvular lesions, 3 with non-cardiac focal infections), treated by H. Kenter[620] with autogenic training (no medication), disappearance of premature beats occurred in 15. Extrasystoles in the three patients with focal infections also disappeared, however, only after the sources of the infections were treated successfully. Similar results have been observed by H. Binder,[1923] J. A. Laberke,[771,2042] H. Kleinsorge and G. Klumbies[662] and D. Müller-Hegemann.[994]

When patients are unaware of their extrasystoles, their attention should not be drawn to this disorder while they are undergoing clinical investigation. For the same reason, the Third Standard Formula should be postponed until after practice of "My forehead is cool," or not be mentioned at all. In others, who are already worried about their heart (e.g., infarctophobia) individually adapted sequences of standard formulae with slow step-by-step progress during heaviness and warmth training and subsequent emphasis on the Fourth Standard Formula ("It breathes me") appears to be the most favorable approach.

Premature contractions in patients with a history of myocardial infarction (see p. 51, 57) may or may not respond to autogenic training (see Case 16, p. 58). However, even in cases with organically determined extrasystoles, a decrease of premature beats has been noted.[2065]

Normalization of pulsus bigeminus (when each normal beat is succeeded by a premature contraction and its compensatory pause) during autogenic training also has been reported (see Fig. 8).[620] Such effects should not be misunderstood as indicating that autogenic exercises can normalize disturbances of cardiac mechanisms which are due to, for example, digitalis intoxication.

Auricular Fibrillation

Of clinical interest are observations indicating that autogenic training may be even helpful in coping with functionally determined episodes of atrial fibrillation.[885,1952,2122] H. Kenter[620] reported two cases with non-organic paroxystic atrial fibrillation. Since no cause could be found, H. Kenter tried autogenic standard exercises. The paroxysms of fibrillation disappeared in both patients (control 24–36 months).

Paroxysmal Tachycardia

Episodes with rather sudden onset of rapid supraventricular or ventricular contractions (100–250 per min.) due to impulses released from an ectopic focus (atrial, ventricular, or AV node), and which are uninfluenced by rest, exercise or posture, can be reduced or eliminated by autogenic training.[141,160,581,617,620,621,649,658,760,761,771,885,888,896,994,1106,1182,1927,1952]

The possible involvement of heart disease (e.g., ischemic, coronary occlusion, overdosage with digitalis), the unpredictibility of onset and the variability of the duration of these sometimes very distressing attacks, call for a thorough clinical evaluation before autogenic approaches are used. When organic heart disease has been excluded and the arrhythmia is *supraventricular* (atrial, nodal), the standard sequence of autogenic exercises can be applied. Likewise, it is possible to approach episodes of usually *supraventricular* paroxysmal tachycardia encountered in patients with accelerated AV conduction (Wolff-Parkinson-White syndrome). Regular medical supervision, control of training symptoms, periodic evaluation of blood pressure and heart rate reactivity, before and after each standard exercise (see Case 13, Fig. 14, p. 73), are considered necessary for patient-adapted management of autogenic training.

When patients without attendant heart disease are digitalized (see Case 13), or have been taking barbiturates regularly, a slow and progressive withdrawal of these drugs, during slowly advancing phases of heaviness and warmth training, is indicated. As these patients kept practicing three to eight sets of standard exercises per day, their apprehension subsides, the attacks tend to become less frequent and milder,[160,581,620,760,761,771] they need less medication[896,994,1927] and start feeling progressively better.

Case 11: A 20-year-old laboratory technician was unable to continue her work because in increasing episodes of paroxysmal tachycardia. Her first attack had occurred during a traumatizing conflict situation four years earlier (for details see Ref. 658, p. 5). For 16 weeks, including hospitalization, she had been treated with various drugs (e.g., digitalis, barbiturates, tranquilizing medication) without success. At rest, her heart rate was about 80 per min., during attacks electrocardiographic recordings revealed a supraventricular tachycardia at a frequency of 190 per min.

It was decided to hospitalize the patient, and to stop all medication. Then, autogenic standard training was started. The paroxysmal tachycardia subsided, and after six weeks she was discharged. No further episodes of tachycardia occurred during an 18-month control period.[658]

Case 12: A 30-year-old income tax inspector suffered for years from episodes of paroxysmal tachycardia which were associated with feelings of weakness, marked perspiration, nausea. During the attacks the patient was afraid that he was about to die. Because of this he had seen twenty different physicians within a four-year period. Repeated examinations did not reveal any organic heart disease. He responded well to the reassuring presence of physicians and sedative medication.

Already during the initial phases of autogenic standard training the patient felt relaxed and generally more comfortable. The paroxysmal tachycardia disappeared and he had no further complaints during a 30-month control period.[141,617]

Case 13: A 44-year-old housewife (anxiety reaction, moderate depression, multiple allergic reactions, migraine type headaches, respiratory disorder, effort syndrome, dysmenorrhea, peripheral circulatory disorder, varicose veins, multiple pains and aches in various bodily areas, tinnitus, and attacks of paroxysmal auricular tachycardia with q.d. digitalis medication for six years; B.P. 112/60; E.C.G.: sinus bradycardia, rate 50 per min., rather low QRS voltage).

Six years earlier the patient had suffered a major attack of auricular paroxysmal tachycardia (210 per min.), which lasted for about 30 minutes. Since this episode, she took digitalis medication (Crystodigin 0.1 mg., q.d.), and her weekly attacks decreased in frequency. She had noted bouts of tachycardia, mostly occurring during the night, when on occasion she forgot to take her daily pill. Lately she had reduced the dosage to five tablets per week.

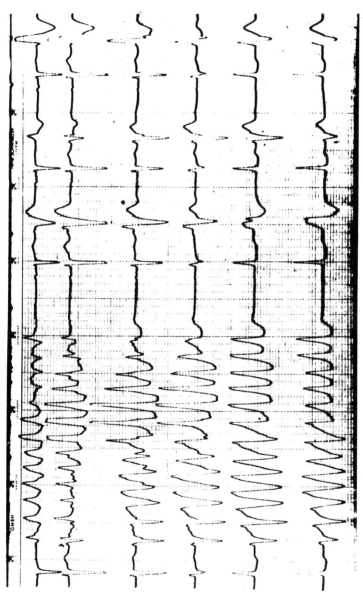

Fig. 8. Progressive normalization of ectopic paroxysm in a patient with mitral valvular disease, during passive concentration on "My arms and legs are heavy," and "Heartbeat calm and regular" ("Mein Herz arbeitet gleichmässig, ruhig und sicher"). *Top:* A sequence of rapid (220 per min.) ventricular contractions subsides (leads

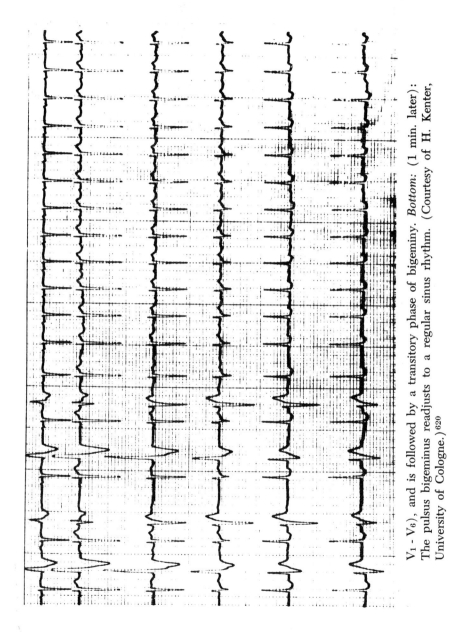

V_1 - V_6), and is followed by a transitory phase of bigeminy. *Bottom:* (1 min. later): The pulsus bigeminus readjusts to a regular sinus rhythm. (Courtesy of H. Kenter, University of Cologne.)[620]

With the beginning of autogenic training the digitalis medication was reduced to 0.1 mg. every second day. Heaviness training was normal. Warmth exercises were started at the beginning of the second week. On the 14th day, three minutes after a set of heaviness and warmth exercises, she experienced a brief episode (45 sec.) of paroxysmal tachycardia (rate: 192 per min.).

At the beginning of the third week the digitalis medication was lowered to 0.1 mg. every third day. The training progress remained normal.

The Third Standard Formula: "Heartbeat calm and regular" was introduced on the 22nd day.

During the preparatory discussion, this academically very well educated patient localized her heart in the epigastric area. Anatomical explanations helped her to localize the heart. However, during subsequent exercises she had considerable difficulties in establishing mental contact with her heart. The cardiac area was perceived as "just a space—nothing particular." Only after eleven days was she able to establish and maintain efficient mental contact with her heart. Meanwhile the digitalis had been reduced to 0.1 mg. every fourth day. No unfavorable cardiac or circulatory symptoms were noted. The Fourth Standard Formula was introduced during the sixth week, and digitalis limited to 0.1 mg. every fifth day. No untoward reactions occurred.

On the 54th day the digitalis medication was stopped, and the patient started with the Fifth Standard Exercise.

During this training phase, three weeks after the digitalis medication was stopped, an electrocardiographic control revealed a normal pattern with two favorable changes:

(a) an increase of QRS voltage, and (b) a regular heart rate of 65 per min.

During a twelve-month control period no further episodes of paroxysmal tachycardia were reported.[896]

The less common form of *ventricular* paroxysmal tachycardia is more serious (e.g., cardiac failure) and often associated with organic variables (e.g., ischemic heart disease) or overdosage with digitalis. Since very close clinical supervision is indicated in all cases, it is suggested that a very slow step-by-step application of autogenic training be started only when the patient is hospitalized and other variables (e.g., ECG, blood pressure, psychodynamic) are favorable. Existence of arteriosclerosis and ischemic heart disease in older patients indicate avoidance of prolonged passive concentration on heaviness and warmth in the limbs in order to circumvent unfavorable circulatory reactions resulting from an undue increase of peripheral blood flow. The emphasis is rather on carefully adapted approaches aiming at an increase of blood flow in the heart (e.g., "My heart is slightly warm," "My heart is agreeably warm") and prolonged phases of passive concentration on the Fourth Standard Formula ("It breathes me"). If and when a reduction or progressive elimination of supportive medication is permissible, must be decided from case to case.

Treatment results obtained with autogenic training are influenced by many variables (e.g., age, co-existence of other conditions, localization of ectopic focus, motivation to practice autogenic exercises regularly and frequently, post-traumatic reactions[360,898]). For example, H. Kenter[620] applied autogenic standard exercises to 8 patients with paroxysmal tachycardia. In five cases the disorder disappeared within 3–4 months (2 yr. control). The other three did not improve satisfactorily and required treatment by medication during attacks. J. Bobon, M. Breulet, M. Degossely and M. Dongier[160,1927] started autogenic training with 7 patients. Three dropped out before they learned the standard series of autogenic exercises and in the other four patients a 56 per cent decrease of attacks was noted. Similar improvements in eight cases were observed by A. Jouve and M. Dongier.[581]

Heart Block

Further research is required to determine the usefulness of autogenic training in coping with various types of heart block.[614,614a] However, since disorders of conduction and depression of impulse formation are often associated with ischemic heart disease (see p. 51), an increase of vagal tone, refractoriness and fatigue resulting from disorders of atrial rhythm (e.g., paroxysmal tachycardia), autogenic training with emphasis on improvement of coronary blood flow, may prove to be helpful in certain conditions.

With the increasing use of implantable pacemakers in patients with depression of impulse formation and conduction defects, autogenic training has found another field of application (see Case 14). The regular practice of case-adapted autogenic exercises appears to facilitate readjustment of cardio-circulatory functions and may be of decisive help in reducing unfavorable psychodynamic repercussions (e.g., anxiety, social withdrawal) related to the implications that one's life depends on the pacemaker (e.g., fear of damage to the pacemaker by accidents). It is in this connection that W. Schumacher's observations[1550] are of particular interest:

Case 14: A 28-year-old barber (history of diphtheria at age 5 and subsequent bradycardia: 40-50 per min., 32-33 per min. when hospitalized) suffered an atrioventricular block. He underwent operation and an electric pacemaker was implanted. The patient's recovery was uneventful and satisfactory. However, after this operation he did not feel well (pacemaker adjusted to 70 per min.). He complained about dizziness, fatigue, mild headaches, anxiety, perspiration, lack of self-confidence, insecurity, etc. He did not trust the pacemaker and was afraid he would die suddenly. In view of his anxiety reaction he was hospitalized again and underwent psychotherapy. After six weeks he appeared to have

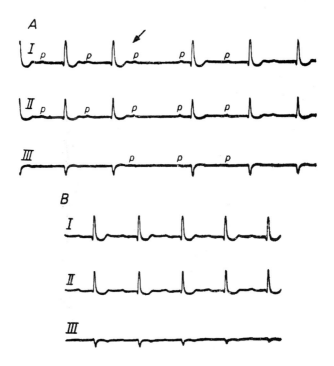

Fig. 9. Normalization of an incomplete AV block with dropped beats (Wenckebach phenomenon) during autogenic training in a female, hypertensive patient with obsessive-compulsive tendencies. A. Before autogenic training (see Wenckebach phenomenon). B. During autogenic training with disappearance of the incomplete AV block. (Courtesy of A. Katzenstein and St. Nitschkoff, Institut f. Kortiko-Viszerale Pathologie u. Therapie, Berlin-Buch.)[614,614a]

no particular complaints, was discharged and soon started again working as a barber. Several months later he was hospitalized because of a duodenal ulcer. A psychoanalytical approach was abandoned after about 10 hr. Then a more pragmatic two-stage procedure was adopted: (a) a series of 12 rest-hypnoses of about 15 min. each, with calming and encouraging support, and (b) subsequent introduction of autogenic training (heart exercise excluded). He progressed through the heaviness formulas in two weeks without difficulties. A modified Second Standard Formula (". . . is agreeably warm") was added, and the Fourth to Sixth Standard Formulae followed. During this period the patient felt progressively better and his anxiety subsided. After four weeks he felt well, he had regained his self-confidence, showed initiative, independence and even got slightly drunk on one occasion (never happened before). Another episode of gastric ulcer followed three months later.* After this he adapted

* The application of the Fifth Standard Formula to patients with a recent history of peptic ulcer is considered unfavorable.

to his 'weak stomach' and continued working as a barber. For 18 months he did not experience any further anxiety. When unexpectedly the power of his pacemaker started to drop and an exchange of batteries was necessary, he accepted the operation readily, and meanwhile helped himself with autogenic training.[1550]

ISCHEMIC HEART DISEASE

The application of autogenic training to patients suffering from various consequences of inadequate blood supply for the heart (e.g., angina pectoris, myocardial infarction, cardiac failure, arrhythmias) must be evaluated on clinical grounds in each case.

The clinical usefulness of autogenic training centers around two major areas: (a) non-specific psychophysiologic relaxation, and (b) promotion of desirable physiologic changes involving cardio-circulatory variables (e.g., decrease of vascular constriction, increase of coronary blood flow, peripheral vasodilatation, decrease of hypertension).[2181] Numerous clinical observations (see references of following sections, and p. 68) and a few experimentally oriented studies (see p. 119; Vol. IV) have contributed to our understanding of the clinically very favorable potentialities of autogenic approaches. In this connection it is, for example, of specific interest, that P. Polzien, in a group of 35 patients with repeatedly confirmed ST segment depression and lowering of the T wave (without any other cardiocirculatory disorder) observed an elevation of the ST segment and increase of the T wave by 0.05 mV or more in 28 patients during passive concentration limited to heaviness formulas of the First Standard Exercise (see Vol. IV).[1073,1083] Of clinical interest, as far as the prophylactic value of autogenic training is concerned, are studies by W. Luthe[885,892,2070] and Y. Aya[1910] showing significant lowering of elevated serum cholesterol levels in patients who practiced autogenic training (see Figs. 10, 24-28; and Vol. IV). In good correspondence with these findings are clinical observations by J. A. Laberke[760,761,2042] indicating that patients with angina pectoris are significantly less prone to develop myocardial infarction when they practice autogenic standard exercises (see p. 56).

It is understood that patients with evidence of ischemic heart disease require careful differential diagnostic evaluation, close medical supervision and, in cases where autogenic training is adopted as part of the treatment program, a case-adapted, well-controlled application of autogenic formulae.

ANGINA PECTORIS

Since attacks of various forms and degrees of ischemic pain do not permit a clear distinction between angina pectoris and myocardial infarc-

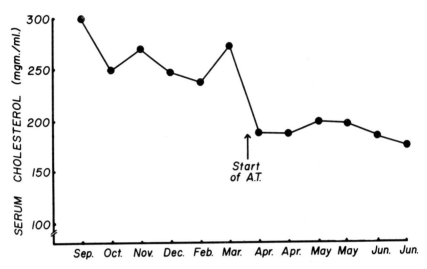

Fig. 10. Lowering of serum cholesterol after a patient with myocardial infarction started practicing autogenic standard exercises regularly. (Courtesy of Y. Aya, Oskar Vogt Institute, Kyushu University, Fukuoka.)[1910]

tion, the application of autogenic training to patients with angina should be undertaken with the same care and respect as in cases with infarction.

Clinical and experimental observations indicate that autogenic training is useful during the following three treatment phases of ischemic heart disease:

1. During the prophylactic phase, in order to forestall early development of ischemic heart disease in "coronary prone individuals."

2. After appearance of angina (as a valuable adjunct in combination with other forms of conventional treatment) during early stages of oncoming attacks.

3. During long-term therapy, in combination with other conventional means of therapeutic management.

Prophylactic application. Ideally, the regular practice of autogenic standard exercises should be started as early as possible and become a routine means of self-protection in "coronary prone persons." This view is based on the multidimensional psychodynamically and physiologically oriented stress-neutralizing effects of autogenic training, as they are presented in the various sections of this book. Better adjustment of blood pressure, of cardiac activity, of coronary and peripheral circulation, buffering and reduction of psychologic stress, as well as lowering of serum cholesterol (see Subject Index, p. 117, 121) are some of the factors which are considered helpful in delaying or preventing undue acceleration of progressive atheromatosis, the onset of angina pectoris and the possibility of myocardial infarction.[479] Apart from the daily benefits resulting from a regular practice of standard exercises, a well trained person has better possibilities of adjusting favorably to ischemic conditions in case they should develop.*

After appearance of angina pectoris. When occlusive coronary artery disease has advanced to the point of producing a relative imbalance between oxygen supply and oxygen needs of the myocardium, the use of autogenic training may be considered.

Since a patient's first episodes of anginal pain are conventionally followed by a thorough clinical evaluation of his condition (e.g., participation of anemia, thyrotoxicosis, valvular disease, arrhythmias) there is little possibility that autogenic training is applied to anginal patients who are not yet under medical care. However, even when new patients with angina pectoris claim that they have been investigated in the past, autogenic training should not be started without carrying out another reassuring clinical evaluation. Participation of psychodynamic disorders (e.g., anxiety reaction, depression, accumulated aggression, infarctophobia) require adequate therapeutic management. Furthermore, since unpredictable massive autogenic discharges (e.g., anxiety, motor, sensory, palpitations, difficulty of respiration, dizziness) may occur in trainees with a history of severe accidents (e.g., car crash, sports), a careful screening of the patient's history is required in this direction (see Case: 19/I, p. 83; Case 20/I, p. 84; Case 13, p. 45).

In simple cases of angina pectoris, when reliable collaboration of the patient is ascertained and regular medical supervision and control is possible, autogenic training may be started.[1952] The emphasis is on a slow step-by-step progress through the heaviness formulae of the First Standard Exercise. Training protocols require periodic discussion, about once a week. The use of case-specific medication (e.g., nitroglycerin, tranquilizers) should not be discouraged. Since anginal attacks are more likely to occur in a recumbent than in a sitting posture, preference must be given to practice of autogenic exercises in the reclining chair posture and the simple sitting posture (see Vol. I). The use of passive concentration on a peaceful background image is considered helpful for many patients. However, patients with obsessive manifestations (e.g., chronic sexual deprivation), anxiety states, grief reactions and post-traumatic psychodynamic disorders may experience difficulties in finding or holding

---

* The American Heart Association and other organizations interested in the prevention of heart disease appear to be blissfully unaware of one of the most effective approaches in their own field.

a peaceful background image. When such difficulties are noted, the use of a peaceful image should be immediately stopped, and passive concentration strictly limited to the autogenic formulae. In cases where this rule is not observed, the therapist may unexpectedly find himself confronted with complicated tension and anxiety-producing dynamics of spontaneously developing processes of autogenic abreactions. In such instances tranquilizing medication is useful. When trainees with angina pectoris have difficulty in finding or maintaining a peaceful image, or when passive concentration on standard formulae is frequently disturbed by powerful interferences of disagreeable thoughts, it is advisable to practice series of very brief (15–30 sec.) exercises until it becomes easier for the patient to maintain passive concentration for longer periods.

Problems requiring careful differential diagnostic evaluation may arise from autogenic discharges involving the heart or chest (e.g., pain, pressure, constriction, palpitation, shortness of breath, dizziness, epigastric discomfort, nausea). After clinically significant changes have been excluded and the nature and pattern of such discharge modalities has been determined, it is important to explain in detail the harmless and rather beneficial nature of such training symptoms.

Periodic control of heart rate and blood pressure reactivity before, during and after autogenic exercises is recommended. Unwanted circulatory reactions (e.g., sharp drop of blood pressure, bradycardia, tachycardia, flushing of face) require prompt attention. Individual adaptation of formulae, duration of passive concentration, number of exercises per set (e.g., two instead of three) help to avoid unfavorable reactions.

The warmth formulae of the Second Standard Exercise are not introduced as long as a trainee shows undue vasomotor reactions or other undesirable training symptoms (e.g., paradox reactions, increase of heart rate, increase of blood pressure, feelings of anxiety, strong motor discharges, dizziness, onset of headaches).

When the trainee's progress is uneventful, the warmth formulas (starting out with the right arm) are introduced one by one at weekly intervals. When unduly strong circulatory reactions are observed, slower progress with reduced warmth formulas (see Vol. I) is indicated. Reflectory connections between the left arm (proximal portion) and coronary blood flow are of particular importance for anginal patients. During advanced phases of warmth training, a step-by-step (l. hand, l. wrist, l. forearm, l. elbow, l. upper arm, l. shoulder) procedure of passive concentration on warmth in the left arm has been recommended.[639,662,1182] According to H. Kleinsorge[639] and G. Klumbies[662] electrocardiographic evidence (e.g., elevation of ST segment) supported the assumption that an increase of coronary blood flow can be achieved indirectly by passive concentration on warmth in the left arm (with emphasis on the proximal arm and shoulder portions).

The Third Standard Formula ("Heartbeat calm and regular") is usually postponed until the end of the standard series of autogenic exercises.[756, 864,1002,1003,1424] Depending on the psychophysiologic reactivity of each case, modified heart formulae are used (e.g., "Heartbeat calm and easy"). [574,755,757,758,760] The relieving effect of the heart formula may be reinforced by passive concentration on "flowing warmth to the heart"[987,994] or, "My heart is agreeably warm." Trainees who use these organ-specific approaches usually note an agreeable sensation of warmth in the cardiac area.[896] This effect supports the hypothesis that passive concentration on warmth in the cardiac area improves coronary circulation and contributes to widening of inter-coronary collateral channels in patients with coronary artery disease.

The Fourth Standard Formula ("It breathes me") usually follows after satisfactory progress with the warmth formulae of the Second Standard Exercise has been made. This formula is generally appreciated by the trainee because of its calming and relieving effects. In certain patients, favorable training effects can be enhanced by reducing passive concentration on warmth in the limbs (with exception of the left arm) to very short periods, and by remaining for longer periods with the Fourth Standard Formula.

The Fifth Standard Formula ("My solar plexus is warm" has occasionally caused some undesirable reactions.[1175,1424] Sometimes these are related to disagreeable modalities of autogenic discharges (see Tables 4-6; Cases 10, 24, 25), sometimes there is indication that changes of the gastrointestinal motor pattern or hemodynamic changes (see Case 48), are involved. When, during or after the introduction of "My solar plexus is warm," undesirable training reactions are noted, it is preferable to practice this formula only for very brief (e.g., 10–20 sec.) periods. In anginal patients with a history of gastritis, peptic ulcer, or association of anginal attacks with epigastric pain,[1175] it is preferable not to use the Fifth Standard Exercise. Furthermore, it is suggested that passive concentration on abdominal areas be avoided, when these have been involved in accidents or relevant traumatisms (e.g., "hit into the abdomen with brief loss of consciousness at age 13").

The Sixth Standard Formula ("My forehead is cool") may activate disturbing autogenic discharges (e.g., headaches, throbbing, pressure, anxiety, dizziness) in patients with a history of accidents involving the cranial region. However, a modified standard formula: "My forehead is *agreeably* cool," may be tried.

Although it can not be expected that significant organic changes can be reversed, clinically encouraging and sometimes surprisingly good results in patients with advanced coronary sclerosis have been observed.[141,156,160, 161,302,410,574,581,620,639,646,649,658,659,662,669,755,757,758,760,761,771,773,883,885,888,930,935, 994,1001,1003,1072,1163,1171,1175,1182,1433,1528,1927,1952,1979,1986,2042]

With regular and frequent practice of case-adapted autogenic exercises, most patients note definite improvement after four to eight weeks. Associated disorders as, for example, headaches and sleep disturbances subside; various other disorders (e.g., constipation, shortness of breath, belching, "gas pains") tend to disappear; apprehension, tenseness and anxiety decrease; anginal attacks occur less frequently and are less severe.[160,302,410,581,658,757,760,1163,1433,1927,2155] During more advanced phases of autogenic standard training, patients are able to control tachycardia and many learn to intercept oncoming attacks without the help of nitroglycerin.[620,760,935] For example, H. Kenter[620] reported on a group of 42 stenocardiac patients, who were treated only with autogenic training (no medication). In 34 cases the anginal symptoms disappeared. H. Kenter also noted that small groups of four to five outdoor patients did better than small groups of hospitalized patients.[620] J. H. Schultz,[1377] who treated 80 anginal cases (27 of predominantly organic and 53 of predominantly vasomotor nature) reported no success in 27 cases, very good results in 38, and moderate but significant improvements in 15 patients. Similar results were observed by J. A. Laberke,[757] A. Jouve and M. Dongier,[581] and J. Bobon, M. Breulet, M. Degossely and M. Dongier.[160,1927]

Long-term therapy. Together with other conventional measures (e.g., weight reduction, dietary adaptation, elimination of smoking, moderate physical exercise, avoidance of stressors, drugs) the regular practice of case-adapted daily programs of autogenic exercises is considered a valuable adjunct in long-term therapy. Apart from multidimensional psychophysiologic relaxation, the emphasis is on case-adapted passive concentration on warmth in the cardiac area. Regular promotion of favorable hemodynamic and metabolic functions (e.g., lowering of elevated levels of serum cholesterol[885,892,1910,2070]) are essential elements of an efficient long-term treatment program (see Figs. 24-27). In this connection J. A. Laberke's observations of two groups of clinically comparable anginal patients are of clinical interest. Thirty-one practiced autogenic training, while the other group of 30 patients relied on medication only. In the control group of untrained patients there were four infarctions within one to four years of observation. No infarctions occurred during the same period in the patients who practiced autogenic training.[760,761]

The long-term use of autogenic training by patients with ischemic heart disease is, however, associated with certain problems. Firstly, certain patients feel so well that they are prone to forget about their organically determined limits of permissible activities.[574,1175,1433] J. H. Schultz[1433,1528] observed a few cases who died at later points without forewarning. The same category of patients also tends to reject periodic medical controls, and they also tend to stop practicing autogenic training because they think the time-consuming exercises are not needed anymore. Secondly, a number of patients give up autogenic training because friends, nurses,[620] dentists or other physicians with inadequate, outdated, or incomplete knowledge of autogenic training discredit the method. Thirdly, and this is a conclusion from more recent observations,[896] there is a reasonable probability that spontaneous and abortive brain dynamics of autogenic neutralization are triggered by certain events, and that the usually disagreeable psychophysiologic consequences of this motivate the patient to stop autogenic training and resort to drugs.

Considering the pathologic implications of ischemic heart disease, and the known problems associated with long-term practice of autogenic training, it is a medical responsibility to impress the anginal patient with the need for periodic medical control and guidance. The patient should feel invited to call any time when unusual training symptoms or other phenomena are noticed. Particular attention is indicated when anginal patients have been involved in recent traffic accidents or mortality of persons close to the patient has occurred.

MYOCARDIAL INFARCTION

Clinically controlled observations of patients who suffered myocardial necrosis, and who learned autogenic training towards the end of a satisfactory recovery period (see Case 15; Case 17) has encouraged the clinically controlled application of case-adapted autogenic exercises in this area.[141,144,160,302,315,410,503,618,620,771,888,935,994,1111,1175,1424,1433,1923,1927,1952,2217, 2266,2297,2321]

Until further clinical information is available autogenic training should not be used during doubtful or impending infarction,[1175] during and after acute episodes, and in the presence of complicating disorders (e.g., arrhythmias, pulmonary embolism; extension of the infarct to the endocardial surface with systemic embolism). The question of how soon after a myocardial infarction autogenic training may be started, varies from case to case, depending on the clinical development, the nature of the myocardial lesion and medically satisfactory recuperation of each patient.[1433]

When autogenic training is applied, the same principles as described for angina pectoris (p. 53-57) must be observed. However, clinical controls are more frequent, and vigilant supervision is required.

After myocardial infarction has occurred, autogenic training has been found particularly helpful in reducing episodes of cardiac pain and anxiety of suffering another infarction, thus helping to break up a vicious circle of unfavorable negative reinforcement.[141,144,160,302,410,503,618,620,771, 888,935,1923,1927] H. Kenter[618,620] treated 27 patients with infarctophobia successfully with autogenic training. None of these patients suffered a myocardial infarction during a 5–7 year control period.[620]

Other clinical observations indicate that even in patients with marked organic lesions, carefully adapted autogenic exercises can help decisively to improve a patient's condition (see Case 15, Case 16).

Case 15: A 55-year-old female patient: paroxysmal tachycardia, severe myocardial damage, left ventricular hypertrophy and ventricular premature contractions (13 per min.).

The patient's heart disorder had deteriorated over a four-year period. She was unable to carry out light work at home, and for the last two years she spent most of the time in bed. Drug treatment (e.g., digitalis, quinidine) was of only transitory benefit. A combined approach consisting initially of (a) rest-hypnoses with prolonged periods of sleep, (b) autogenic training, and (c) gradual withdrawal of all medication was applied. This initial treatment program resulted in a progressive improvement. The second phase of treatment emphasized frequent practice of autogenic standard exercises in combination with gradually increasing physical activity. Electrocardiographic controls verified progressive normalization with disappearance of the previously existing disorders of cardiac mechanisms. The patient improved to the point where she was able to carry out routine housework. She continued practicing autogenic training three times a day at home, and felt well for about one year. She was then asked for a control check-up to be carried out in a small neighborhood hospital. There, against her wish, she was treated again with medication. This was followed by rapid deterioration and she was transferred to our hospital (University of Leipzig). By following the same treatment program, as outlined above, the patient improved and regained a satisfactory condition permitting her to carry out household activities as before.[994]

Case 16: A physician with myocardial infarction (8 years earlier) followed by dilatation and period of sinus arrhythmia, noticed frequent onset of retrosternal pressure, bradycardia and arrhythmia while practicing standard exercises. Occasionally these symptoms became so disturbing, that he preferred to interrupt the exercise. On other occasions, however, he had noticed that the formula: "Heart calm, regular and warm" ("ruhig, regelmässig, warm durchströmt das Herz") seemed to reduce, dissolve and eliminate such cardiac symptoms when they were already present during the Second Standard Exercise (Warmth).

Considering the question of whether autogenic training might be contraindicated in his case, and respecting his wish to continue practicing standard exercises, it was suggested (a) to change the standard sequence of formulas by putting the Third Standard Exercise (Heart Formula) at the end of the entire Standard Series, and (b) considering the patient's observation, namely that his complaints had frequently started with the Second Standard Exercise (Warmth), he was advised to reduce passive concentration on the Warmth and the Solar Plexus Formula to three mental repetitions (instead of six times as he had done previously). Observing these technical changes, no further disturbing phenomena were noted.[1424]

Case 17: A 65-year-old unmarried teacher (homosexual, obsessive dynamics) suffered a myocardial infarction. After being discharged from the hospital, her previously very active life changed into a pattern of isolation and seclusion. Another infarction occurred six months later. When she was seen, she conveyed that her daily life was overshadowed by constant anxiety. She did not see any friends, she had given up her teaching position, and she was no longer interested in reading. After three months of autogenic training her life pattern had reverted completely. She practiced her exercises regularly with a lot of good will, but, as badly as possible and without attaining profound relaxation. In spite of these shortcomings, the exercises helped her to resume a normal pattern of daily life. The electrocardiographic changes normalized and the anginal attacks disappeared completely.[1163,1171]

CARDIOVASCULAR COMPLAINTS AND PSYCHOREACTIVE DISORDERS

In this section an attempt is made to discuss the application of autogenic training to patients who do not suffer from any heart disease but who have complaints involving the heart and cardiovascular functions. Conditions which, for example, have been termed "cardiac neurosis," "neurocirculatory asthenia," "functional heart disease," "psychophysiologic cardiovascular reaction," "effort syndrome," "somatization reaction affecting circulatory system" are considered.

Clinically and therapeutically it is important to attempt a differential diagnostic distinction between complaints arising from disorders which are exclusively, dominantly, partly or largely not associated with combinations of a variety of psychodynamic disorders and normal processes of reactive brain discharges (see Table 4, p. 37; Table 5, p. 38).

Since intercurrent events (e.g., traffic accidents, sudden death in family), intervening infections, endocrine (e.g., hyperthyroidism) and other pathologic factors, as well as the variable nature of participating psychodynamic disorders (see Table 6, p. 61) may significantly modify a trainee's reactivity to autogenic training (see Fig. 9/I), vigilant consideration of differential diagnostic perspectives are of particular importance in the therapeutic management of patients with psychodynamic disorders and cardiovascular complaints.

Within the same categories of psychodynamic disorders, the intensity, frequency and overall pattern of auotgenic discharges may vary con-

siderably with, for example, the number and traumatizing impact of accidents (e.g., drowning episodes, sports, traffic); the frequency and intensity of identification with dying or deceased persons (e.g., brother,
uncle, father) and influences resulting from religious education (see
Table 6, p. 61; Fig. 6; 9/I).

W. Luthe and M. Morissette[977,2065] ran into interesting difficulties while
attempting to test the hypothesis that patients with cardiovascular complaints (e.g., palpitations, cardiac pain, spasms in left chest), as noted
during the initial psychosomatic evaluation, experience autogenic discharges of cardiovascular modalities (e.g., palpitation, pounding, heart
pain, spasms, pulsations) more frequently than other patients who initially did not have any cardiovascular complaints (see Fig. 6, p. 39).
While screening the clinical material in order to match the subjects of
both groups (with and without cardiovascular complaints), it became
evident that the patient's initial cardiac complaints appeared to be of
less importance than expected, and that the intensity, frequency and
overall pattern of cardiovascular discharges appeared to occur more frequently in patients with a particular fear of "sudden death," punishment
by God, damnation and eternal sufferings in hell (as verified by brain-
directed dynamics during autogenic abreaction; see Case 38/I). This
observation led to a modification of initial planning. It appeared necessary to compare four groups (see Table 6). Here again, difficulties were
encountered while attempting to match a suitable number of patients
composing each group. From among 150 cases with verified "ecclesiogenic anxiety," only a small number had no cardiovascular complaints.*

The results (see Table 6) indicate that there is no significant difference
between cardiovascular discharges noted by trainees without "ecclesiogenic anxiety,"[2066] whether they initially have cardiovascular complaints
or not. Quite different is the reactivity of trainees with "ecclesiogenic
anxiety." This group (N = 30) notes a significantly (P < .001) higher
incidence of cardiovascular modalities of autogenic discharges in general.
Furthermore it is of clinical interest, that the group of trainees (with
"ecclesiogenic anxiety") who initially had pronounced cardiovascular
complaints noticed a significantly higher (P < .001) incidence of discharge modalities more directly related to cardiac structure or function,
than the group without relevant complaints. There is no significant difference between the pulsation scores, although pulsations are noted sig-

---

* This observation corresponds well with relevant clinical observations concerning
the incidence of cardiovascular complaints in psychosomatic and neurotic patients:
96 per cent in a group of 50 catholic priests; 57 per cent in catholic patients (W.
Luthe[2065,2066]), and according to H. Enke,[1087, p. 56] 19.4 per cent (N=273) in a predominantly non-catholic, however, ethnically different group of patients.

TABLE 6. *Cardiovascular Discharges during Heaviness Exercises in Psychosomatic Patients with and without Cardiovascular Complaints**

Groups of Patients	With Cardiovascular Complaints or Symptoms				Without Cardiovascular Complaints or Symptoms			
	Age	Total score: CV discharges	Pulsation score†	Total CV score minus pulsation score	Age	Total score: CV discharges	Pulsation score†	Total CV score minus pulsation score
With "ecclesiogenic anxiety" (N=15)	33.3	215	72	143	30.1 (N=15)	128	68	60
Without "ecclesiogenic anxiety" (N=15)	33.7	52	23	29	34.0 (N=15)	50	26	24

* The study is based on a comparison of four reasonably well matched groups (sex, age, occupational level of activity) of 15 subjects each. The two groups with "ecclesiogenic anxiety" are composed of patients in whom (during autogenic abreactions) fear of damnation with eternal sufferings in hell ("sudden death") was found to play a particularly important role (see Case 38, Vol. I). Such dynamics, as related to ecclesiogenic education, were not observed in the control group.

† Since pulsations are not necessarily directly related to the heart but may be viewed as a circulatory phenomenon, the pulsation score was treated separately.

nificantly more frequently ($P < .001$) by trainees with "ecclesiogenic anxiety," than by trainees of the corresponding control groups.

Differences of reactivity during autogenic standard exercises, as for example found in trainees with "ecclesiogenic anxiety," imply practical consequences as far as taking the patient's case history (e.g., accidents, undue reinforcement of anxiety by religious education), application of autogenic therapy and therapeutic management (e.g., supportive drugs) in general, is concerned.

In many patients with cardiovascular complaints, the heaviness training serves as a valuable screening period.[617] When the patient's case history reveals unfavorable and habitually complicating factors (e.g., severe accidents, repeated loss of consciousness, unduly strong fear of "sudden death," negatively oriented religious education), it is advisable to proceed slowly with the heaviness and warmth formulae. In most cases it may be advantageous to drop or to postpone the Third Standard Formula ("Heartbeat calm and regular"). When the heart formula is used, effective support by relevant discussions (see below) is required (see Case 18/I, p. 76; Case 13, p. 45). When undesirable reactions occur, it is generally preferable to drop the heart formula (see Case 19/I, p.

83; Case 20/I, p. 84), and to proceed with the Fourth Standard Exercise (see Case 21/I, p. 95).

In cases with a variety of cardiac symptoms, such as palpitation, extrasystoles and "nervous tachycardia," a reduced step-by-step approach (e.g., right hand, forearm, whole arm) is required if the trainee notes an increase in heart rate or disagreeable palpitation and "pounding" during passive concentration on heaviness and warmth. During heaviness and warmth training the sequence of the trainee's topographic orientation should be arranged in such a way that passive concentration on heaviness or warmth in the left arm is preceded by sufficient training of the other limbs. A preferable sequence is: (1) right arm, (2) right leg, (3) right side, (4) left leg, (5) both legs, (6) left arm, which sequence is later summarized by "My arms and legs are heavy" or respectively "My arms and legs are warm."

When organic disease of the heart can be excluded, and there is sufficient evidence that the patient's complaints are of a psychoreactive nature, it is advisable that the taking of any specific drugs be discontinued when autogenic training is initiated. It is equally important for successful treatment with autogenic training to reassure the patient with cardiac complaints that the clinical evaluation did not find any organic or other disease, but that it is known that certain brain functions (e.g., spontaneous brain discharges), undue concern, vigilant supervision of one's heart and other psychodynamic functions may produce such and such complaints, and influence or interfere with the normal self-regulatory mechanisms of cardiac activity.[1986] Patient-adapted discussions of this nature are of particular importance, because the practice of autogenic exercises is frequently associated with a transitory increase of some of the symptoms the patient is complaining about (see sections on autogenic discharges; Table 1/I, p. 21; Table 6/I, p. 143; Table 4, p. 37; Table 5, p. 38; Table 6, p. 61). For this reason the therapist must be familiar with the nature, the occurrence and the psychophysiologic aspects of autogenic discharge activity. This also implies that differential diagnostic problems can be dealt with more efficiently. The reassuring knowledge that even disagreeable autogenic training symptoms are not coming from a diseased heart, but are actually due to self-regulatory transitory processes of unloading from certain parts of the central nervous system, is an important base for the patient to maintain a passively accepting attitude when such symptoms occur during or after autogenic exercises.

In case the patient is not familiar with these aspects, he may get apprehensive about disagreeable discharges, and by trying to fight the brain's physiologically determined desire to unload, more tension and anxiety may result,[804] thus leading to a reinforcement of negatively oriented vicious circles. The patient may then have the impression that autogenic training makes his condition worse, and consequently he tends to break off further treatment.[160,1927] Doubtful patients should be encouraged to have another ECG in order to convince them that the heart action is normal.

An inspection of Table 1/I, p. 21, and Table 5, p. 38, leads to the conclusion that the Third Standard Formula stimulates certain modalities of disagreeable discharges in a higher number of psychosomatic and neurotic patients than do other formulae. For this reason, a careful patient-adapted evaluation should determine whether this formula is used in the usual standard sequence, at the end (after VI), or not at all. Many patients who have become familiar with their brain's pattern of autogenic discharges, and who have learned to maintain an attitude of passive acceptance will make faster progress by using the Third Standard Formula ("Heartbeat calm and regular") after six to eight weeks of heaviness and warmth training. However, even in these cases the trainee with psychoreactive cardiac complaints, vasomotor instability, infarctophobia and relevant anxiety reactions (e.g., post-traumatic; "ecclesiogenic anxiety," fear of sudden death and eternal punishment by terrible sufferings in hell[2065,2066]), reassuring support and regular supervision is required.

In a number of cardio-neurotic patients, D. Langen found it helpful to postpone the Third Standard Formula until after the patients had gained a sufficient neutral attitude by using the Intentional Formula "Whatever the situation, heart does not matter" ("Herz in jeder Situation vollkommen gleichgültig").[804]

After three to five weeks of regular training (heaviness and warmth) most patients note some significant improvement. They report that they feel much calmer and that their sleep is better. Hypochondriac attitudes (e.g., frequent observation of heart rate) subside. Palpitations, "jumps" or "skips," attacks of tachycardia, pain in the heart region and feelings of oppression in the chest are less frequent and less disturbing. A number of concomitant symptoms characteristic of a neurotic pattern, such as respiratory disorders, meteorism, constipation, nausea, dizziness, headache, ringing in the ears, sighing, faintness, flushes and irritability, tend to disappear spontaneously or fade away gradually. The respiratory exercise ("It breathes me") reinforces the effects of the heaviness and warmth training. Many trainees find this exercise particularly relieving, and some tend to give up therapy after this training phase because they have regained self-assurance and well-being. However, it should be emphasized that the patients should continue doing the exercises for at least five to

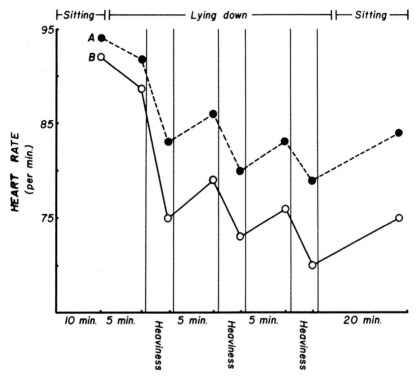

FIG. 11. The effect of heaviness exercises (90 sec. each) upon sinus tachy-cardia in a 24-year-old student. (A) "My arms are heavy" (first week), (B) "'My arms and legs are heavy" (second week).

eight months. The solar plexus exercise and passive concentration on "My forehead is cool" should be practiced, while the heart exercise may not be mentioned at all. The patient should be invited to participate in regular control sessions, and the therapist should follow carefully the patient's notes on the training symptoms.

The therapeutic results reflected by Table 7, correspond well with ob-servations by other authors.[2,3,96,129,130,141,203,269,274,275,302,312,319,378,410,444,466,] [514,525,532,574,602,606,647,649,657,756,757,771,852,885,888,994,1024,1072,1163,1182,1200,1528,1547,] [1566,1923,1927,1932,1950,1951,1952,1954,1979,1986,2042,2122,2181,2194]

J. A. Laberke[771] who reported on 740 patients suffering from various cardiocirculatory disorders, and who learned autogenic training, observed that the method is of decisive help in about 80 per cent of these patients. Independently, T. Abe, S. Iwabuchi, Y. Ishibashi and K. Kihara[2,3] who applied autogenic training to 900 psychosomatic and neurotic patients arrived at the same conclusion (80%) for the group of patients with cardiocirculatory disorders and psychoreactive cardiac complaints.

TABLE 7. *Therapeutic Results in Patients with Psychoreactive Cardiac Complaints*

Authors	Diagnosis	No. of Patients Practicing AT Adequately	Cured or Very Good Results	Significant Improvement	Some Improvement	No Change	Remarks
J. Bobon et al. 160, 1927*	Neurotic, psychoreactive	18	4	11		3	+7 other patients dropped out early
M. Demangeat and J. Darquey 265, 270, 273	Anxiety reaction, psychoreactive	28+	11	10	7		+12 outpatients; 16 hospitalized patients, received supportive medication
Th. Kammerer et al. 360, 416, 612	Neurotic, psychoreactive, 3 post-traumatic anxiety reaction	16	5	8		3+	+post-traumatic reactions
H. Kenter 617	"Cor nervosum"	40	39			1+	+developed cyclothymic depression 2 wk. after starting A.T.
H. Kenter 618, 620	Infarctophobia	27	27				4–6 yr. control, no myocardial infarction
Y. Sasaki 2122	Neurotic, pyschoreactive	4	1	1	2		
Total Results		133	87	30	9	7	
			88%			12%	

*Reference numbers in this column refer to bibliography.

Case 18: A 34-year-old physician who had noticed episodes of extrasystoles, was concerned about the possibility of myocardial infarction. Repeated electrocardiographic controls were normal. In spite of this and in spite of reassuring statements made by cardiologists he remained fearful of an impending myocardial infarction. A variety of distractive activities (e.g., sports, pleasure) and the use of sedative medication did not help. Maintaining a sceptical attitude he finally started practicing autogenic training. During the sixth week, after the Fourth Standard Exercise ("It breathes me") had been introduced, the physician radiantly informed his colleague that the new exercise enabled him to control his "heart attacks" quickly and reliably.[617]

Case 20: A 52-year-old teacher, who for twelve years had suffered from disagreeable awareness of extrasystoles (vagotonic ECG with sinusbradycardia and hypertrophy of the left heart without definite damage of the myocardium), reported normal progress during the heaviness and warmth phases of autogenic therapy. The subsequent introduction of the heart exercise resulted in an increase in the patient's awareness of the extrasystoles. Thereupon, passive concentration on the heart was discontinued and instead "It is breathing me" was introduced as the next exercise. When abdominal warmth was experienced regularly, passive concentration on the heart was possible without any disagreeable side- or after-effects. The extrasystoles disappeared; simultaneously, normalization of a slight hypertension and of dyspneic tendencies was noted. Residual symptoms: feeling of oppression during periods of atmospheric disturbances.[1384,1377]

Case 21: A 55-year-old female patient (diagnosis: "cardiac insufficiency, cardiac asthma") had been treated for a number of years without satisfactory results. Electrocardiograms were repeatedly negative; no symptoms of decompensation. There was shortness of breath while going upstairs and after mild physical exertion. The apneic symptoms persisted while the patient was sitting in a chair and were found to be related to emotional factors. Closer observation revealed that the apneic symptoms subsided periodically (e.g., during interesting conversation, while washing the hands, etc.). Diagnosis: neurotic respiratory disorder.

After a relatively short period of autogenic training the respiratory disturbances disappeared, and the patient surprised her associates with an unexpected degree of efficiency.[1148]

Case 22: A 66-year-old patient began to suffer agonizing states of fear when looking out of the window. This anxiety symptom developed after the patient's third myocardial infarction. It also became impossible for him to use the lift, and he needed help in going downstairs. In addition, the patient reported occasional attacks of dizziness while in his apartment. The patient showed a well-balanced personality, and occupied a responsible position; after superficial exploration the possible involvement of a neurosis was excluded. Quick relief, without loss of time, was indicated. Analytic approaches and hypnotherapy were considered contraindicated because of the age, the danger of death, and the attitude of the patient.

After three weeks of autogenic therapy, with relatively good progress during the initial period of the standard training, the symptoms faded away. The patient had no further complaints until he died one year later.[1675]

LEFT MAMMARY PAIN

Training problems may result when a dull ache accompanied by sharp, stabbing or shooting pain in the neighborhood of the left breast (occasionally referred down the left arm) appears or is activated after treatment with autogenic training was started (see Case 23). Since this common symptom of left mammary pain may be superimposed upon organic heart disease, may be mistaken for angina pectoris, may be associated with other cardiac modalities of autogenic discharges, or may involve accident-related autogenic discharges (e.g., dog bite) or other organic factors (e.g., unusually hard nodular structures in l. breast), a very careful differential diagnostic evaluation is required (see Case 23).

After participation of organic disease has been excluded, these patients should proceed with the *regular sequence* of standard exercises. In several cases with intercurrent episodes of left mammary pain, W. Luthe[896] observed progressive disappearance of these symptoms within 2 to 20 weeks of regular practice of autogenic standard training.

Case 23: A 44-year-old housewife (anxiety reaction, moderate depression, multiple allergic reactions, migraine type headaches, respiratory disorder, effort syndrome, dysmenorrhea, peripheral circulatory disorder, varicose veins, tinnitus, attacks of auricular tachycardia with regular q.d. digitalis medication for six years; B.P. 112/60; ECG; sinus bradycardia, rate 50 per min., rather low QRS voltage; history of prolonged pulmonary tuberculosis and pneumothorax; several accidents, dog bite left upper lat. chest; deep long cut with glass in *left* arm, cholecystectomy, anal fistulectomy).

During and between autogenic standard exercises (during gradual withdrawal of digitalis), the patient noted increasing occurrence of pain in the neighborhood of the left breast. These symptoms were noted for the first time during a camping trip two weeks earlier (see also Case 13, p. 000). The following excerpts from the patient's training protocols may convey some of the differential diagnostic problems associated with "left mammary pain," cardiac disorders and relevant modalities of autogenic discharges:

During Heaviness Exercises (examples):
   (a) Not much heaviness anywhere. Itching fingers, soles of feet, arms, everywhere off and on. *Short stabbing pain in left chest near midline.* More air in stomach (not unusual for me). Yet feeling relaxed.
   (b) Heaviness: right arm good, both arms good, both legs fair. *Pain in left upper chest close to midline,* just ventral to the tense spot in the back.
   Note: Awoke with *pain in left chest near armpit,* could feel blood pulsate in chest.

(c) Right arm heavy even before formula. Arms and legs heavy. *Slight pain inside of left breast* (sensitive to touch again). Exercise "feels good."

After adding Warmth Exercises (examples):
(d) Right arm heavy before formula. Arms and legs more evenly heavy. Right arm very heavy and warm. Some *pain in left breast.*
Note: Woke up with *slight pain in side of left breast.*
Remarks: The pain in the neighborhood of the left breast disappeared for several weeks. No relevant complaints were noted after adding the Third and Fourth Standard Formulas. Then, it started again.

After adding the Fifth Standard Formula (examples):
(e) Heaviness and warmth according to formulae, but during the resp. formula I could feel some *dull pain in the left side of my left breast.* Also still discernible after the exercise—it had disappeared for a few days, but had reappeared this morning.
(f) *Left breast started hurting* during exercises. After starting on the resp. formula, there was a rather *sharp pain in left breast, subsiding to dull pain,* which remained and became somewhat stronger after the exercise. Outside of the exercise I noted *pain of the left breast* on three different days. In spite of the dogbite and the (?) lump in that side, I have no special associations to that pain, and it is also not directly in the spot of either of those two, and sometimes wanders around a little, but it always keeps to the *left side of the left breast.*

Remarks: In the interim, physical, hematological, electrocardiographic and radiologic examinations (e.g., large granular breasts) had been carried out. All findings were within normal limits. The progressive withdrawal of digitalis medication (see p. 45, 48) was followed by functional improvements in the ECG. With these negative findings the following possibilities remained:
(a) Left mammary pain;
(b) Spontaneous and autogenic discharges possibly related to a dog bite in the neighborhood of the left breast; or, related to being hit accidentally (e.g., elbow of husband during sleep) in the same area.[2065]

References: 2, 3, 96, 115, 129, 130, 141, 149, 156, *160,* 161, 203, *265,* 269, *273, 274,* 275, 299, 302, 312, 315, 319, 360, 378, 410, 444, 466, 479, 481, 503, 514, 525, 532, 571, 574, *581,* 602, 606, *612,* 614, 614a, *617, 618,* 619, *620,* 621, *639,* 646, 647, 649, 657, *658,* 659, 662, 669, 670, 755, *756, 757,* 758, *760, 761,* 762, *771,* 773, 804, 852, 871, *872,* 877, *883, 885, 888,* 892, 896, 930, *935,* 970, 977, *987, 994,* 1001, 1002, 1003, 1024, *1065, 1073,* 1082, *1083, 1086,* 1093, 1106, 1111, 1148, *1163, 1171,* 1175, 1182, 1200, 1263, 1264, 1265, 1268, 1288, 1291, 1299, 1300, 1308, 1384, 1424, 1433, *1528,* 1537, *1541,* 1547, *1550,* 1565, 1566, 1574, 1608, 1616, 1622, 1625, 1765, 1787, 1923, *1927,* 1932, 1950, 1951, 1952, 1954, *1979,* 1986, 2028, *2042,* 2047, 2065, 2066, 2070, 2122, 2155, 2181, 2194, 2216, 2217, 2257, 2266, 2276, 2297, 2308, 2321, 2358, 2447.

ALTERATIONS IN BLOOD PRESSURE

With due consideration of non-functional pathologic variables (e.g., renal disorders, coarctation of the aorta, toxaemia of pregnancy, Cushing's syndrome, pheochromocytoma, thyrotoxicosis, atheroma of the aorta, aortic incompetence, arotic stenosis) it has been emphasized that the regular practice of autogenic standard exercises over prolonged periods has beneficial effects on a variety of physiologically and psychodynamically oriented functional variables which may participate in causing or amplifying certain hyper- and hypotensive[244,1787,2065] conditions. It is in this sense that autogenic training has been applied either as an adjunctive measure in the treatment program of certain organically determined forms of hypertension (e.g., atheroma of the aorta, thyrotoxicosis), as a prophylactic approach (e.g., evidence of hereditary predisposition, arteriosclerotic factors), and as a therapeutic mainstay when, after exclusion of other causes, unusual instability of blood pressure and hypertension is assumed to be due to psychophysiologically oriented functional variables (e.g., emotional stress, accumulated aggression, resentment, feeling menaced or trapped).

Although many etiologic and pathophysiologic aspects of various forms of alterations in blood pressure remain to be clarified, clinical and experimental studies of patients practicing autogenic training have indicated a number of physiologic and psychologic changes which appear to be of particular value in the treatment of hypertensive patients. Physiologically, the vasodilatory and circulatory effects (see Fig. 15; Fig. 5/I, 7/I), associated with passive concentration on the different standard formulae and certain organ-specific formulae, appear to include a number of desirable variables, which are known to participate in lowering elevated blood pressure readings. Furthermore, of perhaps even more clinical importance is the multidimensional psychophysiologic shift towards a pattern of reactivity and relevant functional changes the direction of which is diametrically opposed to the pattern of changes elicited by stress.

In the treatment of hypertensive conditions, clinical observers have reported variable results. Depending on participation of known and unknown etiologic variables, the clinical results vary between excellent and an apparently complete failure of response.[115,323,678,1800] However, it is generally agreed that the effectiveness of autogenic standard exercises increases as the hypertensive condition is due to functional factors of psychophysiologic nature.[56,96,269,339,418,823,852,1494,1495,1668,1951,2079] In many cases of essential hypertension (primary hypertension, hypertensive vascular disease) marked improvement has been noted after four to eight weeks of regular standard training.[115,160,247,323,481,678,758,760,870,872,873,877,878,] [879,880,935,987,1377,1625,1787,2122,2178] Readings taken before and after one set of standard exercises usually show a 5–12 per cent reduction of diastolic values, and a 5–25 per cent decrease of systolic blood pressure (see Fig. 14). In some cases, the systolic blood pressure may even drop 30 to 50 mm.Hg within a few minutes, during one exercise.[870,987,] [1377,1452] Studies involving larger groups of patients suffering from essential and other forms of hypertension have shown failure rates between 10 and 50 per cent.[160,323,678,1377,1927] The incidence of early dropouts in hypertensive trainees is known to be unusually high (25 to 70 per cent) and constitutes a particular problem for the therapeutic management of this category of patients.

While investigating various aspects of hypertension, G. Klumbies and G. Eberhardt[323,678] applied autogenic training to a group of 83 male hypertensive patients. Fifty-seven patients discontinued their treatment during initial phases of autogenic training. This unusually high rate (69 per cent) of early dropouts was viewed as being related to (a) the fact that the hypertensive disorder did not cause any subjective complaints, (b) that most of the dropouts were rather young (below age 26), and (c) that the treatment program was intentionally limited to the learning, practice and control of autogenic exercises (excluding individual discussions of a psychotherapeutic nature). The remaining 26 (17 below age 26) learned all standard exercises and participated in periodic control sessions over a period of 5–15 months. In this group, blood pressure readings were taken repeatedly before starting autogenic training and during subsequent control periods (see Fig. 12). The most significant decrease of systolic and diastolic readings occurred during the first month of autogenic training (see Fig. 13). Further decrease continued during the second, third and fourth month, with little or no change occurring during subsequent periods. In correspondence with other observations,[56,160,] [407,409,418,535,873,878,879,935,1538,1927,2122] G. Klumbies and G. Eberhardt noted considerable variations of the individual treatment response (see Fig. 12) with more marked decreases of the systolic component (average decrease 35 mm. Hg, single cases up to 55 mm. Hg): The decrease of the diastolic values was 18 mm. Hg on the average, with some cases reaching a reduction of 30 mm. Hg.[678] Normalization of blood pressure deviations was noted in 22 of the group of 26 patients. The authors emphasize that the treatment with antihypertensive drugs is less time consuming for both the therapist and the patient. However, group training (up to 10) is time-saving, and in view of the beneficial short- and long-range effects of the regular practice of autogenic standard exercises and the elimination of unfavorable side-effects caused by antihypertensive drugs (e.g., im-

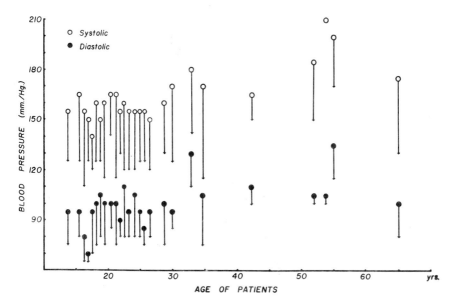

Fig. 12. Changes of systolic and diastolic blood pressure in a group of 26 hypertensive patients. The graphic representation of changes in each patient is based on arithmetical means of repeated readings carried out under comparable conditions on different days, before and towards the end of a four-month treatment period with autogenic training. (Courtesy of G. Klumbies and G. Eberhardt, University of Jena.[323,678])

potence, gastric distress, diarrhea, psychic disturbances), autogenic training appears to be the method of choice for many patients suffering from forms of essential hypertension.

A more detailed study of the effects of the different standard exercises on blood pressure and cardiac activity has revealed that there are persons in whom a set of three heaviness exercises induces a gradual and significant increase in diastolic and systolic blood pressure (see Fig. 14). In a number of subjects, it has been observed that disturbances in passive concentration (intruding thoughts, sleep, snoring, minor movements) tend to coincide with a slight increase in diastolic and systolic blood pressure.[535] These observations indicate that the effect of the exercises on the trainee's blood pressure should be determined at regular intervals. Until further information is available, it is advisable to discontinue autogenic therapy in cases in which correct and undisturbed exercises cause a significant increase in the blood pressure. In this respect, it must be kept in mind that there is experimental evidence that any minor voluntary

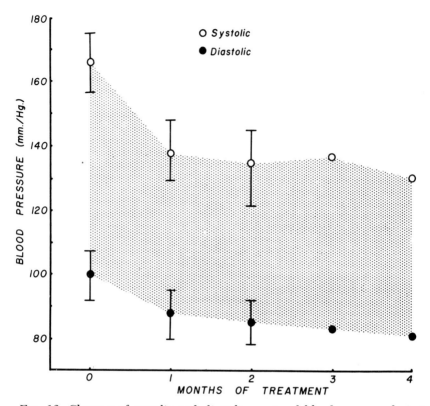

Fig. 13. Changes of systolic and diastolic range of blood pressure during a four-month period in a group of 26 hypertensive patients practicing autogenic standard exercises (based on arithmetical means of repeated reading in each case, taken before the beginning of A.T. and towards the end of each subsequent month; standard deviations as indicated). (Courtesy of G. Klumbies and G. Eberhardt, University of Jena.[323,678])

motor activity (e.g., moving a hand, talking, etc.) as well as various modalities of autogenic discharges (e.g. intruding thoughts) and transitory states of sleep occurring during the exercises may reduce the beneficial effect of the autogenic exercises and may even provoke unwanted physiologic changes.[535] Clinical observations also indicate that the duration and sequence of the standard exercises should be adapted to the patient's functional state. Regular control of training symptoms is required.

In most patients suffering from hypertension, normal training symptoms and average progress is usually noted during heaviness and warmth training. Reduced step-by-step exercises (see Vol. I) are indicated in cases in which disagreeable side-effects are noted, such as congestion of

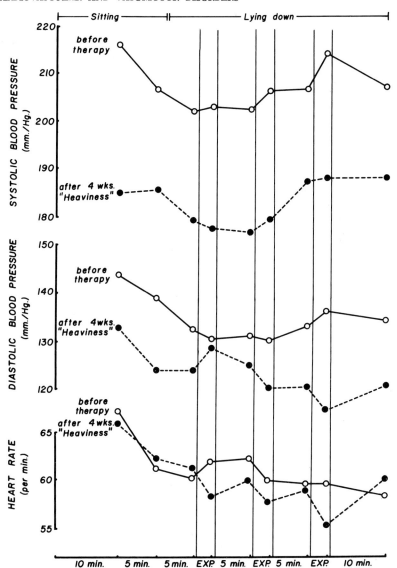

FIG. 14. The effects of heaviness exercises upon the blood pressure and heart rate of a 57-year-old teacher with hypertension of about 15 years' duration. Mean values of readings taken on three different days before (solid lines) and three different days after (broken lines) four weeks of heaviness training. The decrease in systolic blood pressure is about 12% (P <.01). The response of the diastolic blood pressure is less marked and about 5.5% (P <.01). The response of the heart rate is typical but not statistically significant.

the cranial region and palpitation. Slow progress is also advisable when the heaviness and warmth exercises cause a decrease in blood pressure which exceeds 15 per cent of the patient's average readings. Introduction of the third standard exercise ("Heartbeat calm and regular") has frequently led to training difficulties. Trainees have noted that feelings of uneasiness, tenseness or even anxiety developed during passive concentration on the heart. Although the psychophysiologic mechanisms involved are not yet entirely understood, there is some evidence that the trainee's feeling of uneasiness and anxiety is related to a relatively strong and sudden decrease (20 per cent or more) in blood pressure during this exercise.[987] As a consequence of such experiences, trainees tend to develop resistance to autogenic therapy.

Because of these observations it is advisable to postpone the heart exercise till the end of the standard series and to introduce "It breathes me" in its place. This exercise is followed by passive concentration on abdominal warmth. After the solar plexus exercise has been practiced successfully, a specific modification of "My forehead is cool," namely:

"My forehead is agreeably cool. My head is clear and light."

may be introduced. This formula and "It breathes me" appear to have a particularly pleasant and relieving effect on trainees suffering from hypertension. It is suggested that passive concentration on these two formulae be emphasized and prolonged during each set of exercises. Finally, passive concentration on the heart may be introduced by using a modified heart formula:

"Heartbeat calm and easy."

At this period of autogenic therapy, after the other five exercises have been mastered satisfactorily, passive concentration on the heart is usually possible without causing any uncomfortable side-effects.

Since the psychoreactive and physiologic effects of autogenic training develop slowly over a period of months, patients suffering from hypertension should practice the exercises for long periods. Although it can hardly be expected that the condition will be cured, it is considered a valuable gain if the blood pressure decreases and can be kept down, so that a patient remarks casually "Doctor, I do not know what has happened to me, but I cannot get angry any more."

Case 24: A 55-year-old patient with marked arteriosclerotic symptoms and variable hypertension (155/110–180/120) complained of increasing nervousness, insomnia, disturbances in concentration, and irritability with outbursts of temper. During the initial phases of autogenic therapy the patient had considerable difficulty with passive concentration on heaviness and warmth. However, after a few weeks of heaviness and warmth training the patient felt much calmer. Subsequently, the heart exercise was introduced. During this phase of therapy the patient developed resistance to the autogenic exercises and finally did not want to continue doing them. A discussion revealed that the patient experienced feelings of anxiety as soon as he started with passive concentration on the heart. The patient had tried to suppress the anxiety, without success. A subsequent control of blood pressure during the first three standard exercises (horizontal position) revealed that the trainee's blood pressure dropped down to 120/70 and lower during passive concentration on the heart formula. The patient's feelings of anxiety (with localization in the cardiac region) were found to coincide with the decrease in blood pressure. After this observation, passive concentration on the heart formula was discontinued. Marked improvement in the patient's condition was observed after autogenic therapy had been limited to regular practice of the heaviness and warmth exercises.[987]

Case 25: A 56-year-old female patient (anxiety reaction, labile hypertension, marked underweight) who had already consulted many physicians. A clinical evaluation did not reveal other abnormalities. With autogenic standard exercises the blood pressure dropped from initial readings of about 240/130 to 150/70 and occasional readings of 180/80 (2 years control).[1163,1171]

Since norepinephrine-producing pheochromocytomas are much more frequent than previously suspected, a more systematic screening of hypertensive trainees who do not show satisfactory responses to autogenic training, is suggested (see Case 23/I, p. 97; Case 54, p. 139). This precaution is particularly indicated in presence of paroxysmal hypertension, which may or may not be triggered by autogenic discharges.

In hypertensive patients who do not show a satisfactory response to autogenic training,[115,1175,1800,2122] case-specific combinations of antihypertensive and tranquilizing drugs can be added after involvement of a pheochromocytoma has been excluded. Although systematic research is lacking, there are isolated clinical observations[935,2065] indicating that autogenic training appears to enhance the antihypertensive action of certain drugs in certain patients, thus permitting a desirable low dosage treatment over more prolonged periods. It is in this connection that the experimental studies carried out by D. Langen, J. M. Hohn, W. Vogel and G. Schwarz,[527,528,814,1558,1747] and especially the summation of vasodilatory and circulatory effects resulting from combinations of autogenic training with relevant drugs, are of particular clinical interest (see Vol. I).

Repeated observations of a significant increase of diuresis in trainees practicing autogenic exercises for prolonged periods, undergoing autogenic abreaction or practicing autogenic verbalization[418,895,897,898,901,1927] provided indication that circulatory and other renal functions appear to undergo certain changes, which may be of special value in the treatment of hypertensive patients. Considering relevant experimental findings which indicated that passive concentration on organ-specific formulae (e.g., "My stomach is warm"; "My lower abdomen is warm") produce an increase of blood flow (e.g., fingers, gastric mucosa, colon wall), trials with passive concentration on "My right kidney is heavy,"* "My left kidney is heavy,"* and "My kidneys are heavy"* were started.[2065] It is hypothesized that this organ-specific approach may amplify desirable circulatory effects (e.g., decrease of resistance of blood flow) already produced by the standard formulas by enhancing disturbed conditions of blood flow in renal vessels.

References: 56, 96, 115, 156, *160*, 244, 247, 269, 302, *323*, 339, 407, 409, 410, 418, 482, 535, 581, 602, 639, 658, 662, *678*, 758, 760, 771, 823, 852, 870, 872, 873, 876, 877, 878, 879, 880, *883*, 887, 888, 896, 935, 987, 994, 1163, 1175, *1182*, 1314, 1377, 1433, 1452, 1494, 1495, 1528, *1537*, 1538, 1541, 1625, 1668, 1784, 1787, 1800, *1927*, 1951, 1979, 2065, 2079, 2122, 2178.

Disorders of Peripheral Circulation

The normalizing influence of autogenic exercises on autonomic self-regulation, and the possibility of increasing at will the circulation in the extremities, makes autogenic training a valuable therapeutic tool in the treatment of various disorders of peripheral circulation (e.g., intermittent claudication, Buerger's disease, ischemic neuritis, Raynaud's phenomenon, scleroderma, frostbite, cold feet).

The effects of autogenic training on peripheral circulation have been studied repeatedly (see Fig. 5/I). Plethysmography (see Subject Index, Vol. IV) and measurements of skin temperature (see Figs. 14a, 15; 7/I) have verified that it is possible to increase the peripheral blood flow by passive concentration on topographically oriented heaviness and warmth formulas.[1747]

Vasodilatation, reduction or elimination of reflex vasospasm, muscular relaxation, favorable action on vasospastic humoral factors (e.g., epinephrine) and circulatory variables (e.g., cardiac function, blood pressure) as well as the reduction of elevated levels of serum cholesterol (see Figs. 10, 24–28) are some of the clinically desirable factors which make autogenic training a valuable therapeutic tool in the treatment of disorders which affect the blood supply to the extremities. Furthermore, it is of clinical interest that recent studies, carried out by D. Langen and J. M. Hohn[527,528] verified that autogenic training enhances or amplifies

---

* These organ-specific formulas should not be used until further information is available.

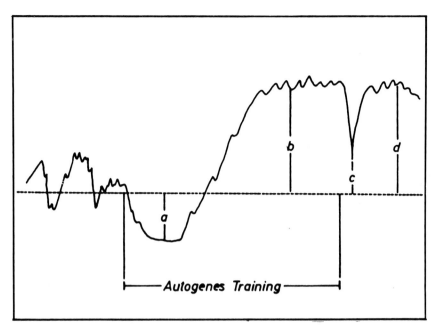

Fig. 14a. Typical pattern of temperature changes (heat conveyance measurement; thumb) during the practice of heaviness and warmth exercises. The beginning of autogenic training is associated with a reactive "initial drop" (a). Then a relatively steep and progressive increase of temperature, the "main reaction" (b), is noted. The termination of autogenic training produces a reactive, however, transitory, decrease (c), which is followed by an "after-reaction" (d) with slow readjustment towards pre-training levels of temperature. This readjustment phase may last about 3-30 mins. (Courtesy of W. Vogel,[2436] University of Tübingen, and D. Langen, University of Mainz.[814,1747])

the effects of certain vasodilatory drugs (e.g., Complamin,* Hydergin, Opilon†).

Clinical and experimental observations indicate that there are different forms of passive concentration which enhance peripheral circulation to a variable degree. The mildest vasodilatatory effect is produced by passive concentration on heaviness over brief periods (1–3 min.). Heaviness exercises prolonged over periods ranging from 3 to 15 minutes induce more intensive changes in blood flow in the extremities.[303] Further reinforcement may be brought about by passive concentration on warmth, which,

---

* 7–(2Hydroxy 3 (N-2-hydroxy-ethyl-N-methylamino) propyl)-1, 3 dimethylxanthine, pyridine-3-carboxylate).

† Acetoxythymoxy-ethyl-dimethylamine.

if sufficiently prolonged, may finally cause a sense of fullness and a dull ache in the hands and feet. In addition to this, a more localized increase in circulation is made possible by focussing mental contact on circumscribed areas (e.g., calves) of the extremities. From a physiologic point of view, there is experimental evidence to support the assumption that the peripheral vasodilatation induced by passive concentration on heaviness and warmth is due to autonomic changes which reduce the overactivity of the sympathetic nervous system and retard the reflex vasoconstriction. The clinical value of this effect is enhanced by the fact that the peripheral vasodilatory changes are not immediately reversed when the trainee terminates the exercise. According to the data collected by Polzien,[1067,1072] there is a gradual return to normal skin temperature over periods of 10 to 20 minutes.

Another valuable effect associated with the peripheral increase in blood flow is the simultaneous reduction in pain. Diffuse pain produced by reflex vasoconstriction and the resulting ischemia are reduced as the circulation improves under the influence of the first two standard exercises. This effect has some similarity to the relief of vasoconstriction produced by paravertebral block of the appropriate sympathetic ganglia. Passive concentration on heaviness and warmth has been also effective when pain in the extremity is associated with local circulatory dysfunctions caused by nerve injuries after amputation.[1804]

Considering the information which evolved from experimental studies, autogenic training is indicated for peripheral vascular disorders which may be either organic or functional in origin (e.g., thromboangiitis obliterans).

In patients suffering from Buerger's disease with gradual or sudden onset of coldness, numbness, tingling or burning, evidence of reflex vasospasm (e.g., in arms, legs) and sensation of pain or tightening as it occurs in intermittent claudication, autogenic training with emphasis on warmth in the affected areas is recommended.[658,994,1069,1377,1527,1528,1746,2177] Since trophic changes (e.g., skin, deeper tissues; ulceration, gangrene) are usually starting in the distal parts, it is of particular clinical interest to remember that P. Polzien (see Vol. IV) found a higher and more prolonged increase of skin temperature in distal parts (e.g., fingers) than in more proximally oriented areas (e.g., hand, forearm, upper arm).[1067,1069, 1072,1076,1082,1085,1747]

In patients with intermittent claudication, the emphasis may be simply on "Both legs are warm" (see Case 26).[2177] When additional reinforcement appears indicated, the organ-specific formula used by H. Hoffmann,[523] "My calves are warm," may be applied. Hoffmann's patients reported satisfactory results after six to twelve weeks of regular training.

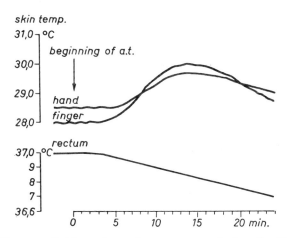

FIG. 15. Changes of skin and rectal temperature during the First Standard Exercise. The graphic representation summarizes the data reported by P. Polzien.[1066,1067,1069,1072,1076,1082,1085] (University of Würzburg)

Case 26: A 60-year-old male patient suffered from intermittent claudication, which limited his walking time to about 20 minutes or less. With autogenic standard training and emphasis on the formula "Both legs are warm" (Beine strömend warm"), he became able to increase his walking time to about 30 min.[1527]

Conditions manifested by an intermittent abnormal degree of vascular spasm of the distal arteries (*Raynaud's phenomenon*), which are secondary to other conditions (e.g., endocrine, collagen disease, obliterative arterial disease), or which may be triggered by cold or emotional reactions have been treated with autogenic standard training.[160,244,581,658,994,1175,1927,2122] Referring to the variability of clinical improvements,[160,1927,2122] M. Sapir, F. Reverchon, R. Philibert and I. Javal[1175] emphasized that the patient's response to autogenic training is largely influenced by participating psychodynamic factors.

Other functional circulatory disorders associated with decreased blood flow in the limbs as, for example, *acrocyanosis,* cold clammy feet[274,275,302,411,1528] and cold hands tend to improve progressively as the patient advances through the standards exercises (see Case 26, p. 79). Organ-specific formulae are usually not necessary. Good results have been also noted in cases suffering from *causalgia,* when persistent burning pain is associated with dystrophic and vasomotor changes are related to injury (e.g., amputation).[594] Likewise, autogenic standard training has been recommended in cases suffering from erythromelalgia.[244,1746,2177]

The usefulness of heaviness and warmth exercises during prolonged exposure to cold has been documented by a number of trainees[328,329,1528, 1566] and by experimental studies carried out by G. Schwarz and D. Langen.[1558] The reports state that trainees were able to prevent injury from cold by passive concentration on warmth, whereas other persons exposed to the same conditions appeared to be less protected against cold and were more liable to tissue damage.

Case 27: A well-known sportsman who had learned autogenic training for the purpose of improving his performance was caught by an avalanche. He and his companions were buried under the snow in below 30 C. temperature and had to stay motionless for several hours until they were rescued. The advanced trainee applied the autogenic approach and focussed on warmth in nose, fingers, toes and ears in rotation. He was the only person who escaped without frostbite or any other injury from the cold.[1377]

References: 156, 160, 244, 274, 275, 302, 305, 328, 329, 409, 410, 411, 418, 523, 581, 594, 602, 639, 647, 658, 662, 771, 872, 877, 883, 888, 994, 1067, *1069, 1072, 1076, 1082,* 1085, 1101, 1163, 1175, 1182, 1377, 1433, 1527, 1528, 1537, 1541, *1558,* 1566, *1747,* 1927, 1979, 2065, 2122, 2177, 2216, 2255, 2308.

HEMORRHOIDS

Successful attempts have been made in the application of autogenic principles to the treatment of hemorrhoids.[866] The organ-specific approach focussess mainly on three factors: (a) local relaxation of muscular elements, (b) activation of local and regional circulation, and (c) reduction in itching and/or pain in the pars externa sphinterica ani.[410,411,658, 662,1524,1528,1541]

The organ-specific training begins with passive concentration on: "My anus is heavy." During this phase of the exercise a number of typical training symptoms have been observed. The first category of symptoms refers to variable and usually not easily describable symptoms of local relaxation. The second category of symptoms are paresthesias, for example, tingling and pins-and-needles feeling which tend to be localized in certain circumscribed areas of the genito-anal region (see Fig. 16, a and b). These symptoms, which are conceived as being related to dilatatory vasomotor reactions, may or may not be accompanied by phenomena of erection (pelvic nerve). A further reinforcement of the local and regional responses is brought about by focussing upon: "My pelvis is warm." However, before the trainee starts using this formula, it should be pointed out to him that the formula aims at an increase of blood flow ("flowing warmth") in the depth of the pelvis and that the mental contact should be established accordingly. When mental contact is established with the tegumentary area only, the blood flow-activating effect in the depth of the pelvis appears to be reduced. During this second phase of the organ-specific training, agreeable sensations of flowing warmth are experienced in the pelvic region.

The third phase, which should only be practiced after passive concentration on the first two formulae has become effective, aims at relieving the pain caused by the hemorrhoids. In analogy to the formulae applied in certain skin disorders (e.g., pruritus of the vulva) the trainee focusses upon: "My anus is cool." When mental contact is effective the training symptoms are fairly well localized (see Fig. 16) and the sensations are similar in quality to those experienced during the sixth standard exercise.

This organ-specific approach should always be applied in combination with at least the first two standard exercises. With respect to the circulatory factors involved, it is advisable to limit the increase in peripheral circulation by modifying the second standard formula (e.g., "My arms and legs are *slightly* warm"). Furthermore, the trainee should be advised not to practice the fifth standard exercise when he intends to induce an effective increase in the circulation of the pelvic region.

The combined standard and organ-specific exercises should be terminated in the usual way (flexing the arms, breathing deeply, opening the eyes). In well-trained persons the after-effects of the organ-specific formulae are usually quite marked. After one week of regular training, patients have, for example, noted that the feeling of agreeable flowing warmth in the pelvis persisted for as long as 40 minutes. After three weeks of regular training, circulatory after-effects occasionally last up to two hours. The after-effects of the formula, "My anus is cool," are less marked and of much shorter duration.

The approach has been successful in less severe cases and in uncomplicated conditions where no other organic disease has been involved. Eight patients obtained complete relief within two to six weeks of regular organ-specific training. In three cases the patients' complaints started anew several months after they had stopped practicing the exercises. When the exercises were recommenced, however, the hemorrhoidal complaints disappeared within about two weeks.

BLUSHING

The abnormal and specific vasomotor reaction which leads to blushing in average siuations is usually found in association with other symptoms of increased vasomotor irritability (e.g., dermographia, fainting). The disorder has been conceived as a disturbance in the person's psychophysiologic adaptation to certain environmental situations. Both the increased vasomotor irritability and the person's fear that blushing may occur subside under the influence of autogenic standard therapy (see

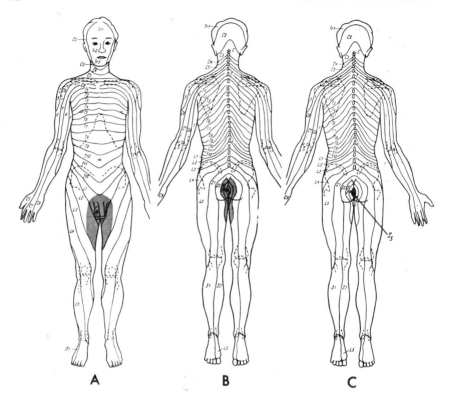

FIG. 16. Localization of paraesthesias in the genital and anal regions during passive concentration on "My anus is heavy" (a and b) and "My anus is cool" (c). Drawings from: Hansen, *Sensibilitätsschema*, 3rd Ed., G. Thieme Verlag, Stuttgart.

references p. 83). After two to three months of regular training the patients tend to note that they are less emotionally involved and remain, without effort, much calmer in situations which previously induced blushing.

In addition to the standard exercises, two specific formulae have been used:

"My neck and shoulders are warm," and
"My feet are warm."

These two formulae are considered as physiologic extensions of the standard warmth training and are designed to divert the abnormal circulatory changes to areas of the body which are acceptable to the patient. In well-trained patients these formulae have been found effective. Under everyday circumstances the patient learns to control blushing by "switching on" "My feet are warm" as soon as a situation arises where blushing may occur.[760,1377] The physiologic effect of this formulae may be supported by adding "My forehead is cool."

Case 28: A 24-year-old salesman complained of frequent blushing, which had started when he was in elementary school. Recently, the patient had developed strong feelings of guilt because he felt that he did damage to his father's business when serving clients by blushing when he had to talk to them. The patient's mother suffered from the same disturbance. Other complaints of the patient were enuresis nocturna until the age of eighteen, frequent masturbation as a teenager, increased vasomotor irritability, and slight tremor of hands. Autogenic therapy was instituted. After five months of regular training the patient reported that he was cured. Under circumstances in which blushing tended to occur, "my unconscious sends the wave of blood down into my feet instead of up into my face." Control period two years.[1377]

Another means of coping with blushing is composed of two successive steps. First, the patient relaxes the muscles around his neck and shoulders by applying: "My neck and shoulders are heavy." This brings about a sensible relief in tension and, in its physiologic aspect, acts as a preparatory phase for the more specific step: "My neck and shoulders are warm." This formula may be applied when premonitory symptoms of blushing develop.

References: 81, 115, 156, 274, 275, 302, 360, 410, 541, 612, 658, 662, 760, 761, 877, 883, 888, 1178, 1234, 1377, 1528, 1537, 1541, 1590, 1718, 1720, 1723, 1763, 2217.

HEADACHE AND MIGRAINE

The therapeutic results of the autogenic approach in the treatment of migraine and different forms of headache are variable. In a relatively few cases, no improvement is noted after several months of standard training. The majority of patients, however, report that the frequency and intensity of headache or attacks of migraine is much lower than before therapy (see references p. 89). A number of patients report that they have been cured after practicing the autogenic standard exercises for several months.[259,261,986] There are also a number of observations that trainees with periodic attacks of migraine can learn to intercept the onset of an attack by starting autogenic exercises as soon as prodromal symptoms (e.g., visual scotoma, hemianopsia, paresthesias, nausea, etc.) develop.[534] In some instances, patients succeed in stopping an acute attack by applying autogenic training after the early stages of the attack are established.

These clinical observations indicate that autogenic training may be primarily regarded as preventive therapy.

Since migraine and different forms of headache are often associated with emotional factors (e.g., conflicts, anxiety, worry, sexual incompatability) and a variety of functional disorders (e.g., constipation, indigestion, deviations in blood pressure, dermographia, cold feet), emphasis should be placed on practicing the first five standard exercises. The application of the sixth standard formula ("My forehead is cool") requires caution. Since the functional disorders may involve localized vasodilatation or vasoconstriction, and since there often exists a particular irritability of the patient's cranial vasomotor system, it is advisable to proceed carefully and slowly.

For the same reason a modified formula, namely, "My forehead is slightly cool," should be applied, and for brief periods only (20–30 seconds). When the trainee repeatedly notes a conspicuous increase in pain during passive concentration on this reduced formula, it is probable that vasospastic mechanisms are involved.[1148] In such cases, any further passive concentration on a formula which aims at cooling a cranial region should be avoided. Instead, passive concentration on "flowing warmth in nape and shoulders" should be practiced. This approach has been found relieving by many patients suffering from migraine and certain forms of headache.[523]

Patients who note that the formula "My forehead is slightly cool" is agreeable and reduces headache may after a short time use the original formula of the sixth standard exercise: "My forehead is cool." These trainees, however, should be warned not to use any similar formula without having discussed their intention with the therapist. Patients who have aimed at reinforcing the physiologic effects of the sixth standard formula by applying, for example, "My forehead is cold" or "ice-cold" have experienced an increase in headache or dizziness and nausea.[1377] Mueller-Hegemann[987-989] observed that the beneficial effect of "My forehead is cool" can be amplified by a preceding phase of passive concentration on relaxation of the facial musculature.

Case 29: A 20-year-old girl started suffering from attacks of unilateral migraine after a series of emotionally traumatizing events. For seven years numerous drugs were used but without lasting improvement. After six months of regular practice of autogenic standard exercises the attacks of migraine had disappeared. No further complaints were noted during a 3 year control period.[658]

Case 30: A female patient started suffering from frequent attacks of unilateral migraine with scintillating scotomas and vomiting after she learned that her husband had died in action. For ten years various drugs were tried without producing any lasting change. The patient started practicing autogenic training, and the frequency of the attacks subsided significantly to about one episode per month. She also learned to intercept attacks of

a manner that the thyroid could function with a higher degree of efficiency (e.g., making better use of the iodine available).[890] These early observations were confirmed during subsequent studies (experimental procedure as described in ref. 890) involving larger groups of patients[890, 2065] (see Fig. 23; Vol. IV).

The results obtained so far indicate, in a general sense, that the regular practice of autogenic training facilitates unknown autoregulatory processes which promote an adjustment of disturbed thyroid activity in two directions: (a) a lowering of initially elevated PBI and TI values (see Fig. 20, and Fig. 23, p. 118), and (b) a marked tendency of initially low PBI values to shift towards higher levels (nutritional iodine deficiency and organic pathology excluded) and a physiologically more favorable pattern of thyroid activity. In this connection it is of interest to note that similar autoregulatory two-way adjustment reactions during treatment with autogenic training have been observed in relevant deviations of other physiologic functions (e.g., heart rate, blood pressure, serum cholesterol). However, in a small number of cases the usual pattern of progressive readjustment did not occur, or was transitorily reversed or arrested (see Fig. 20, Fig. 23). In some of these instances trainees were passing through a period of strong emotional stress when the PBI and TI determinations were arranged. In other cases autogenic training had not been practiced regularly, and several times no plausible explanation could be found.

In euthyroid patients whose initial PBI values were already located in what appears to be a physiologically favorable "central adjustment zone," no particular pattern of changes, except for a tendency of the PBI values to remain within the range of the adjustment zone (4.8–6.2 μg./100 ml.), was noted (see Fig. 21).

From the clinical observations reported, it may be concluded that autogenic training is a valuable approach in the therapeutic management of those functional disorders of the thyroid which are not associated with specific organic disease (e.g., toxic nodular goiter, neoplasm, simple colloid goiter, myxedema with nutritional iodine deficiency, congenital defects, thyroiditis, lymphadenoid goiter).

References: 51, 161, 261, 262, 389, 410, 411, 418, 602, 658, 662, 877, 878, 883, 885, 888, 890, 891, 1041, 1071, 1072, 1077, 1084, 1377, 1524, 1528, 1537, 1541, 1591, 1787.

FIG. 23. Pathologically high levels of total iodine (TI) and "high normal" values are lowered during autogenic therapy. There is also some indication that initially "low normal" TI values increase slightly. No consistent pattern of changes is noted when initial determinations showed physiologically favorable TI levels.

Disorders in Lipid Metabolism

Disturbances of lipid metabolism as associated with increased or normal serum lipids may involve hereditary factors (e.g., familial pre-beta lipo-proteinemia, familial fat-induced hyperlipemia, hypercholesterolemia with hyperglyceridemia), or may be related to other pathologic processes (e.g., biliary cirrhosis, hypothyroidism, diabetes, pancreatitis, nephrotic syndrome). Furthermore it is known that the complexity of physiologic variables (e.g., endocrine) which participate in lipid metabolism are also influenced by unknown regulatory mechanisms responding to psychologic stress. It is in this connection, and with specific reference to the literature, which suggests a statistical relationship between serum cholesterol levels and the incidence of arteriosclerotic heart disease, that clinically and experimentally (see Vol. IV) oriented studies of the psychophysiological effects of autogenic training are of practical therapeutic interest.[892,1910,2070]

Stimulated by clinical observations indicating that the regular practice of autogenic training has a normalizing effect on certain hyperthyroid conditions, W. Luthe began a study of serum cholesterol. In a first report on a group of 20 psychosomatic and neurotic patients who were tested under standard conditions (e.g., 8:30 a.m., after 14 hr. fasting, routine tests, research project unknown to the laboratory personnel) before starting autogenic training, and after variable periods (e.g., 2–50 months), W. Luthe[892] summarized the findings as follows:

1. Statistically, there was no significant difference between a group of ten patients who had received medication (e.g., imipramine, meprobamate, chlordiazepoxide) for transitory periods and the group of ten patients who did not receive supportive medication.

2. In both groups there was a significant difference ($P < .01$) between the first and the second determination of serum cholesterol ($F = 9.04$).

3. There was no apparent correlation between the time interval (between the two determinations), and relevant changes of the serum cholesterol values.

4. There was no correlation between the changes of serum cholesterol values and the age or sex of the patients.

5. There was some indication that patients whose condition requires transitory support by imipramine, meprobamate or chlordiazepoxide are liable to show a tendency towards higher and more fluctuating levels of serum cholesterol.

6. The results indicated that initially high serum cholesterol levels decrease more markedly than initially low values.

These findings were confirmed as the investigation was continued with a larger group of patients (see Fig. 24-25).[2070]

The changes of serum cholesterol values seen in Fig. 24-26 indicate that there appears to be a biologically determined "adjustment zone" located between 150–200 mg./ml., towards which initially elevated serum cholesterol levels adjust (see Fig. 24 and Fig. 25). Values which initially were already located within the range of the "adjustment zone" (see Fig. 26) show relatively little changes. Only in four out of 45 patients did the serum cholesterol readings drop transitorily below 150 mg./ml. (see Fig. 24-26). Furthermore it was observed that control tests taken during periods of particular stress showed an increase of serum cholesterol values (see Fig. 25 and Fig. 26).

Additional information which appears to be of particular clinical interest resulted from a study of a group of patients who (a) gave up the regular practice of autogenic training for certain periods, (b) interrupted treatment and came back after variable periods, or (c) practiced autogenic exercises very irregularly (see Fig. 25). In these patients a significant increase (P < .01) of serum cholesterol levels was noted. However, as these patients resumed the regular practice of autogenic standard exercises, the elevated serum cholesterol levels decreased again. These observations indicate that the *regular* practice of autogenic training is essential in the promotion of those metabolic functions which participate in maintaining physiologically well-adjusted levels of serum cholesterol. It is in this respect that clinical observations by Y. Aya[1910] in patients suffering, for example, from myocardial infarction are of particular interest for therapeutic programs aiming at the prevention, the delay of onset and the slowing down of coronary heart disease (see Fig. 10, p. 52) and atherosclerosis obliterans.

In attempting to obtain more information about the effect of autogenic exercises on metabolic functions determining the serum cholesterol level, Y. Aya[1910] carried out a pilot study with ten psychosomatic patients (e.g., same food program, same experimental procedure) who had practiced autogenic training (heaviness, warmth) for only three weeks (see Fig. 28). Determinations of serum cholesterol values from samples taken directly after termination of a 20-minute period of autogenic training did not show a consistent pattern of changes. In contrast with these findings are values from blood specimens obtained thirty minutes after termination of autogenic training which showed a reactive lowering in 9 cases and no change in one trainee (see Fig. 28). Y. Aya's data seem to indicate that relevant metabolic adjustment reactions due to autogenic training involve a latency period. Further studies of this nature, however,

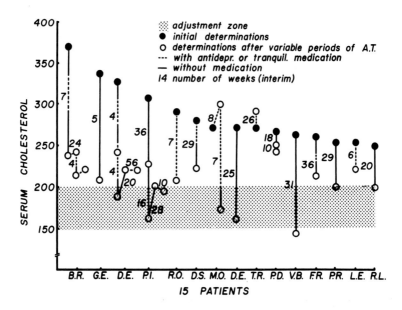

FIG. 24. Lowering of serum cholesterol in patients suffering from hyper-cholesteremia (normal range: 150–250 mg./ml.).

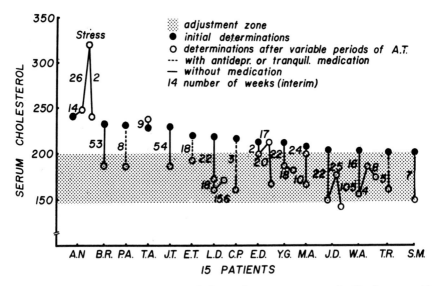

FIG. 25. Lowering of serum cholesterol in patients with "high normal" values (normal range: 150–250 mg./ml.) before starting autogenic training.

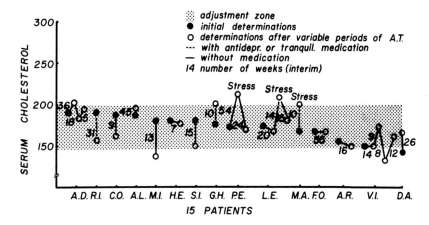

FIG. 26. Changes of serum cholesterol levels in patients with normal or "low normal" values (normal range: 150–250 mg./ml.) before starting autogenic training.

including carefully matched control groups of non-trainees practicing simulated exercises, and others who apply active concentration, would be of clinical interest (see also Vol. IV).

Considering the known correlations between the rate of incidence of coronary disease and the level of serum cholesterol (or related lipids) it is hypothesized that the regular practice of autogenic standard exercises may play a valuable role in the prevention of early onset and undue acceleration of arteriosclerosis and associated forms of heart disease.

TETANY AND RELATED DISORDERS

Syndromes characterized by increased excitability of the nervous system with motor disturbances as, for example, carpopedal spasms, laryngospasms and convulsions, are primarily a problem of clinical investigation and subject to medical treatment. However, when the serum Ca ion levels are normal, when other sources of disturbances in inorganic metabolism (e.g., loss of hydrochloric acid by repeated vomiting, excessive ingestion of alkalis like sodium bicarbonate, metabolic alkalosis with hypokalemia), and alkalotic tetany due to hysterical hyperventilation are excluded, the use of autogenic training may be considered as a complementary form of medical treatment. Patients with functional, idiopathic tetany, and others considered to be suffering from latent tetany[302,410,411,646,662,664,1591,1787] have lost their susceptibility to attacks after practicing autogenic exercises regularly.[639] H. Kleinsorge and G. Klumbies[658] reported for example:

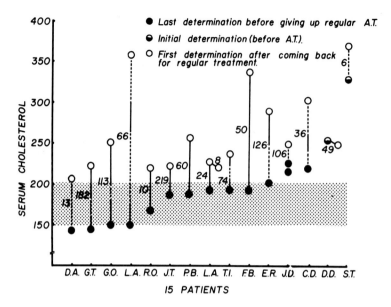

FIG. 27. Increase of serum cholesterol levels (normal range: 150–250 mg./ml.) in patients who (a) interrupted treatment, (b) stopped practicing autogenic training for other reasons, or (c) practiced autogenic training very irregularly.

Case 43: A 35-year-old widow with four children had her first episode of tetany two years before she was admitted for clinical evaluation (Dept. of Medicine, University of Jena). After investigation (normal serum Ca levels) she was diagnosed as normocalcemic tetany with disturbances of coronary circulation.

The patient learned autogenic standard exercises with emphasis on warmth in the limbs, and became able to intercept and eliminate any further attacks.[658]

Case 44: A 39-year-old secretary suffered from attacks of tetany with subsequent diarrhea, whenever she became very nervous and excited. Calcium medication had no effect. After clinical investigation (*diagnosis:* psychogenic tetany), autogenic training was applied. After ten weeks, the patient was without complaints. She had no further attacks for several months. Then, there appeared to be a slight relapse. However, the patient managed to intercept oncoming attacks successfully by practicing autogenic training whenever she felt any "warning" symptoms.[658]

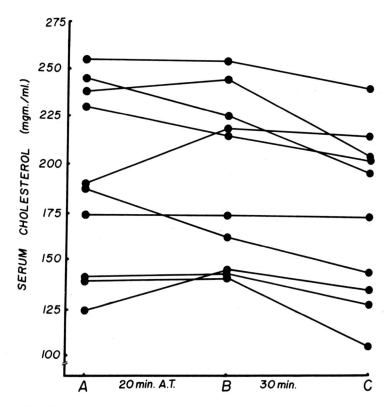

Fig. 28. Changes of serum cholesterol values in ten psychosomatic patients (short-term trainees, 3 weeks A.T.).

A. Before starting passive concentration on heaviness and warmth formulas (normal range: 120–220 mg./ml.).

B. After a 20-minute period of autogenic training.

C. Thirty minutes after termination of autogenic training. A comparison of B and C shows a decrease of serum cholesterol values in nine trainees, and no change in one. (Courtesy of Y. Aya, Oskar Vogt Institute, Kyushu University, Fukuoka.[1910])

6. Musculoskeletal Disorders

The clinical usefulness of autogenic training in the treatment of a variety of musculoskeletal disorders is largely based on the following factors:

(a) muscular relaxation;
(b) improvement of local circulation;
(c) decrease or elimination of pain;
(d) reduction of unfavorable reactivity to emotional stress;
(e) possibly favorable effects on deviations of certain metabolic and endocrine functions;
(f) reduction or elimination of relevant pharmaceuticals;
(g) promotion of the patient's active participation in his treatment.

While these therapeutic variables are considered valuable in breaking up or reducing the self-reinforcing potency of vicious circles of pathophysiologic and psychodynamic nature, autogenic training remains an adjunctive approach to be applied in combination with other forms of case-specific medical management.

As a rule, autogenic training should not be introduced to a patient before a differential diagnostic evaluation (e.g., infectional arthritis, osteomyelitis, neoplasms) has been carried out. After a case-specific treatment program has been determined, it is considered essential that patients who improve with the regular practice of autogenic exercises, are advised to maintain contact with the attending physician for periodic medical control.

ARTHRITIS AND RELATED DISORDERS

Arthralgia due to gonococcal, tuberculous or other infections, neurogenic arthropathy (e.g., tabes dorsalis, syringomyelia), neoplasms of the joints, bursitis and many other conditions (e.g., leukemia, purpura, neuritis, Reiter's syndrome) which may be associated with pain in or around joints are primarily, if not exclusively, subject to clinical evaluation, control and relevant forms of medical treatment.

So far, the regular practice of autogenic exercises has been found helpful in relieving complaints associated with various forms of *rheumatoid arthritis* involving the spine (rheumatoid spondylitis: i.e., von Bechterew spondylitis[449,569] ankylosing spondylitis, spondylitis ankylopoietica), or multiple joints (e.g., atrophic arthritis, proliferative arthritis).[141,1042,1822, 1952,1957,1958,2008,2192] Patients suffering from complaints related to *degenerative joint disease* (e.g., osteoarthritis,[141] senescent arthritis, hypertrophic arthritis) as, for example, pain and limitation of movement associated with a cervical root syndrome[222,490,1174,1528,1746,1952,1978,2008] also noted marked relief (see Case 45).

Myalgia, stiffness and pain in the joints or tenderness of adjacent structures as occurring in chronic or periodic (e.g., damp and cool temperature) *non-articular rheumatism*, fibromyositis, pleurodynia, lumbago[739, 1171] and torticollis are also known to respond well to autogenic training.[1171,1915,1952,2178] There is no information about effects of autogenic training in patients suffering from gout.

Although systematic clinical studies concerned with application of autogenic training to larger groups of patients with rheumatoid arthritis are not yet available, reports on isolated cases and small groups agree in a number of respects.

The "do it yourself" nature of autogenic training is considered to be better adapted to the arthritic patient's tendency to deny help from others, than, for example, psychoanalytical therapy or related approaches which favor direct expression of feelings. Other favorable therapeutic aspects are related to the patient's active participation in his treatment and the direct experience of agreeable muscular relaxation (see Case 45, p. 126), reduction of pain (see Case 47, p. 127) and improvement of sleep during the heaviness training.

Several observers emphasize the beneficial effects of the Second Standard Exercise, which gains particular therapeutic value as the patient gradually succeeds in increasing the blood flow in circumscribed regions and experiences the agreeable feeling of warmth in affected joints and adjacent areas. The patient's experience of symptomatic relief resulting from autogenic training helps to promote the therapeutically desirable frequent practice of autogenic exercises. As the patient discovers that he can use rest periods and medically imposed confinement to bed for a productive purpose, and thus reduce engagement in worries, his chances of improving more rapidly with less medication appear to be enhanced. Of further advantage at a psychophysiologic level is the stress-neutralizing effect of autogenic exercises. This is of particular clinical interest, since emotional stress is a potent variable in the course of rheumatoid arthritis, and it is known that exacerbations tend to coincide with, for example, suppressed feelings of grief or mobilization of accumulated intense feelings of hostility.

Since rheumatoid arthritis is frequently associated with peptic ulcer, it is not advisable to use the Fifth Standard Formula ("My solar plexus is warm") in patients with a history of gastritis or ulceration.

When musculoskeletal disorders involve the spine (e.g., rheumatoid spondylitis, degenerative disease, arthritis due to trauma), topographically more specific formulae may be added to enhance the effects of the usual pattern of standard exercises. D. Hammer,[449] for example, who treated five cases with von Bechterew spondylitis (ankylosing spondylitis, spondylitis ankylopoietica, spondylitis rhizomelica, Marie-Strümpell arthritis), observed particularly beneficial effects when passive concentration on warmth along the spine was combined with the warmth formulas of the Second Standard Exercise. Satisfactory results with patients suffering from attacks of lumbago, increasing stiffness of the spine, limitation in chest expansion, kyphosis with muscular tension and pain associated with various degrees of ankylosing spondylitis have been also reported by K. A. Jochheim[569] and others.[739,1042,1528]

Muscular spasms, pain and variable limitations of movements not due to bony ankylosis but associated with degeneration of the articular cartilage and formation of bony outgrowths at the edges of the affected joints (osteoarthritis, hypertrophic arthritis), also respond well to autogenic training (see Case 45).[1163] In these conditions, which are characterized by degenerative processes affecting the joints (osteoarthritis, hypertrophic arthritis, senescent arthritis), the regular practice of autogenic training also exerts desirable effects on frequently encountered co-existing disorders, such as obesity (see p. 32), hypercholesterolemia (see p. 119) and essential hypertension (see p. 69, 73). Even in advanced cases of, for example, destructive tuberculosis of the spine,[1528] frequent practice of autogenic exercises may contribute to the reduction of muscular tension and to relieve associated nerve root pressure and thus help to reduce the sufferings of the patient (see Case 47).

Case 45: A 36-year-old female patient (osteoarthritis, cervical area of spine, brachial neuralgia l.) reported: "For three years I had been suffering from pain in my left shoulder. In October 1955, the pain became so strong, that I could not move my arm anymore. Traction was applied to my neck. But, after this, the pain kept coming back. Since I learned the heaviness and warmth exercises of autogenic training, I have no pain anymore. Generally I feel much better" (3 months control).[141]

Case 46: A 30-year-old, married, female patient had suffered a severe episode of rheumatic arthritis at the age of 12. From this resulted ankylosis of both shoulder joints with inability to carry out normal arm movements. Compensatory movements involving the upper spine and both shoulders were associated with tension, muscular spasms and pain. However, the patient actually came for treatment of bronchial asthma, which had started ten years earlier. After a brief problem-focussed discussion (e.g., resistance) and subsequent hypnosis, the asthmatic attacks stopped. After several hypnoses (heaviness, rest, sleep) the patient continued with autogenic training. During several control interviews analytically oriented, psychotherapy was not applied. As the patient kept practicing her autogenic exercises regularly, it was noted that the dynamics of the patient's family changed progressively towards a more positively oriented relationship. Apart from this, and rather as a side-effect, the patient noted that the tension, the muscular spasms and the pain in the shoulder-neck area had considerably improved. This improvement was of such a nature that the patient became able to carry out movements which she could not do before treatment. Others had the impression that she now was able to move her arms, when in fact she could not.[1822,2192]

Case 47: A 28-year-old female patient suffered from spinal tuberculosis, with collapse and wedging of the affected vertebrae. This was associated with total paralysis and continuous pain. Regular and frequent practice of standard exercises decisively helped the patient to remain calm and to reduce her sufferings from pain.[1528]

In musculoskeletal disorders affecting the joints or adjacent parts of the extremities, the emphasis is on frequent practice of the first two standard exercises (heaviness, warmth) with relatively prolonged passive concentration on those formulas which include the affected areas (e.g., "My right leg is very heavy"; or later: "My right leg is warm"). Additional reinforcement of desirable training effects are obtained by using topographically more specific approaches which usually follow at the end of the habitual pattern of heaviness formulae (e.g., after "My arms and legs are heavy," "My right knee is very heavy"). Similarly, it has been found helpful to use topographically oriented activation of local blood-flow in affected areas by adding complementary organ-specific warmth formulae (e.g., "My right shoulder is warm," "My right knee is warm") at the end of the habitual pattern of warmth formulae composing the Second Standard Exercise (e.g., after "My arms and legs are warm").

When the spine is involved, as, for example, in ankylosing spondylitis or osteoarthritis, it is indicated that topographically specific heaviness and warmth formulae which cover the entire length of the spine be added (e.g., "My spine is very heavy" follows "My arms and legs are heavy," and "my spine is warm" follows after "My arms and legs are warm"). Better effects are obtained[896] when passive concentration on these organ-specific formulae are used in combination with what may be called *dynamic mental contact.* In distinction from the habitually applied static form of mental contact (e.g., "My right arm is heavy"), *dynamic mental contact* implies that the mental contact does not remain fixed on a given topographic area, but shifts progressively over the different sections of a given area. In this case (e.g., "My spine is very heavy," "My spine is warm") the mental control travels repeatedly down the spine, always starting with the cervical section and moving to the coccygeal part, while the mental process of passive concentration on, for example, "My spine is very heavy" continues.

NON-ARTICULAR RHEUMATISM

The numerous conditions characterized by stiffness, aching or soreness, local tenderness and tearing pain which may appear without clearly definable cause in almost any part of the locomotor system remain subject to medical investigation and treatment. When infections (e.g., influenza, meningitis, tonsillitis, Bornholm disease, epidemic stiff neck), metabolic disorders (e.g., elevated uric acid levels, excessive intake of certain food), endocrine deviations (e.g., hypothyroidism, hypopituitarism) are excluded, psychogenic causes (e.g., anxiety reaction, emotional conflicts, hysteria), and the application of autogenic training may be considered. However, since it has become evident[2065] that muscular spasms, pain, and tenderness in circumscribed areas are frequently linked to specific minor or major traumas in the patient's past (e.g., hit by a baseball, slipping and falling against the corner of a table, being dropped as a small child and hitting the edge of a chair, bicycle accidents, hit by a ski pole or hockey stick, car collisions), and that relevant modalities of autogenic discharges may occur during autogenic training, it is advisable to take a detailed medical history with emphasis on minor and major traumas in each case. It has often been observed that trainees who noted onset or increase of pain, muscular spasms, tearing, pressure-like sensations and phenomena "like rheumatic pain," suddenly remembered a forgotten incident which appeared to be related to the specific area of autogenic discharge. Unless the related trauma was severe and complex (e.g., car collision with loss of consciousness), such autogenic discharges and the "non-articular rheumatism" tended to subside progressively and finally disappear completely as autogenic exercises were practiced regularly over long periods.[2065]

In other instances, when onset of rheumatic pain is thought to be associated with the weather (e.g., dampness, rapid changes of temperature), it has been observed that "the weather" loses its complaint-related importance[143] as the muscular spasms and rheumatic pain subside and other improvements (e.g., sleep, digestion, headaches, apprehensiveness, depressive dynamics) improve.[896,1952] In such cases it is recommended that any previously used medication (e.g., analgesics, barbiturates) be reduced and eliminated as quickly as possible and to stop the unenlightened application of physiotherapy.[1746,1915]

When hysterical or psychotic dynamics are involved, the limitations of autogenic training and the indication of more complex forms of treatment must be considered (see Vol. III).

LOW BACK SYNDROME

The use of autogenic standard exercises and organ-specific formulae in patients complaining about pain in the lumbar, lumbosacral, sacroiliac or coccygeal region of the back may vary with the particular nature of the participating causes. Generally, it is advisable not to start autogenic training before the frequently underestimated complexity of differential diagnostic problems has undergone careful evaluation. Intervertebral disk abnormality, spinal tumors (e.g., neurofibromas, meningioma), local mechanical defects, pancreatic disease, infections, pelvic metastases, post-traumatic reactions, specific disease of the vertebrae, structural inadequacies, proctalgia fugax[1068] (see Case 61, p. 147), sexual deprivation, menstrual disorders, underlying psychodynamic disorders (e.g., depression, anxiety reaction, psychotic dynamics)[1163,1171,1915] and other etiologic variables may participate in various combinations. Since therapeutic requirements and prognostic perspectives differ widely with the causative variables, an indiscriminate application of autogenic approaches as "a cure for the low back pain" is medically not acceptable.

However, once the nature of the etiologic variables and relevant treatment programs have been determined, autogenic training, organ-specific formulae, intentional formulae, or methods of autogenic neutralization (e.g., post-traumatic syndromes) may prove to be very helpful in combination with other forms of treatment.[739,1068,1163,1171,1528,1746,1915,1952,2178] A general and topographically specific reduction of muscular tension together with stress-neutralizing effects at a psychophysiologic level as it already results from the regular and frequent practice of heaviness exercises are desirable treatment factors for many cases. This is particularly so when sprains of the lumbosacral or low lumbar joints, herniation of an intervertebral disc, or collapse of vertebrae are associated with congestion of or pressure on the nerve roots (e.g., lumbago-sciatic syndrome) and prolonged periods of bed rest are required.[896] As muscular spasms in affected areas subside under the influence of passive concentration on heaviness (e.g., standard heaviness formulae plus "My spine is heavy," see Vol. I) circulatory functions have better possibilities to adjust to local requirements. The subsequent practice of the warmth formulae composing the Second Standard Exercise tend to promote muscular relaxation and adjustment of circulatory variables. The additional use of topographically specific warmth formulae (e.g., "The lower part of my spine is warm" or, "My pelvis is warm") may be very helpful in many instances. However, in order to avoid undue congestion in affected areas (e.g., increase of pain), case-specific evaluation and, for example, adjustment of duration of exercises is recommended.

Unless there are contraindications (e.g., co-existing gastritis, peptic ulcer, brain-injury) these patients should be encouraged to learn all standard exercises.

When disturbing modalities of autogenic discharges (e.g., pain, nausea, dizziness) are frequent and do not subside within a reasonable period of regular practice of autogenic training (e.g., 2–4 months), as is frequently the case in post-traumatic reactions, decisive improvements are usually obtained with intensive use of autogenic abreaction and progressive neutralization of the accident and related dynamics of disturbing material (e.g., fear of death, sufferings in hell, grief reactions, accumulated aggression).

References: 141, 190, 222, 449, 569, 739, 1042, *1068*, 1163, *1171*, 1174, 1528, 1822, *1915*, 1952, 1957, 1958, 1978, 2008, 2178, 2192.

7. Hemophilia

Observations by W. Luthe[896] of three adult male patients with classical hemophilia who learned autogenic training may be considered of interest for further research. Two cases were observed during the practice of the First Standard Exercise only, while the third case learned four standard exercises and was under observation for about nineteen months (see Case 48, Fig. 29). In all three cases autogenic training was started under continuous clinical control while the patients were hospitalized with manifestations of bleeding (hematoma formation, hemarthroses, arthropathy). The heaviness exercises produced the usual effects, such as muscular relaxation, reduction of discomfort in various muscles, alleviation of pain in affected joints (e.g., knee, elbow, ankle), decrease of apprehension and better sleep, in all three cases. There was no evidence of clinically unfavorable side-effects of autogenic training.

Case 48: A 36-year-old patient with classical hemophilia (hemoarthroses, arthropathy, intra-muscular hemorrhages, valgus deformity of knees and ankles) and a long history of various hemorrhagic episodes with hospital admissions. Over the years the patient had become addicted to codeine-containing medication (e.g., taking about 12 to 15 "292"s, six "293"s per day). The patient had difficulty in walking because of pain in his left knee and r. ankle joint, and used a cane. He complained about lumbar back pain, anorexia, frequent nausea, heartburn, abdominal discomfort, missing heart beats, disturbed sleep, periods of panic with generalized perspiration, trembling hands, pain in left upper arm, chronic constipation, multiple phobic reactions, feelings of guilt and depression about not being able to work and letting his wife down.

The patient learned autogenic training without experiencing any particular difficulties. Frequent and intense motor discharges occurred during heaviness training, but subsided progressively during warmth training with case-adapted reduced warmth formulae ("slightly warm"). The Third Standard Formula "Heartbeat calm and regular" was omitted because of the patient's unfavorable tendency to watch his heart for "missed beats" and "palpitations." The Sixth Standard Formula was not used in order to avoid an increase of frequently occurring sensory and motor discharges involving the cranial region (see examples of the patient's training protocols).

Formula	Reports on the effects of the exercises
	First week
	October 19
"My right arm is heavy." (45 sec.)	a) I had a funny sensation about my eyes in the middle of the exercise. Slight heaviness in right arm.

131

Formula	Reports on the effects of the exercises
"	b) Right arm a bit heavier. I don't feel so tight in my stomach.
"	c) In the top part of my mouth I felt a sort of throbbing. Felt relaxed. Electric waves were going down my legs. My legs appeared to be relaxed.

October 22

"My right arm is heavy . . . My left arm is heavy . . . Both arms are heavy." (90 sec.)

a) Twitches behind right and left eyeball. Feel more relaxed.

b) Twitch on left temple. Feel more relaxed in my stomach. My legs are relaxed and feel comfortable. There was a funny sensation on my right temple and the slight headache I had has disappeared. Now (after termination) I can move my legs without pain.

"

c) I seemed to go deeper, my respiration and my heart slowed down. There is a tingling sensation in my legs, a very nice feeling, as if they were new. There is also some tingling in my arms, and I have a nice peculiar feeling over my left skull, like after washing my head, I feel more relaxed.

Second week

October 29

"My right arm is heavy . . . My left arm is heavy . . . Both arms are heavy . . . My right leg is heavy." (120 sec.)

a) Face twitching. Muscles in right leg above knee felt as if it was moving, with a nice feeling in leg. Had a feeling as if my heart and breathing slowed down. After exercise had a tight feeling in both legs and I was very relaxed.

October 30

"

a) Face twitching very heavy. Had a feeling like a cold wave passing down both legs. Both my legs felt quite light after exercise. Had a funny feeling in my scalp as if it was tight and tingling, ending at the back of my head near my neck. Felt very relaxed after exercise.

November 1

"

a) Face twitching very heavy, also jaw going from side to side, had cold feeling go down my legs. Left arm twitched around my wrist. Scalp twitched from back to front. After exercise was over, my body felt very light

Formula	Reports on the effects of the exercises

Formula

Reports on the effects of the exercises

and when I picked up objects they seemed lighter.

Third week
November 6

All heaviness formulae plus "My neck and shoulders are heavy."

c) Face twitched a little. Head, arms, shoulders and top of body moved and twitched quite a bit, also left hand jumped up and down on bed very fast. Could feel stomach twitch, had current wave in legs and feet. When I finished the exercise I had a feeling like shutting off a current.

After three weeks of heaviness training, the patient commented: After the exercises I feel relaxed and calmer. The tight feeling in my heart is gone and the tingling sensation in my legs and feet stays on. The tense feeling in my neck is gone and the tight feeling behind my eyes is gone. My sleep is better, I can go back to sleep readily after a smoke. I often get hungry after the exercise, generally I get hungrier faster and eat more. The "292" pills are about 50 per cent down. My stomach relaxes very easily and my palpitations have disappeared. Lately, when I get this bleeding-like sensation in my right elbow, it goes away by doing exercises. The petechiae I get, usually announcing a hemorrhage, now with the exercises go away. I used to get jumpy legs with cracking of the bones and pain with hot flushes and burning sensations which were frequently followed by a hemorrhage and stiffness. This does not occur anymore, when my legs started jumping, recently, it was associated with relaxation.

After adding the formulas of the Second Standard Exercise:

Fifth week
November 18

"My arms and legs are heavy . . . my neck and shoulders are heavy . . . my right arm is slightly warm . . . my left arm is slightly warm."

a) Arms and legs are heavy and relaxed. My face twitched a little. Had tingling in both legs like an electric current. Had feeling like pins and needles go over my scalp in a wave. Also felt my body was smaller. After exercise still had tingling in legs and felt sleepy.

Formula   **Reports on the effects of the exercises**

Sixth week

November 29

The patient's progress continued. He felt particularly proud that he had not taken one codeine pill during the last four weeks. He said he did not even feel a need for them. He took an aspirin only once. He had much less pain and discomfort in his knees and ankle joints and was walking better. He still had some heartburn occasionally, and his appetite was not completely back to normal. Since the patient was still apprehensive while walking, being afraid to have pain in his legs again, and his attention appeared to increase the tension in his legs, it was suggested that he use "My neck and shoulders are very heavy" while walking. For further support the following physiologically oriented Intentional Formula, "My legs work automatically—pain does not matter," was added to the regular pattern of standard formulae.

December 2

"My arms and legs are heavy . . . my neck and shoulders are heavy . . . my right arm is slightly warm . . . my left arm is slightly warm . . . both arms are slightly warm . . . my right leg is slightly warm . . . my left leg is slightly warm . . . both legs are slightly warm . . . my legs work automatically —pain does not matter."

a) Arms and legs were relaxed and heavy. Had heavy tingling feeling in both legs. Also had feeling as if my right leg was stretched, but it did not hurt, it felt nice. After exercise I was relaxed and felt better.

b) Had pulling on right leg again. It was as if somebody was holding it with a hand on each side of it, and pulled, very nice feeling, Also very relaxed feeling and marked tingling in both legs. After exercise I felt very relaxed.

Seventh week

December 9-12

Did not do any exercise in this period. I found that my legs hurt more when I did not do the exercises.

After adding the Fourth Standard Formula:

Formula   **Reports on the effects of the exercises**

Ninth week

December 23

a) Arms and legs are heavy with slight tingling and pulling in right leg. Warm feeling in both legs. Had feeling as if I was not doing the breathing. Stiff feeling in chest, as if chest was hard.

Eleventh week

January 5

a) Arms and legs are relaxed with slight tingling and warm feeling in both legs. Slight pulling feeling in right leg. Had stiff feeling in my chest. Also feeling as if each part of my body came together and was very firm. After exercise both legs were warm. Had feeling as if the exercise could go on and on.

After adding the Fifth Standard Formula:

Thirteenth week

January 15

a) Arms and legs are heavy and relaxed with faint tingling and warmth in both legs. Also had feeling like a current go to my rectum. Had tight feeling in chest. My stomach felt relaxed. After exercise had tingling in legs.

Fifteenth week

January 29

a) Arms and legs are heavy and relaxed with faint tingling in both legs also slightly warm. Had faint tingling around rectum. After exercise my stomach felt relaxed, less pain in legs.

February

The patient suffered from influenza and felt very ill. He did not practice any autogenic exercises for over two weeks. Then he experienced a minor episode of intramuscular bleeding. He immediately recalled that he had not done his exercises for a while and felt that it was better for him to practice autogenic training regularly.[2065]

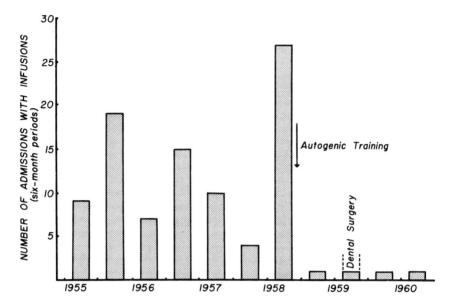

FIG. 29. Decrease in hospital admissions (Case 48) after application of autogenic training.[2065]

Summary of therapeutic development over a period of 19 months:

1. Reduction of pain and discomfort in previously affected joints and sites (e.g., l. knee, r. ankle, l. upper arm, back), with easier and longer periods of walking and standing.

2. Relatively fast and progressive reduction and, finally, complete withdrawal of the codeine-containing medication to which the patient had been addicted.

3. A 90 per cent decrease of hospital admissions (44 during a 19-month period before starting autogenic training; 4 during 19 months with autogenic training; see Fig. 29).

4. Marked improvement or disappearance of various psychophysiologic reactions (e.g., sleep disorder, anorexia, nausea, heartburn, constipation, palpitations, "missed beats").

5. Decrease of anxiety, situation-related apprehensiveness and depressive manifestations, with a favorable shift towards more initiative (e.g., the patient started a small business together with his wife).

These observations indicate that autogenic training may be a very valuable adjunctive approach in the treatment of hemophilic patients. However, further research during systematic application to larger groups of patients is required. The unexpected and drastic decrease of bleeding episodes associated with the regular practice of standard exercises appear to be of particular clinical and theoretical interest.

8. Disorders of the Genitourinary System

The applicability and the effects of autogenic standard exercises and relevant organ-specific formulas in the field of genitourinary disorders await systematic exploration.

There are as yet no studies concerned specifically with the effects of the standard exercises on renal function. However, clinical observations indicate that autogenic standard exercises seem to promote diuresis in certain trainees. Particularly in patients who practice autogenic standard exercises for prolonged periods (e.g., 20–30 min.), and in about 20 per cent of trainees who undergo autogenic abreactions it has been noticed that certain patients (who had been to the bathroom shortly before) were forced to terminate the autogenic exercise because their bladder had filled up again (see Case 49).

Case 49: A 40-year-old male patient (personality disorder, sexual deviation, multiple psychophysiologic reactions, history of recurrent duodenal ulcer).

Considering previous experiences, when he had to interrupt prolonged exercises because of an increasing urge to urinate, the patient went to the bathroom before getting ready for an autogenic abreaction. After 42 minutes the patient anounced that his bladder was prompting again. However, he did not want to interrupt the autogenic dynamics at this point and continued. About twenty minutes later he felt so disturbed by the increasing need to void that he decided to empty his bladder without getting up. Using a urinal, while his eyes remained closed, he voided 22 ounces and continued autogenic neutralization.[896]

DISORDERS OF MICTURITION

Various functional disorders of urination, involving nervous control of the bladder and disturbances of sphincter functions have been reported to respond favorably to autogenic approaches.[602] Functional incontinence, nocturnal enuresis (see Vol. III), frequency of micturition, nocturia, functional dysuria and psychogenically determined inabilities to urinate (see Case 52) have readjusted to normal. Depending on the particular nature of such psychophysiologic disorders, case-specific adaptation of autogenic standard training and eventual combinations with organ-specific approaches or Intentional Formulae must be emphasized.[2217,2365]

In psychophysiologic reactions associated with pollakiuria and nocturia, the progressive readjustment of emotional reactivity, as it occurs during the regular practice of autogenic standard exercises, is usually associated with the disappearance of the unduly frequent desire to urinate.[302,410] When insomnia occurs in association with nervousness, and frequency persists during the night (psychophysiologic nocturia), the addition of a case-adapted combination of organ-specific modifications of the Fifth Standard Exercise (e.g., warmth extending to bladder region) and relevant Intentional Formulae may be indicated (see Case 50).[1377]

Case 50: A 40-year-old engineer had suffered for many years from a disturbingly frequent urge for urination and defecation at all hours of the day and night. After ten weeks of standard training the patient reported: "Before I go to sleep I relax my abdomen and focus particularly on warmth in the abdominal region. For the last five weeks I have also applied an Intentional Formula which aims at maintaining deep breathing throughout the night. Abdominal complaints have all disappeared and I no longer need to go to the bathroom during the night." (Follow-up: 5 years.)[1377]

Similarly, disturbing spasms of the bladder[750] (see Case 51), cystalgias (without pathologic findings),[1101,1163,1171] and other psychophysiologically determined disorders of the bladder and the urethral region[741] have been reported to respond favorably in most cases.[410] It is, however, helpful to remember the case of a female patient reported by R. Lemke,[828] who complained about vague pain and discomfort in the bladder region and who did not respond to autogenic training. Later, this patient was diagnosed as suffering from schizophrenia.

Case 51: A 68-year-old chemist (arteriosclerotic heart disease) who suffered from difficulties of urination and disagreeable spasms of the bladder, particularly during the night. Urological investigation: no positive findings, no hypertrophy of the prostate. While the patient practiced standard training regularly, his complaints disappeared and he slept well again.[750]

Different forms of functionally determined difficulties in urination have also responded to autogenic approaches. Of particular interest are cases with postoperative urinary retention and patients with psychodynamically determined difficulties in urination under specific circumstances (situational urinary retention).[302,410] Even in cases where underlying fear of castration or homosexual dynamics participate in, for example, bringing about the inability to urinate in presence of others (e.g., public toilets), autogenic training has been successful in helping these patients to overcome their difficulty (see Case 52).

Case 52: A 26-year-old male patient who, since adolescence, suffered from inability to urinate outside of his home. He was always afraid that a stranger might watch him. This interfered with his social life. He never dared to be absent from his home for more than a few hours. Apart from this difficulty, his socio-professional adaptation was very good. With the help of autogenic training, and by induction of generalized relaxation while voiding, he became able to urinate at any place, after a few weeks.[302]

Information about the usefulness of autogenic approaches in instances of postoperative urinary retention stems from trainees who had practiced autogenic training regularly before they underwent surgery (see Case 53, Case 54). The avoidance of catherization and the prophylactic value of preventing cystitis and ascending renal infections by facilitating spontaneous bladder emptying through autogenic training is perhaps one of the clinically most valuable potentialities of autogenic therapy.[282,1163,1171]

Case 53: Postoperative urinary retention. Dr. U. Diesing reported[282] that after a successful abdominal operation (appendectomy, resection of Meckel's diverticulum), he was unable to void. Since his bladder continued filling up and his voluntary efforts, hampered by postoperative pain, remained for eight hours without results, it was suggested that he be catheterized if voiding did not start within another hour. In this situation, Dr. Diesing, who had practiced standard exercises for several years, started passive concentration on standard formulae. Then, without thinking of any specific verbal formulation, he used the solar plexus exercise as a point of departure for passive imagination of a feeling of warmth with a "flowing" quality, radiating downwards to the pelvis, the bladder and the genital region. Somatization of this approach occurred within a few minutes. This was followed by and became associated with an increasing urge to void. Actual voiding of 290 cc. of urine occurred soon after. Subsequently, no further episodes of urinary retention were experienced.[282]

Case 54: A 49-year-old theologist (anxiety reaction of long duration, obsessive-compulsive and phobic reactions, moderate depression, multiple psychophysiologic reactions) while undergoing autogenic therapy was found to have higher blood pressure values after 26 months of treatment than during his initial psychosomatic evaluation (see Case 23, Vol. I) and later controls (see Fig. 10, Vol. I). Clinical investigations carried out at this point had indicated an egg-size mass in the area of the right kidney. Surgery (Wednesday) verified that this tumor was a pheochromocytoma.

During the first three postoperative days no particular difficulties were encountered. However, on the evening of the third postoperative day (Saturday), the hospital chaplain told the patient that his heart had failed during the operation, and that while efforts were made to revive him, he, the chaplain, had applied extreme unction.

This revelation was quite a shock to the patient, who now also understood why he was still in the intensive care unit, hooked up to an oscillograph. He now also remembered that another priest had given him a detailed description of how he had applied the last rites to a patient who was operated and who had died because of heart failure. This story, presented to the patient 48 hours before his own operation, had helped to increase his anxiety.

The next day (Sunday) the patient was unable to void, catheterization (940 cc.) became necessary. Although some intermittent voiding occurred, catheterization (800 cc.) had to be repeated the following day (Monday).

On Monday afternoon the patient called the therapist's office. After he had told his story, he was instructed to practice autogenic standard exercises very slowly for prolonged periods, with emphasis on passive concentration on warmth radiating down into the bladder area with the Solar Plexus Formula as a point of departure. Using this approach the patient described his experience as follows:

"First I tried a hot sitz-bath. It gave me some relief, but nothing happened. I gave it up. For the night I also left the nightlamp on in my room; this also helped temporarily. It was the autogenic training which was decisive. During the night from Monday to Tuesday, I practiced for several hours, almost continuously, with the urinal between my legs. I worked very slowly taking about 50 minutes for one exercise. During the first two nights it was the formula "My solar plexus is warm," which was effective. It started suddenly with short micturitions, which were repeated quite often. Sometimes urination was drop by drop, becoming easier in the process. They had worked close to the solar plexus, that's why. . . . Then, it was the formula "Heartbeat calm and regular" which became effective. I think this had something to do with what I was told about my heart. Then, during the following days, it was the Intentional Formula "Je regarde l'aquarium et je laisse les autres s'emmerder" which was particularly effective. This formula triggered an easy and abundant micturition. This formula was once suggested by the therapist in order to regain some distance from the habitual environment and the hostility it generated in me. In my present situation this formula was associated with the following images: an aquarium which actually was a hospital made out of glass, with rows of beds on each story, and operated patients who suffered from urinary retention; they were almost out of their urinals; and I, standing there, I urinated with a tremendous stream on the aquarium making it almost invisible. While this image was in my mind, suddenly the sphincter relaxed and abundant micturition occurred. Sometimes I burst out in laughing." No further catheterization was required.[896]

DISTURBANCES OF SEXUAL FUNCTION

Experienced clinicians have reported encouraging results with autogenic approaches in the management of various manifestations of psychologic impotence.[302,360,410,475,595,596,612,643,1163,1171,1175,1528,1693,1699,1723,1758] Hasty emissions, premature ejaculation, functional disturbances of erection and inability to ejaculate during coitus may result from interfering inhibitions involving different combinations of psychodynamic variables. It is for this reason that the application of autogenic approaches (e.g., standard exercises, Intentional Formulae, Special Formulae, Autogenic Neutralization) requires a particularly thorough, case-specific adaptation based on a judicious psychodynamic evaluation. In certain cases a detailed sex education and the regular practice of the Standard Exercises may be sufficient by themselves (see Case 55). Observations reported by different authors (see references, p. 143) indicate that adequately applied autogenic training is successful in lessening interfering inhibitions without approaching the underlying psychodynamic problems (see Case 56). Improvements of sexual performance have also been observed in certain cases with systemic disorders such as diabetes mellitus, alcoholism and excessive fatigue. Therapeutically less favorable are cases who suffered traumas (particularly when the cranial region was involved), whose inability to perform the sexual act is associated with forceful patterns of obsessive nature or severe anxiety reactions of long duration (e.g., ecclesiogenic syndrome).[360] However, even in such complicated conditions, unexpected improvements may occur with autogenic standard training. Since the autogenic standard approach is inoffensive, its application as an initial phase (at least six months) of psychotherapeutic management has been recommended.[595,596,1163,1171,1528,1693,1723]

Case 55: A 30-year-old male patient suffered from premature ejaculation, which made it impossible for him to engage in intercourse. During sexual engagement, he tried to overcome the obsessive thoughts and apprehension related to his difficulty by unduly active, voluntaristic approaches.

Autogenic training permitted him to remain calm, to reduce his apprehension and to avoid functionally disturbing effects resulting from the interference of active, voluntaristic dynamics during intercourse. He regained normal sexual performance with satisfactory ejaculation function.[302]

Case 56: A 26-year-old, nice, soft and somewhat immature boy, who had married a more intelligent, very maternal girl. He loved and admired her, but he could not satisfy her. Although the Oedipus situation was quite obvious, the intellectual and cultural level did not encourage extensive psychotherapy. Autogenic training was started and after a while the couple had found its modus vivendi: in bed with his wife looking on sympathetically, he proceeded by first starting doing his autogenic exercises for a few minutes thus preparing himself for a performance which was satisfactory for both partners. It is not thought that this procedure solved the underlying problems, but, nevertheless, it served the purpose (12 months control).[1163, 1171]

In male trainees, good results have been observed in patients suffering from impotence due to anxiety-inhibition mechanisms of a relatively simple nature. Premature ejaculation and hasty emissions also tend to respond well if linked to affective-emotional factors. Depending on the individual case, it has been found helpful to apply the standard exercises in combination with an intentional formula which aims at a neutralization of the psychophysiologic process and/or a reduction in the trainee's anxiety and apprehensiveness.

Case 57: A 49-year-old teacher with strong feelings of anxiety and guilt about sexual intercourse considered himself an unmanly and inadequate sex partner because of hasty emissions which he felt himself unable to control. The condition had been present from the time of his marriage many years previously. Other complaints: hay fever, feelings of professional inadequacy (anxiety and insecurity, lack of firmness and consistency in school), inhibition of self-expression, uneasiness in groups, inhibited contact with other people, extreme self-consciousness, and a gloomy and pessimistic attitude in general.

After three weeks of standard training (heaviness): "Intercourse has become slower and more satisfactory."

Fifth week: (heaviness and warmth): "Feel much better, less insecure and inhibited with other people. Decided to join the teacher's bowling league."

Sixth week: (heaviness and warmth): "Last intercourse was more satisfactory because of delayed emission and less anxiety."

Tenth week: (heaviness, warmth, heart): "The emissions do not come quickly any more; intercourse is much more satisfactory than in the past. Less anxiety, fewer guilt feelings. While playing golf I get better shots when I relax in between by focussing on "My shoulders are heavy." Social contact much better."

Eleventh week: (heaviness, warmth, heart): "In general, I feel more confident and play better golf. My breathing is better than before. I feel this particularly when singing at church. More recently my feelings toward my wife have become more tender. After the exercises I even feel that my eyes are relaxed."

Fourteenth week: (heaviness, warmth, heart, respiration): "Sexual intercourse more satisfactory. My contact with other people is much better. I am more at ease, friendlier and less irritated. I am planning schoolwook leisurely. I do not feel harried anymore and there is less dread of going back to school this year. The onset of hay fever was late this year; it bothers me much less (last year I had to take antihistamine drugs). The exercises, particularly the last one ("It breathes me"), give me quite a relaxed feeling."

However, in each case of impotence or premature ejaculation a detailed evaluation of the variables involved (e.g., relative sexual deprivation, fear of causing undesirable pregnancy, fear of venereal disease, practice of coitus interruptus, castration anxiety, masturbatory guilt, sadistic desire to soil the woman) is advisable.[2178] It cannot be expected that an indiscriminate application of several weeks of heaviness and warmth exercises[115,2079] will result in normalization of a sexual disorder which has come about as a result of an intricate interaction of a variety of psychodynamic and environmental variables.

When impotence persists in the absence of any evident organic condition, and after autogenic standard exercises have been practiced regularly for six to eight months, therapeutic combination with autogenic neutralization (autogenic abreaction, autogenic verbalization) may be indicated. These approaches permit efficient brain-directed neutralization of underlying disturbing material (e.g., anxiety, ambisexual or homosexual dynamics, aggression, traumas, fear of pregnancy or venereal disease, ecclesiogenic anxiety and feelings of guilt).[2065,2066,2068]

Vaginal spasms,[302,410,602] dyspareunia,[302,410,930,1101,1758] and frigidity[302,360,595,596,612,1758] have also been reported to improve or normalize during autogenic standard exercises. However, similar to sexual disturbances in the male, it is essential to emphasize a thorough sex education and to carry out a detailed psychodynamic evaluation in each case. In many cases autogenic training is rather a valuable adjunctive approach, which may help to pave the way for the readjustment of marital problems,[1723] but which cannot be expected to dissolve deeply rooted psychodynamic disorders.

References: 115, 218, 282, 302, 312, 360, 410, 418, 475, 516, 541, 595, 596, 612, 643, 741, 750, 828, 852, 877, 888, 896, 930, 1100, 1101, 1163, 1171, 1175, 1190, 1528, 1541, 1693, 1699, 1723, 1758, 1902, 2048, 2065, 2066, 2068, 2069, 2079, 2122, 2178, 2208, 2217, 2330, 2365, 2425, 2426.

9. Gynecologic Disorders

In patients who were treated with autogenic training for non-gynecologic reasons it was occasionally observed[1568] that improvement or disappearance of certain co-existing gynecological disorders occurred as a therapeutic side-effect. Such observations stimulated a more systematic application of autogenic approaches in those gynecologic patients who are classified as belonging to the "functional group."

The largest group of authors reported on improvements of menstrual disturbances (see references, p. 148). A variable 40 to 70 per cent of patients suffering from primary and secondary dysmenorrhea tend to respond favorably. Premenstrual and menstrual cramp-like pains in the pelvis, the thighs and the lower back become less troublesome or disappear completely. There are less complaints of malaise, nausea, weakness, cold sweats and disagreeable vasomotor changes. Patients who previously had to rely on drugs feel that they can manage well without medication. Associated phases of increased irritability, depressive reactions, emotional outbursts, headaches, nausea, slight edema and other symptoms which are considered as being characteristic for premenstrual or menstrual "tension" become less marked or subside completely.[1953,2047,2064,2065,2092] Whether these improvements are also associated with favorable changes of previously existing disturbances of the electrolytic balance has not been investigated.

Different authors agree that better results are obtained when autogenic standard training is combined with passive concentration on warmth in the pelvic region.[217,219,302,410,538,1101,1226,1433,1528,1738] Different approaches ranging from a rather non-specific promotion of circulatory dynamics in the abdominal cavity to formulae aimed at "warmth" in topographically circumscribed areas, can be distinguished:

1. Topographically non-specific approaches:
   (a) "My abdomen is warm"[1101,1226] instead of "My solar plexus is warm."
   (b) "My solar plexus is warm" and in addition to this, "My lower abdomen is warm."[217,218,219,538,1226,1738]
2. Topographically more specific:
   (a) "My uterus is warm" ("Utérus chaud et calme").[302]
   (b) "My ovaries are warm" ("Meine Eierstöcke sind ganz warm").[1226]

Case 58: A 36-year-old patient (married to a gynecologist) had suffered from dysmenorrhea since the onset of menstruation at the age of 15. The patient began autogenic training because of gastric complaints and reported:

"The monthly complaints consisted mainly of painful spasms, which preceded the actual onset of menstruation, for many hours or even a whole day. Since I began practicing autogenic exercises two to three times daily the duration of premenstrual painful spasms has been reduced to only two hours. After this 'first stage of labor,' menstruation is now smooth and accelerated without particular pain. During subsequent menses, when training was further advanced, the menstrual flow started without any premonitory symptoms. I now can relax and open my uterus by focussing upon it during the exercises. I don't need to take drugs any more."[1377]

Case 59: A 32-year-old physician reported: "Under the influence of autogenic exercises the pains which regularly occur during the onset of menstruation disappear within a few minutes."[1377]

While there appears to be agreement between different authors that the therapeutic effects of standard exercises are enhanced by additional emphasis on warmth in areas of the lower abdominal region, it must be mentioned also that there is a lack of reliable experimental data. The formulae mentioned above are considered as tentative approaches of an empirical nature. It is not clear if the implied degree of topographic precision (e.g., "My ovaries are warm"[1226]) is of more therapeutic value than less specific approaches (e.g., "My lower abdomen is warm"). Obviously further research is needed. It is in this context that an investigation carried out by Y. Ikemi, S. Nakagawa, M. Kimura, H. Dobeta, Y. Ohno and M. Sugita[546] is of specific interest. The investigators found that passive concentration on "My lower abdomen is warm" produced a gradual increase of blood flow and activation of the peristaltic activity in the sigmoid colon (see Vol. IV).

J. Cepelak and Z. Tumova[217,218,219,538,1738] applied autogenic standard training, with additional emphasis on warmth in the lower abdomen, and observed favorable effects on cases suffering from dysfunctional bleeding, persistent pain in the pelvic area (without detectable lesions), pelvic congestion and cases diagnosed as chronic "adnexitis" and "pelvipathia vegetativa."[1088,1101,1102] J. N. Wagner[1758] reported onset of normal menstrual flow after seven weeks of autogenic training in a neurotic patient who had suffered from secondary amenorrhea for seven years. Related psychophysiologic reactions and disturbances as, for example, dyspareunia, vaginal spasms, sexual frigidity, sterility, climacteric disorders, pruritus vulvae (see Index; Case 63), leucorrhea, non-specific pelvic pain and cystalgia.[602,888,889,925,1101,1102,1758,2114,2124,2177]

Encouraging results in trainees suffering from certain forms of sterility have been noted. For example, Y. Sakakura, S. Iwabuchi and T. Murata[2114] reported on a group of 22 patients who were believed to suffer from infertility because of anxiety-related functional disturbance of tubal patency (control by utero-tubal insufflation). After treatment with auto-genic training in combination with a limited number of simple psychiatric interviews and group hypnosis, eight of these patients became pregnant within one year, and five others later.

In a group of 60 patients suffering from a variety of gynecologic dis-orders, H. J. Prill reported disappearance of relevant complaints in 19 (27.5 per cent) cases, significant improvements in 29 (42 per cent) and little or no improvements in 21 (30.5 per cent) patients.[1101] Autogenic exercises are also helpful when abdominal cramps, nausea and painful uterine contractions start after insertion of intrauterine devices (see Case 60).

Case 60: A 24-year-old nurse (anxiety reaction, peripheral circulatory disorder, mild depression, multiple phobic reactions, history of multiple accidents and emotional traumas), who participated in a course of autogenic standard training, decided to have an intrauterine loop installed. After in-sertion of the intrauterine device she experienced onset of disagreeable painful cramps in the lower abdominal (uterine) area.

The patient continued her regular pattern of autogenic exercises and noticed that abdominal spasms, painful cramps and uterine contractions subsided progressively during the heaviness and warmth exercises (see below). This beneficial effect lasted for about two to three hours after each set of exercises. When the painful spasms reappeared, she practiced another set of autogenic exercises and obtained prompt relief.

During heaviness and warmth training:

April 5, 1968   (a)   Position comfortable, feeling of apprehension and anx-iety. Frontal headache, concentration difficult, feel-ing of aggression. Abdominal pain: uterine contractions, very disagreeable.

                (b)   Less apprehension and less anxiety. Respiration regu-lar. Abdominal pain and uterine contractions dimin-ished.

                (c)   Relaxation. Abdominal pain and uterine contractions stopped. Headache disappeared. Feel comfortable and rested.

April 6, 1968   (a)   Some anxiety, position comfortable, fluttering of eye-lids. Concentration easy, no distractions. Pain in lower abdomen, uterine contractions.

                (b)   Relaxation, feel fine. Abdominal pain and contrac-tions diminished, feel sleepy.

                (c)   Relaxation. Pain and contractions stopped. Concen-tration easy. Sleep.[2065]

Of particular therapeutic concern is the group of patients who suffer from chronic recurrent diffuse sacral aching and variable forms of persistent low back pain involving the lumbar or sacrococcygeal region (see also p. 128-130). In these cases, after a careful evaluation of possible participation of pelvic or extrapelvic diseases has been carried out, and physical findings are inconsistent, diffuse or absent, autogenic approaches are recommended.

In milder cases good results have been observed in the course of the regular practice of standard exercises, with emphasis on prolonged passive concentration on heaviness formulae. In other cases, when standard exercises are insufficient, topographically oriented Special Formulae may be added. Two approaches have been helpful: firstly, passive concentration on "My back is (very) heavy" and secondly, added at a later point, "My back is warm." When using "My back is (very) heavy," it is recommended that the patient be instructed not to limit the mental contact to the lower part of the back, but to include the entire length of the dorsal region. While passive concentration on "My back is (very) heavy" continues, better effects are obtained when the mental contact starts at the cervical portion of the spine, and then wanders progressively and swiftly down to the sacrococcygeal region. After focussing on this area for a brief period, mental contact is shifted again to the upper spine, wanders downward, and pauses at the lower part. This dynamic use of the "mental contact function" during passive concentration on "My back is (very) heavy" yielded better results than the static type of mental contact either when including the back as a whole or when mental contact is specifically limited to the lower part of the back. However, when additional application of passive concentration on warmth is indicated, it is preferable to apply the usual (static) approach, aiming at an increase of circulation in a circumscribed area in accordance with the implications of the formula "My lower back is warm."

Occasionally associated with menstrual complaints, sexual arousal and various forms of pelvic discomfort is a periodically occurring sudden onset of sharp pain (proctalgia fugax[1068]) in the anococcygeal region. It is assumed that this type of coccyalgia is caused by a spasm of muscular components of the pelvic diaphragm (e.g., levator ani). P. Polzien,[1068] who investigated several cases, reported that autogenic training helped decisively in the therapeutic management of such patients (see Case 61).

Case 61: A relatively young female patient, who had her first attack of proctalgia fugax at the age of fifteen, kept suffering periodically from these unpredictable attacks of acute pain. A variety of therapeutic approaches attempted during the past years had remained unsatisfactory.

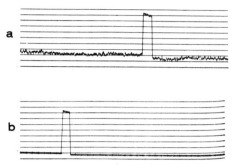

Fig. 30. Muscle potentials (a) during attack of proctalgia fugax, before starting autogenic training, and (b) several minutes later, during passive concentration on heaviness formulae. (Courtesy of P. Polzien, University of Würzburg.[1068])

Rectal examination during one of her attacks confirmed the palpable contraction of elements of the levator ani. Local tenderness and the muscular contraction subsided after digital massage. The patient started practicing the First Standard Exercise (heaviness). She reported that the exercise enabled her to stop the development of an attack. The autogenic approach remained effective during a control period of four years. During two of her attacks, P. Polzien managed to verify changes of muscle potentials after the patient started passive concentration on heaviness formulae (see Fig. 30 a and b).

References: 217, 218, 219, 225, 302, 410, 430, 537, *538*, 602, 610, 858, 859, 860, 863, 925, 1088, 1092, 1095, *1098*, *1100*, *1101*, *1102*, 1184, 1185, 1190, 1191, 1194, 1218, 1220, 1226, 1377, 1433, *1528*, *1541*, 1562, 1738, 1758, 1937, 1953, 2047, 2064, 2065, 2092, *2114*, 2124, 2126, 2177, 2179, 2366.

10. Pregnancy and Birth

Clinical results obtained with autogenic therapy in the field of psychosomatic disorders, together with the growing concern about the physiologic influence of emotional and mental factors on the course of pregnancy and birth, have stimulated a number of obstetricians to combine autogenic training with other modern approaches of prenatal care (see references, p. 159). This development received substantial support from favorable results obtained with related methods (e.g., G. D. Read, I. Z. Velvoski, A. P. Nikolajew, F. Lamaze, L. Chertok[220-232]) which aim at facilitating birth by prompting relaxation and reduction of fear and pain.

Autogenic training offers a number of therapeutic advantages which are as valuable during the prenatal period as during the course of labor, and as during the puerperium. It has been observed that regular practice of the autogenic standard exercises, when started during the early phases of pregnancy, reduces the onset of, or acts as an effective therapy for, minor disorders of pregnancy. Complaints such as nausea, vomiting, constipation, insomnia, shortness of breath, tenseness and irritability become less disturbing or subside more quickly under the influence of the standard exercises. Fear and anxiety also respond very well, unless deep-rooted neurotic mechanisms are involved. Patients with latent tetany and spastic tendencies find the exercises particularly relieving.

H. J. Prill (University of Würzburg, Department of Obstetrics), who applied autogenic training to over 1000 pregnant women,[1101] studied the effects of autogenic approaches in various respects. In 1957 he reported[1093] on the therapeutic effects of heaviness and warmth exercises on a group of 104 pregnant women (see Table 11) who suffered from various disorders (N = 142) of a functional nature. Most of Prill's patients had previously been treated by other means, without experiencing any significant improvement.

Since the average training period of H. J. Prill's patients was rather short (4–12 weeks), it can be expected that the therapeutic results will be much better when autogenic training is started earlier in pregnancy (e.g., third or fourth month). H. J. Prill obtained very little or no improvement in cases with heartburn. This may be explained by relevant anatomicophysiologic implications of progressing pregnancy (e.g., deficiency of cardiac closure, displacement of stomach, gastric hypersecretion). Another relatively poor improvement rate was observed in cases suffering from constipation. Since significantly better results are usually obtained in nonpregnant patients, H. J. Prill hypothesizes that certain constipatory conditions developing during pregnancy may be related to certain physiologic changes of the prenatal phase.[1093]

TABLE 11.   *Improvements of Functional Disorders in 104 Pregnant Trainees*

	Results		
Disorders	Very Good	Moderate	Nil
I. Disorders of the gastrointestinal tract (spasms, gastric hypersecretion, heartburn)	5	7	14
Constipation	5	9	26
II. Circulatory disorders (cold hands and feet, acroparesthesia)	16	4	3
Cardiac disorders of a functional nature	3	2	4
III. Spasms and neurovegetative disorders	4	6	9
IV. Sleep disorders	15	6	4
Total	48	34	60

In addition to the beneficial effects on the patient's prenatal state, passive concentration on the first four standard formulae has been found particularly helpful when applied during the different stages of labor. Apart from the reassuring effect resulting from the patient's knowledge that she has an effective technique at her disposal which almost instantly brings about calmness and relaxation, there are other physiologic changes which provide a favorable counterbalance to certain emotional and organismic phenomena usually associated with pregnancy and delivery. Of particular relevance are the respiratory changes (see Vol. IV), the inhibiting and lowering influence on blood pressure (p. 69) and heart rate (p. 41, 44ff; Vol. IV), decrease in muscular tension, the increase in motor and sensory chronaxy (see Vol. IV), the reduction in perception of pain (see Vol. III), and the delay of fatigue and exhaustion.

Because of the prophylactic and therapeutic value of autogenic training during the prenatal period, it is in the interest of the patient's well-being to begin with the standard exercises as early as possible after pregnancy has been verified. Of the three training postures, particular emphasis should be given to the reclining chair posture. The patient, however, should also practice the exercises in the horizontal position, which may be used without discomfort during the first months of pregnancy. Later, during more advanced stages, relatively high support for the knee joints is required to ensure a maximum of bodily relaxation. During the last two months the reclining chair posture is usually preferred, though many well-trained patients readily learn to perform the exercises while lying on their right side. During the entire period of pregnancy, repeated emphasis on a comfortable and relaxed position of the head, neck and shoulders is advisable. Many patients, particularly during the last three months, feel much more relaxed when an additional pillow is used for extra support.

It is further suggested that pneumograms be taken before and during autogenic therapy. The visible changes in the patient's respiratory pattern during passive concentration on the standard formulae serve as a useful control of the effectiveness of the patient's technique of passive concentration and illustrates better than anything else to the patient that her subjective impressions of certain bodily changes during the exercises are not merely imaginary. Regular readings of blood pressure and heart rate before, during, and after the exercises (see Fig. 12, p. 71); Fig. 14 p. 73; Vol. IV) are advisable. When there is a rise in systolic blood pressure (exceeding 15 per cent) during the exercises, in spite of a correct technique, autogenic therapy should be discontinued.

During heaviness and warmth training, a regular and effective association with a peaceful background image ("I am at peace") may be emphasized (see p. 53; Vol. I; Vol. III). Since the autogenic technique will be applied during labor, it is essential that the patient trains at establishing the autogenic state without delay. Clinical experience has demonstrated that the physiologic changes occur more readily and are most intensive when the first two standard exercises are regularly practiced for brief periods (e.g., 30–60 seconds). Patients who remark that they need more time for experiencing heaviness and warmth should be advised to limit the duration to 30 to 60 seconds nevertheless and to increase the frequency of the exercises, whether they experience heaviness and warmth regularly or not. Only when the exercises have been established in such a way that the patient is able to switch on the specific psychophysiologic state almost instantly may the duration of passive concentration be gradually prolonged.

More recently H. J. Prill[1101] reported that about 20 per cent of pregnant trainees noticed a disagreeable increase of bloodflow in the cranial region while practicing the Second Standard Exercise (warmth). This undesirable circulatory reaction, which may be associated with palpitations, may occur as early as during the initial phases of warmth training (e.g. "My right arm is warm"). In such instances it is suggested that the trainee continue with modified warmth formulae (see Vol. I).

Patients not suffering from periods of uncomfortable palpitation or other cardiocirculatory side-effects of pregnancy should continue with the Third Standard Exercise ("Heartbeat calm and regular"). Others, whose attention is already focussed on the heart because of disagreeable symptoms, would do better to omit the passive concentration on the heart. Instead, regular and prolonged periods of passive concentration of the fourth standard formulae ("It breathes me") should be emphasized.

The respiratory changes induced by the first two standard exercises are significantly reinforced by focussing on "It breathes me" (see Fig. 18, p. 99; Vol. IV) and are regarded as particularly effective in reducing painful sensations and in facilitating the process of birth.

Autogenic therapy during the prenatal period requires periodic supervision. Groups of four to eight patients carefully selected for intelligence, cultural and social background should be invited to meet at regular intervals (e.g., once every second week) for discussion and control training. Other patients who are acceptable to the group and who have delivered with the help of autogenic training are of great help when they are capable of reporting on their experience with the method. Expectant trainees usually notice that the movements of the fetus become more distinctive, active, and frequent during the exercises. Slow or no progress at all occurs most frequently in cases in which there is a lack of the mother's identification with the child or the baby is rejected for one reason or another.[1094]

The autogenic approach is regarded as being of particular value during the first stage of labor. The pattern of passive concentration should be adapted to the rhythm of the pains so that the deepest and most effective phase of each exercise ("It breathes me") coincides with the "fortissimo" of the pain. This technique of "diving through the pains" has been found to reduce the strain of labor significantly. From a comparison with non-trained patients the impression was gained that the well-trained group in general was less tired, calmer and better relaxed during the second stage of labor. Fewer or no analgesics were required for trainees, and the whole process of birth appeared to be facilitated and accelerated.[1094]

Case 62: A 29-year-old multipara, who had a great fear of the birth process, came to learn the autogenic training. Last pregnancy was three years previously, after 34 hours of labor; delivery was by forceps because of secondary weakness of labor and increasing weakness of the baby's heart sound.

Excerpts from the patient's notes:

Sept. 11th: Distinctive heaviness in right arm, tingling in finger tips and feeling of slight swelling in right forearm. I am still very much afraid; nobody who had not experienced my last delivery could take the fear from me.

Sept. 16th: My whole body is heavy and there is some pins-and-needles feeling in both arms.

Oct. 4th: I easily can "switch off," even when my 3-year-old son is around. Everything gets heavy and somehow disperses. First, there is flowing warmth in the arms; sometimes they appear to be swollen and then they almost dissolve. My feet are also getting really warm; this is quite a pleasant experience since I have constantly suffered from cold feet.

Nov. 9th: Now we have discussed the birth process in detail. I feel much better now and I am much calmer. I think this time the whole thing will work out much better. I now know what I did wrong last time.

Nov. 14th: Today we visited Mrs. S., a member of our training group who has already delivered. Mrs. S. was very satisfied with the autogenic relaxation. This had a very reassuring effect on me. If she can do it this way, I should be able to do just as well.

Nov. 21st: The respiratory exercise still does not work as it should. I am still afraid that perhaps I may not get enough air. Heaviness and warmth are established almost instantly. Since I find it difficult to do the exercises while lying on my back, I am now doing them lying on my side.

Dec. 3rd: "It breathes me." I am very glad to have reached this point. The others in my group are far ahead of me. During this phase of the exercises there occurs a funny feeling—as if the body were somehow detached. Now that the exercises work much faster than before, I think I will be able to get deep enough during each pain. Actually I am not afraid any more.

Dec. 6th: Spontaneous onset of labor, 12 days after the "due date." On arrival at the hospital the cervix was dilated four fingerbreadths. The patient reported that the pains had started the night before and that she had begun with autogenic exercises after distractive activities did not help any more. The patient stated that this time she did not aggravate the pains by getting tense, but that each time she somehow "collapsed as if hit by a bullet" and thus succeeded in "diving through the wave of labor." The patient entered the hospital when the pains became more regular and the intervals became so short that she could not reach the "respiratory phase" any more. The patient was quite relaxed: voluntary relaxation was calm and rhythmic. After 90 minutes, there was spontaneous birth of a 3750 gm. female child (left occipitoposterior presentation). No analgesics were required. Quite in contrast to her last delivery the patient was satisfied with her achievement this time. The autogenic exercises were regarded as very relieving.[1090]

H. J. Prill[1090] also reported on the pain-relieving effect of passive concentration in a group of 142 patients with spontaneous births. All patients had mastered at least the heaviness and warmth exercises reliably. Very good and good results were reported by 102 patients; 23 noted moderate effects, and 17 others little or no relief from pain. In four patients of the latter group anomalies were present.

H. J. Prill[1094,1101] confirmed these results in a more recent study covering 302 well-trained patients (see Table 12).

According to H. J. Prill's data, the pain-alleviating effect of autogenic training lasted well through the different phases of effacement and dilatation. About 70 per cent observed a notable relief of pain during the active phase with cervical dilatation up to 7.5 cm. or even complete dilatation achieved.[1101] Similar observations have been reported by Y.

TABLE 12.   *Reduction of Pain during Labor*[1101]

Duration of Alleviation of Pain (cervical dilatation:cm.)	Total Number of Parturient Women		Primipara		Multipara	
	N	%	Total N	Age 30 and over (N)	Total N	Late IIp. (N)
3.5 cm. and less	91	30.1	74	(18)	17	(4)
Up to about 7.5 cm.	132	43.7	102	(34)	30	(7)
Over 7.5 cm. to complete dilatation	79	26.1	46	(21)	33	(3)
Total	302		222	(73)	80	(14)

(43.7 and 26.1 braced together = 69.8)

Okamura and T. Goto[2097] and V. S. Sbriglio[2123,2124] who studied the effect of autogenic training in a group of 137 women.[253] Further studies undertaken by H. J. Prill[1101,2108] indicated that the reduction of pain is largely independent of the intensity of uterine contractions (see Table 13).

In patients having a negative attitude toward the child the pain-relieving effect of the autogenic exercises appeared to be significantly reduced. In this group (N = 41), 12 women felt incapable of using the autogenic technique during the first stage of labor. No failure occurred in the group of women (N = 100) with a positive attitude toward the child. Eighty-three per cent of the positively oriented women reported relief from pain until the opening of the cervix was three to four fingerbreadths or larger. Of the group with a negative attitude toward the child, about 50 per cent experienced the pain-relieving effects of passive concentration to the same extent of cervical dilatation. In another study, H. J. Prill[1090] compared a group of married patients having an above average social level with a group of unmarried patients whose social level was below average (N = 85). The autogenic training period in both groups ranged from eight to twelve weeks. H. J. Prill scored the subjective reports of the patients in respect of the degree of relief of pain experienced during birth which they credited to the autogenic exercises and compared these scorings with the patient's degree of relaxation as observed by a physician. The group of married women showed significantly better results in both categories.

H. J. Prill[1101] also carried out a comparative study of 104 pregnant women who practiced autogenic training and relevant data obtained from a control group of 300 non-trained parturient women. This investigation revealed a number of differences which are of clinical interest. In the group prepared with autogenic training, H. J. Prill found:

TABLE 13. *Intensity of Uterine Contractions and Reduction of Pain*[1101]

Uterine Contractions	Total Number of Parturient Women N	Reduction of Pain (dilatation of cervix)		
		3.5 cm. and less N	Up to 7.5 cm. N	7.5 cm. and over N
Very good contractions, speedy delivery	116	43	50	23
Average contractions (3-4 min./40 sec.)	152	37	67	48
Poor contractions, use of stimulating drugs	34	11	15	8
Total	302	91	132	79

(a) The *mean* duration of the dilatation phase was about three hours shorter. In primiparae the difference was almost four hours (10.7: 14.5 hr.).

(b) The *mean* number of contractions was lower (103: 126).

(c) The *mean* frequency of contractions (per 30 min.) was slightly, but not significantly higher (6.0 : 5.4).

(d) Contractions with a frequency of 40 sec. and above were observed in 13.2 per cent of the patients practicing autogenic training, and only in 5.5 per cent of the non-trained control group.

(e) A calculation of the duration of uterine contraction (number of contractions multiplied by duration of contractions) indicated that the "total contraction time" was 28.6 per cent higher in the non-trained control group.

H. J. Prill, in agreement with observations reported by other authors (see references, p. 156), concluded that autogenic training helps significantly in facilitating, economizing and accelerating the physiological processes of natural delivery.[2108]

A pilot study with a small group of eleven subjects, carried out by Y. Okamura and T. Goto,[2097] indicated that even a very small number of autogenic exercises may (a) shorten the duration of labor (particularly stage one and two), (b) decrease or prevent asphyxia of the newborn, and (c) keep the plasma cortisol at lower levels.

If possible and indicated, it is recommended that passive concentration on standard formulae be resumed after the baby's birth, when the contractions cease for a short interval. This helps the exhausted women to recover and to pass more smoothly through the third stage of labor.

Furthermore it has been noted that the frequent practice of short-period standard exercises has a favorable effect in recovery in general and on transitory sleep disturbances in particular. It is also helpful to remember that cases of postoperative urinary retention have used auto-genic approaches successfully (see Case 53, p. 139; Case 54, p. 139) and that autogenic training has been of valuable help in the promotion of lactation (Janson[253]).

References: 169, 217, 220, 225, 227, 228, *232, 253, 302,* 310, 340, 341, 403, *410,* 477, 478, *538,* 597, 715, 795, 858, 862, 877, 888, 963, 1088, 1089, 1090, 1091, 1093, 1094, 1095, 1096, 1097, *1098, 1099, 1101, 1102,* 1189, 1190, 1191, 1194, 1220, 1226, 1403, 1433, 1465, *1528, 1541,* 1598, 1737, 1738, 1801, 1802, 2046, 2063, 2095, *2097, 2108,* 2109, 2112, 2113, 2123, 2124, 2179, *2225,* 2254, 2277, 2344, *2351, 2354,* 2366, 2391, 2413.

11. Skin Disorders

Autogenic training has been applied in the treatment of various skin disorders and relevant allergic conditions (see references, p. 159). The improvements and cures observed in dermatologic patients, most of whom had already been treated for long periods by other means with only temporary or limited success, are mainly credited to the normalization of autonomic functions resulting from the standard training, as well as to the more direct effect of organ-specific exercises. Depending on the nature of the skin disorder, an organ-specific formula may be used either for increasing the blood flow ("warmth") in certain tegumentary areas of the body or for cooling and/or tranquillizing in general. In four cases suffering from severe neurodermatoses, K. Thomas[1718] successfully applied, for example:

"My skin is soothed, cool and free from irritation."

In patients whose localized disorder had been diagnosed as an allergic condition, H. Kleinsorge[641] gained the impression that organ-specific exercises were much more effective than desensitization or any symptomatic treatment.

Y. Ikemi, S. Nakagawa, T. Kusano, and M. Sugita[547] applied a new approach of systematic desensitization to three patients suffering from contact dermatitis and seven patients with food allergy and skin reactions. Stimulated by the observation that the trainees' reaction to various stimuli was markedly decreased after passive concentration on autogenic formulae, the authors designed a step-by-step program of desensitization by applying auditory, imaginary and actual confrontation with the noxious stimuli during autogenic training (for details see ref.: 542, 545, 547, 891). The results obtained with this method of desensitization were encouraging. Four patients lost their allergic reactions within 8 days, four others after four weeks, and two did not respond.

Certain cases of generalized and localized forms of pruritus as, for example, pruritus of the perianal area, scrotum, vulvar region and pruritus due to urticaria[622,1182,2079] have been reported to respond favorably[168,410,622,739,1101,1182,1528,1981,2085] by combining the standard exercises with passive concentration on coolness in the affected region. In these cases the antipruritic reduction of vasomotor reactions, the decreased need for scratching, the significant improvement of disturbed sleep pattern,[1918,2085] and the progressive elimination of sedative medication were considered to be of particular therapeutic value.

L. Holčik[538] used autogenic approaches in 71 cases suffering from dermatoses (49 chronic eczema, 18 psoriasis, 4 lichen ruber). From his data, L. Holčik concluded that autogenic training helps to accelerate the therapeutic effects of other forms of treatment, and that there is a prolongation of periods without symptoms.[410,538] These observations correspond well with a report by M. Sapir[1163] who obtained good results in cases of allergic and non-allergic type of urticaria,[2176] psoriasis, acne and even pityriasis rosea. Satisfactory improvements of hyperhidrosis,[168,1981] successful reduction of local irritation and pain[1416,1981] and effective "warming" (see p. 79) of exposed areas (e.g., nose, ears, extremities) as a prophylactic measure against frostbite have been also recorded.[1416,1433] A number of authors successfully used various combinations of standard exercises, Special Formulae and Intentional Formulae (see Case 64, 65) in the treatment of warts.[114,213,410,1101,1182,1527]

Case 63: A 46-year-old artist had suffered for 14 years from distressing pruritus of the vulva. X-ray treatment, ten years ago, brought about transitory relief but also caused burns; these were treated successfully but the itching continued. The complaints disappeared under the influence of standard training and passive concentration on organ-specific cooling (follow-up: 6 years).[1377]

Case 64: W. Causse, a dentist, had a cherry-sized verruca vulgaris removed from his right middle finger by cauterization. Within six weeks the wart was back and was even bigger than it had been before. W. Causse, who already practiced the standard exercises, now added the formula, "Day by day the wart is becoming smaller," to his training film. After about five weeks the wart had become significantly smaller. Then W. Causse changed the Intentional Formula and continued applying, "The wart is disappearing completely." After three to four weeks the wart had disappeared and did not return during the subsequent period of two years.[213]

Case 65: A 60-year-old civil servant suffered from intermittent claudication which limited his walking time to about 20 minutes. After he had learned all standard exercises, a Special Formula aiming at flowing warmth in both legs ("Beine strömend warm") was added. With this approach the patient was able to prolong his walking time up to about 30 minutes. The patient also complained about several wart-like filiform epithelial proliferations in the neck area. Although his collar and shirt covered these skin lesions well, he felt quite bothered by their very existence. In an attempt to make these proliferations disappear a two-stage intentional approach was used. First, for four weeks the Special Formula: "Warts are getting smaller" ("Warzen werden kleiner") was added to the Standard Series. Then this formula was substituted by "Warts fall off" ("Warzen fallen ab") for another two weeks. At this point, the epithelial proliferations had disappeared.[1527]

In the field of dermatology clinical observations indicate that the adjunctive application of autogenic approaches facilitates the therapeutic management, accelerates improvements and enhances the results of conventional drug therapy. However, depending on the specific nature of the skin disorder and the underlying pathogenetic dynamics in each case, the results ascribed to autogenic therapy vary considerably. Unexpected, very encouraging results in certain therapy resistant cases suffering from chronic dermatoses, and failure rates of 70 per cent in other cases[3,2079] are stimulating discrepancies which require further clarification by intensive and systematic research.

References: 3, 114, 156, 167, 168, 213, 274, 275, 302, 315, *410,* 538, 541, *542, 545, 547,* 604, 641, 655, *662, 739,* 877, 888, 968, 969, *1101, 1163,* 1171, 1182, 1200, 1307, *1416, 1433,* 1477, *1527, 1528, 1541,* 1566, 1718, 1786, 1928, 1981, 1982, 1983, 1984, 1994, 1995, 2031, 2065, 2079, 2084, 2085, 2110, 2111, 2122, 2176, 2177, 2317.

12. Ophthalmologic Disorders

The application of autogenic approaches in the field of ophthalmologic disorders was stimulated by patients who noticed improvements of their eye disorder while practicing autogenic exercises for other reasons. Such improvements occurred particularly in disturbances which involved vasomotor instability and functional deviations of neuro-muscular elements as, for example, certain forms of strabismus, amblyopia and glaucoma. The ameliorations were observed to coincide with progressive normalization of coexisting disorders as, for example, readjustment of essential hypertension, disappearance of headaches, improvement of respiratory disturbances, smoothing of neurotic reactions and noticeable gains in emotional stability in general.

Encouraged by observations in isolated cases, autogenic training was used more systematically in adults, adolescents and children[1570] with eye disorders considered to benefit from this therapeutic approach.

So far, autogenic standard exercises have been used most frequently in cases of nonparalytic (concomitant) strabismus and latent strabismus which frequently is associated with blurring of vision, headache and diplopia.[706,707,942,943,981,1566,1568]

J. Seabra-Dinis,[1565,1566,1567,1568,2145] M. L. Merces de Mello,[942,943,1568] J. Dos Santos[1568] and H. Moutinho[981,1568] in Lisbon reported satisfactory results in over 100 cases suffering from amblyopia, strabismus (see Cases 66, 67, 68) and blindness (see Case 71, 72). In many cases which did not respond to other previously applied forms of treatment (e.g., corrective glasses, orthoptic training), progressive restoration of muscle balance and normal convergence together with better adjustment of emotional reactivity and relevant psychodynamic disturbances resulted from the regular practice of autogenic exercises.

Case 66: A 25-year-old unmarried couturière with a variable internal non-paralytic (concomitant) strabismus since childhood. After an unfortunate love affair at the age of eighteen the deviation became more marked. She underwent orthoptic therapy on several occasions, however, without result. She never accepted her visual defect, and occasionally went into crises of revolt and despair.

At the age of 24 she started suffering from episodes of nausea and periorbital headaches and went for another ophthalmologic consultation. At this point (June 2) her strabismus was 20 degrees, without simultaneous macular perception. She started practicing autogenic standard exercises regularly. The episodes of nausea and the headaches disappeared during heaviness training. After about four weeks, at the beginning of the Third Standard

Exercise (heart) she noticed that her squint was less marked. The ophthalmologic examination verified a deviation of only 10 degrees. The patient continued to practice autogenic exercises regularly. Ophthalmologic controls at two-week intervals indicated steady progress of improvement. No other means of psychotherapy or drugs, except for encouraging support during her control visits, were applied. After 14 weeks (September) when she practiced all six standard exercises the divergence was reduced to 5 degrees. On September 20 orthoptic motor training (convergence, relaxation) was added. Five weeks later (end of October) the divergence had reached zero intermittently (with simultaneous macular perception). In December her strabismus was adjusted with satisfactory stability. During a three-year control period her binocular vision remained almost perfect.[1568]

Case 67: A 22-year-old female student, suffering since early childhood from a variable divergent strabismus, without simultaneous macular perception (S.M.P.). A variety of therapeutic attempts aiming at restoration of normal convergence had remained without benefit. Strabometric examination (March 29) revealed a 24 degree divergent and a 5 degree vertical strabimus.

Autogenic standard exercises were started. During the first weeks the patient practiced very irregularly, without interest. Only about six weeks later, in May, the patient started experiencing a feeling of heaviness and generalized relaxation. This together with ophthalmographic measurements indicating a progressive diminution of the divergent angle stimulated her to practice more regularly. On June 9, ten weeks after starting autogenic training, the divergent angle was only 10 degrees, without S.M.P. At this point orthoptic exercises aiming at alternation of tension and relaxation of relevant eye muscles, were added. On June 15 the divergent angle had adjusted to zero. The patient also had reached simultaneous mascular perception although only for brief periods at this point.[1566]

Case 68: A 16-year-old male student who suffered from a variable convergent accommodative strabismus of the right eye from early childhood. From age 5 to 9 he had been wearing glasses to correct a slight hyperopia with astigmatism. At the age of nine he put his glasses away because he felt that he did not need them anymore. At the age of fifteen, in the course of a prolonged viral infection, the deviation of the right eye reappeared. This was associated with a variable, however quite disturbing diplopia. He became more nervous, more irritable and further deterioration of his visual disorder ensued. He did not want to wear glasses again, his social activities diminished, and he preferred to stay with his books in his room. Finally convinced that something should be done, he saw a psychiatrist who taught him autogenic standard training (April). He practiced regularly, but without hope or enthusiasm. After about 10 weeks (June) the visual disorder had readjusted. His orthophoria remained unchanged during a control period of two years.[1568]

Primary glaucoma, particularly the chronic congestive forms (chronic wide-angle or simple glaucoma, chronic narrow-angle glaucoma), are reported to respond well, when autogenic standard exercises are used as an adjunctive approach.[102,360,612,939,940,1758]

As in cases suffering from hypertension (see p. 69-75), it is essential that glaucoma patients practice autogenic standard exercises regularly over prolonged periods of time. Although changes of intraocular pressure can be noticed during the first six weeks of autogenic training, stabilization at significantly lower values and even complete readjustment and stabilization at normal tonometric values[939-941] may be expected only after many months of regular use of autogenic training. Depending on the clinical situation of each case, it may be indicated that patients be advised to practice prolonged autogenic exercises (up to one hour) during periods when known stressors exert disturbing influences on the patient's pattern of life. O. Mentz[941] reported that the adequate use of autogenic standard exercises permitted a significant reduction of myotic medication and progressive elimination of tranquilizing drugs in patients who were depending on them before. Perhaps the most challenging task of using autogenic training as an adjunctive form of treatment in glaucoma patients, is the effective mobilization of the patient's motivation to practice the autogenic exercises regularly over long periods of time. Adverse dynamics, as for example related to secondary gains (pension, social insurance claims)[1758] or statements by other physicians and opinions of friends and family members[941] may be difficult to overcome, and may interfere with the patient's motivation to keep practicing autogenic training. When negative, therapy-antagonizing and self-destructive dynamics are manifestations of neurotic disorders, additional treatment with autogenic abreaction, autogenic verbalization or other convenient forms of psychotherapy are indicated.

Case 69: A 52-year-old male patient (primary glaucoma, essential hypertension, functional dyspnea, lumbar back pain) with an intraocular pressure of 26 mm.Hg (l. eye) and 23 mm.Hg (r. eye), started practicing autogenic standard exercises. With the Second Standard Exercise, coinciding with generalization of warmth, the patient noticed that his dyspnea started to improve markedly. After several months at the end of the learning period of the standard exercises, his respiratory difficulties had disappeared. The systolic blood pressure readings which initially varied between 150 and 200 mm./Hg had stabilized at 140 mm./Hg. The intraocular pressure had decreased significantly: 19 mm.Hg (r. eye), 17 mm.Hg (l. eye). However, two years later the patient wrote somewhat triumphantly that he recently had obtained official recognition as being an invalid (pension) and that because of this state of health he could no longer participate in autogenic training sessions.[1758]

More recently, H. Moutinho[981] in collaboration with J. Dos Santos,[1568] M. L. Merces de Mello[942,943,2083] and J. Seabra-Dinis,[1568,2145] started to use autogenic training in selected cases suffering from certain forms of errors of refraction. In cases with myopia and astigmatism encouraging results were observed (see Case 70).

Case 70: A 42-year-old female patient with marked myopia and astigmatism since childhood. Starting at the age of seven, she had been wearing glasses continuously. For the past eight years her lenses were: 12d (right eye) and 11.5d (left eye). After five months of autogenic training the myopia improved and the corrective lenses had to be readjusted to 9d for both eyes.[1568]

J. Seabra-Dinis also recommends the use of autogenic training in asthenopia, and during postoperative phases of cases with retinal detachment, when the patient is confined to bed rest and the eyes are bandaged.[1568]

BLINDNESS

According to observations of K. Thomas,[1710,1714,1718,1720] and the reports by Maria Lucilia Merces de Mello,[942,1568] J. Seabra-Dinis[1566,1568,2145] and K. Hasegawa,[1987] autogenic approaches appear to be particularly valuable in helping the blind to cope with the multitude of physical and emotional stressors resulting from the loss of vision.[162,626] Blind trainees treated by K. Thomas soon noted that the regular practice of the heaviness exercise already brought about a sensible relief in the tension resulting from, for example, intensive use of the sense of touch during prolonged periods of reading Braille. In the course of the standard training, blind trainees emphasized that their tension-producing apprehensiveness, insecurity and anxiety had subsided markedly and that they felt calmer and more at ease in situations which had caused them much emotional distress before they learned autogenic exercises. Furthermore, the trainees had the impression that it was now easier for them to establish contact with other people and that this encouraging experience helped to counterbalance the feeling of loneliness and isolation.

From more detailed studies of a group of 9 cases, K. Hasegawa[1987] concluded that blind persons tend to learn autogenic training much faster than others. K. Hasegawa hypothesized that sensations of heaviness and warmth are more readily experienced by blind trainees because blindness appears to be associated with a greater ability (a) to engage in passive concentration, and (b) to establish and (c) maintain better mental contact with formula-related areas of the body.[1987]

Independently different authors[942,1568,1720] observed and emphasized [626,1554,1987] that the regular practice of autogenic standard exercises helps decisively in re-mobilizing personal initiative and starting or re-summing educational training. Readjustment problems, as they are frequently encountered by blind persons, are overcome more quickly (see Case 71) and autogenic self-determination with or without the supportive use of Intentional Formulae pave the way for a more satisfactory future (see Case 72).

Case 71: A 30-year-old male, married, completely blind patient (I.Q. 110) who had been under observation since the age of nine. Being dissatisfied with earning some money by playing violin in the streets, he recently had begun a training course as a telephone operator. Initially enthusiastic and eager to learn, he however became more irritable, moody and pessimistic as the training course progressed. He displayed aggressive and explosive behavior towards his teacher, his wife and his three children. The new task and the difficulties of readjustment had raised serious doubts about his capacities in his mind. In this situation the patient was taught how to practice autogenic training. Within a period of four weeks he felt well. He regained his usual good mood, showed interest in his professional training and his life became calm again. After four months of regular practice of autogenic standard exercises his facial expression, his posture, gait and motor expression, which was quite rigid and "frozen" before, became smooth, more elegant and more normal in general. After he had noticed the remarkable benefit he derived from doing his autogenic exercises, he started recommending incessantly to his wife, to his children and to all the other blind people that they practice autogenic training.

One of his sons who also suffered from blindness since his birth was even more distorted and spastic, also experienced progressive normalization of his motor pattern after he started to practice exercises regularly.[1568]

Case 72: A 19-year-old male patient who had lost his sight during World War II had learned autogenic training in order to reduce disturbing cramps, spastic phenomena and tension in general. After several months the patient, who had a grade 9 level education, decided that he wanted to become a clergyman. He started studying and managed to pass his high school and university entry examinations with very good marks. In his faculty he became one of the best students.[1720]

In view of these encouraging observations, it is regrettable that only a very limited number of blind persons have been given a chance to learn autogenic training.

Information about the response during autogenic abreaction or the meditative exercises of trainees suffering from various forms of blindness is not yet available.

References: 102, 162, 302, 360, 410, 421, 612, 626, 705, 706, 707, 877, 888, 939, 940, 941, 942, 943, 981, 1433, 1441, 1528, 1541, 1554, 1565, 1566, 1567, 1568, 1570, 1710, 1714, 1718, 1720, 1748, 1758, 1987, 2031, 2145, 2217, 2431.

13. Surgery and Related Disorders

The application of autogenic training during the pre- and postoperative period is considered a complementary measure which helps to reduce the undesirable psychophysiologic consequences of trauma- and situation-related reactions.[465,488,1163,1171,1433,2160,2180]

During the pre-operative period the frequent practice of autogenic exercises reduces psychoreactive stress as related to apprehension, anxiety, fear of mutilation, of loss of part of one's body, fear of possible death, the breaking up of the habitual pattern of daily life and confrontation with many new and disturbing environmental variables.[488,1163,1171,2065]

Patients who have learned autogenic training for other reasons, before surgery was indicated, reported that the frequent practice of autogenic training helped them effectively to pass more calmly through the pre-operative period.[1433,2065] Other trainees who suffered fractures or sprains were able to reduce muscular tension and pain.[1699] Together with conventional measures (e.g., positioning, local cooling), incarcerated hernias appear to have a better chance of being reduced when autogenic exercises are practiced,[488,2065] and generally there appears to be a better tolerance of a variety of disagreeable or painful physical examinations and relevant medical procedure.[853,1389,1433,1528,2065] Similarly autogenic training was reported helpful in coping with certain preoperative problems related to specific medical disorders, as, for example, hemophilia,[526,2065] the consequences resulting from the power failure of an implanted pacemaker (see Case 14, p. 49),[1550] pulmonary tuberculosis[853,2180] or attack of renal colic.[2031]

While the preoperative usefulness of autogenic training is largely limited to a rather non-specific reduction of adaptational and psychoreactive stress, a much more differentiated and more physiologically oriented field of indication exists during the postoperative phase.

In addition to desirable psychodynamically oriented effects which help to promote recovery by buffering postoperative psychoreactive repercussions (e.g., regressive dynamics, neurotic and depressive reactions),[1163,1171,2180] the favorable physiologically oriented effects of autogenic exercises on respiratory, circulatory, digestive and other autonomic functions (e.g., sleep) are considered to be of particular clinical value (see Subject Index).[1403,2180]

More specifically, various authors emphasize the subjectively and clinically beneficial effects related to the reduction of reactive muscular tension and pain in the surgically affected area and its adjacent structures.[19,20,21]

165

Isolated observations of postoperative urinary retention,[282,2065] indicate that autogenic approaches can be effective in situations where other forms of medical treatment did not succeed (see Case 53, p. 139; Case 54, p. 139).

Another area of indication for autogenic training is a variety of psychophysiologic and autonomic disorders related to amputations (e.g., pain, coldness, twitching, paraesthesias)[612,1528] and permanent or transitory loss of function[568] (see also, p. 127; Vol. III and Subject Index). Further research is required to verify the impression that autogenic exercises with emphasis on relevant heaviness and warmth formulae, help significantly to forestall muscular atrophy in fractured limbs which require prolonged periods of inactivity in order to heal properly.[1699]

Of further interest are certain modalities of postoperative autogenic discharges, as for example, are observed in patients after abdominal surgery (appendectomy, cholecystectomy, hernia repair). Generally, a distinction can be made between relatively non-specific forms of discharges which appear to be related to certain pre- and postoperative situations (e.g., anxiety and suppressed crying while being rolled into the operation room, removal of dressings before anesthesia was fully effective, intubation, suppression of postoperative coughing or vomiting because of abdominal pain), and other modalities of autogenic discharges which are specifically related to the surgically affected area (see Table 14).

The occurrence of such postoperative discharges during and after autogenic training is variable. In certain trainees the topographically well-localized discharges may occur even when the operation was performed many years before. In others, no relevant discharges are reported. However, when such postoperative discharges occur, the trainee may be left with the impression that something is wrong, that the symptoms are similar to those experienced before or after the operation, and consequently a growing concern may build up. For this reason it is advisable to screen the training protocols of patients with a history of surgical interventions

TABLE 14. *Post-operative Autogenic Discharges*

Topographically Specific	Non-specific
Sensation of pressure	coughing
Sensation of tearing, pulling	crying (frontal headache)
Sensation of dull pain	feeling of nausea
Sensation "as if stitches were removed"	anxiety
Sensation of numbness	feeling of suffocation
Sensation of tingling	feeling of irritation in throat
Sensation of coldness	
Sensation of tension or twitching	

carefully, and to provide supportive explanations when indicated. However, in all cases with repeatedly occurring topographically well-localized "training symptoms" (e.g., tearing, pain, pressure) a prompt evaluation of the differential diagnostic significance of the patient's observation is mandatory.

Similar to topographically specific postoperative autogenic discharges, are autogenic reactions related to specific medical examinations or procedures which were carried out with insufficient or no anesthesia (e.g., bone marrow puncture, lumbar puncture, cervical dilatation, bronchoscopy, myringotomy, pain after fractures, application or removal of dressings, filling of pneumothorax). While many trainees do not notice such iatrogenic modalities of autogenic discharges, others are concerned about repeated occurrence of sensations like pressure, pulling, pain, numbness, or burning in relevant bodily areas. A relatively small number of trainees was observed, who repeatedly experienced development of pain to such an extent that they had to terminate the exercise. In these cases, when autogenic discharges involve unusually strong pain in circumscribed areas previously affected by accidents, surgery or medical procedures, it has been found that onset of crying is followed by disappearance of the pain. The pain tends to continue or to reoccur until sufficient crying has been accomplished. This brain-directed "pain-crying-relief" phenomenon appears to be a psychophysiologic mechanism which is also of self-normalizing significance in other related areas (e.g., disappearance of frontal headaches after *sufficient* crying; grief reactions).[2065]

The iatrogenic nature of non-specific and topographically specific modalities of autogenic discharges is more clearly revealed during relevant phases of brain-directed processes of autogenic neutralization (see Case 37/I; Case 38/I, p. 205; Case 24/III; Case 73).

Case 73: A 36-year-old housewife (anxiety reaction, multiple psychophysiologic reactions).

The traumatizing significance of various medical procedures and related experiences while being sick, or in hospital, are reflected in the following passages:

". . . again this could be evasion . . . the figure just rolled up on the bed, and it was myself sitting at the Royal Vic with that chest pain . . . again the white of the room, the green of the anesthetist's smock . . . telling them about the nausea waves during the . . . *the spinal* has been given too fast . . . and again I was going to say spinal tap . . . I noticed I said that a couple of times when that came up, the rachie . . . and it is that pain . . . and I am tearing and screaming . . . the sheet, the nightgown, I'm just ripping it off . . . I am clawing my shoulders . . . I want to tear the pain out . . . and I evaluated the doctor taking the case history [thematic shift]."

". . . and it is something about *the kidney stone* . . . I saw the blue pot, I saw him . . . I saw myself getting out from that side of the bed and then I came back . . . I don't know I got into his bed but I know that when the attack stopped, I was in his bed . . . Then I could not but I was trying to control . . . but I remember; there was an animal sound coming out of me from the pain . . . I was surprised at it, I was trying to hold it back . . . and I would hear it . . . so it is having the kidney stone attack . . . it is that lance as I described it . . . like the end of an arrow . . . I am screaming, I am trying to . . . I don't know . . . get at the pain . . . get it out of there . . . the kicking I did . . . I could not control that, but I was trying to . . . now I am not trying to control . . . I have no pain now, I feel funny . . . half dizzy or what? . . . I am still on that bed with the kidney attack . . . my head is spinning . . . it is one shriek . . . P. was trying to hold me; I told him no, it makes it worse . . . physically, sensation just broke, it is going . . . there is now that tingling all over my body . . . the moisture is drying up . . . I feel heavy; legs, arms, tired . . . there is a little of the buzzing in the head, left . . . there is still a bit of the tingling . . . soles of the feet . . . as I was having that, the reel played again, the children . . . the arms are getting this funny sensation again, feeling also . . . the children had come; I can see Mary and John not daring to come into the room . . . P. shouting at them to get back into bed, I hear Mary say; come on, daddy is beating up mommy . . . I said; no, Paul, go tell them, go tell them . . . that vibration, sensation . . . tingling from the knees down . . . I don't know . . . had we connected it with anesthetic? . . . I feel I want to stretch, shake my legs, my arms; I just did with the legs . . . it relieved temporarily and then it . . . the feeling is there again, it is . . . I think it is still Mul . . . I just saw Dr. X. there . . . he thought it may have been a miscarriage and then as I was relating that, I saw myself in the other bed . . . red . . . *the marrow puncture* . . . I want to cry, I don't know why, it is ridiculous . . . I am alone . . . it is after Louisa left; I don't know if she came in to help me undress or not or stayed in the car . . . I am alone and it hurts . . . so there again, I started screaming . . . broke the windows . . . ripped the sheet. I thought I could not even close my purse or bring my fingers together, how can I rip the sheet? It does not matter, I will or did rip it . . . again I want to tear off whatever I had on, I feel just the weight of the clothing on the chest is hurting, I remember saying: it is as if a truck had run over my chest . . . Either, I am visualizing the sternum, I am seeing it, I am feeling it, the way it was . . . there is no actual pain now but there is sensation . . . there is . . . the arms and the legs are increasing or that . . . tingling and heaviness . . . either it is increasing or it had disappeared, it is coming back; I don't know which . . . I was going to say: it has changed, it is not . . . the . . . puncture but it was the same bed and it is that *chest pain* . . . and I was looking at the window and I realized it is when I went to sit up when John came to wake me, John and or Mary, saying: mommy, it is a quarter to eight, hurry up and get up. So when I went to sit up, I could not, it was *the pneumonia.* . . . Realizing that I had been delirious that night, that it was foolish not to call a doctor. Knowing what I know today . . . it could possibly have been a wish to die. I thought: is it to make a martyr of myself? to attract attention but I think that is the top blanket . . . for a desire to die. . . ."[2065]

References: 19, 20, 21, 282, 465, 488, 526, 568, 612, 853, 1163, 1171, 1389, 1403, 1433, 1528, 1550, 1699, 1979, 2065, 2160, 2180, 2321, 2376.

14. Dentistry and Related Disorders

It has been observed frequently that persons who have learned autogenic training feel more relaxed before and during dental appointments. While in the dentist's chair, passive concentration on heaviness in the limbs has been experienced as a very helpful technique to buffer the stressor effects (see Case 74, Vol. III) of uncomfortable, long and arduous sittings. The lessening of tension, the shift towards a passively oriented attitude and the non-specific pain-reducing effect of autogenic standard exercises are associated with a decrease of apprehension and increase of tolerance in general.[39,73,101,216,295,1042,1403,1433,1476,1528,1588,2012,2051,2065,2162,2252,2271,2292]

Drilling appears to be more distant and less bothersome.[1217] Gagging and retching during taking of roentgenograms or impressions can be easily avoided by engaging in passive concentration on "My arms and legs are very heavy." In addition to the non-specific pain-reducing effect of passive concentration on standard formulae with emphasis on heaviness and warmth in the extremities, various combinations of organ-specific formulae were found to be effective in producing a further decrease of pain (see Case 74).

Case 74: Dr. H. Schlicht (neurologist) observed certain effects of autogenic training while he was undergoing dental treatment (upper l. centr. incisor). He experienced the drilling as quite painful, and while his dentist was called away for a few minutes, Dr. Schlicht started practicing the First and Second Standard Exercises, adding the neutralizing Intentional Formula: "Pain does not matter" (*"Schmerz ist vollkommen gleichgültig"*). When the drilling continued a little later, he still experienced the pain; however, the pain appeared somewhat dissociated and Dr. Schlicht felt more like an onlooker than a directly involved participant. After a while, his dentist was called away again, and this time he reinforced the autogenic state by repeating passive concentration on heaviness and warmth. During these exercises the local discomfort, the bothersome effects from the cotton packs in the mouth and the uncomfortable position faded away. He added a Special Formula: "Gums and tooth are cool" (*"Zahnfleisch und Zahn ganz kühl"*) and noticed a transitory feeling of localized coolness. Dissatisfied with this, he changed the approach and adopted "Tooth free of pain" (*"Zahn schmerzfrei"*) for passive concentration. When drilling was resumed, Dr. Schlicht did not feel any pain. He also had the impression that he was much less bothered by the noise of the drilling, which seemed to have become weaker and more distant. The attending dentist was surprised and wondered what had happened to his patient. Normal sensitivity returned at the end of the session, when Dr. Schlicht terminated his autogenic exercises in the usual three-step manner.[1217]

Observations gathered from trainees who applied autogenic standard exercises, Intentional Formulae (e.g., "Pain does not matter") and organ-specific approaches (e.g., "Tooth free of pain") during dental treatment, obtained variable pain-alleviating effects. Furthermore, it was noted that when autogenic training was applied, there was a definite shortening of time during which locally injected (nerve blocking, infiltration) anesthetic solutions were effective.[2065] This phenomenon may indicate that physiologic changes associated with autogenic training (e.g., counteracting drug-induced vasoconstriction) accelerate metabolization, dislocation or dilution of local concentrations of the anesthetic solution (e.g., procaine hydrochloride with epinephrine). Further research is required to add more precision to autogenic approaches in this area.

In contrast to many other bodily areas, it was found that autogenic discharges involving the oral cavity and adjacent internal structures (e.g., teeth, gingivae, tongue, pharynx) are rare. Even in trainees with a history of multiple dental and other oral traumas, no relevant training symptoms were noted. However, during brain-directed autogenic neutralization, traumatizing situations related to dental treatment (see Case 75) and other oral discharges (e.g., pressure, dull pain, tingling, numbness) have been noted in a few cases.[2065] The exceptionally low incidence of autogenic discharges involving the oral cavity invites the hypothesis that there exists a special inhibitory mechanism, which protects the oral cavity against biologically undesirable disturbances from brain-directed discharge activity.

Case 75: A 26-year-old housewife (anxiety reaction, multiple phobic reactions, ecclesiogenic syndrome).

The following brain-directed passages* from a cinerama-type autogenic abreaction, convey the disturbing significance of tension and anxiety producing material accumulated during dental treatment. Note the brain-directed pattern of thematic repetition focussing on pain.

". . . I see myself in the dentist's office at St. Tropez . . . he is treating me very badly and he does not care very much, he does not take any X-rays and I am disgusted to see how all these doctors, all these dentists work down there. . . . I see my father, that evening, taking me to the dentist, I am quite afraid . . . our maid told me that he would come with a big pair of pliers and then would pull my teeth out. . . . I shall see . . . he has a drill and it is hurting very much . . . and I am a little girl, I am very much afraid . . . the next morning I have to go again and he puts me asleep and pulls my teeth out . . . after this I wake up and I vomit blood and I feel quite sick. . . . I feel myself . . . about twelve or thirteen years old, at the dentist's office. . . . I don't want to be anesthetized. . . . I am very afraid of the

---

* Translated from the tape-recorded, original French version.

injection . . . he works on my teeth without anesthesia . . . he is emptying my molars completely, without anesthesia . . . and he touches the nerve . . . oh,, it hurts very very much . . . he gets at the nerve, and it hurts very much . . . it's a stabbing pain in my gums . . . he is hollowing out all my molars without anesthesia. . . . I go into the dentist's office and sit down in the chair . . . he starts drilling and then he is poking in my teeth, he is drilling deeper and all without anesthesia . . . it hurts very very much and it is a sharp stabbing pain . . . and he touches the nerve and I jump because it was hurting so much . . . tears start flowing. . . . I go to the dentist and he is hurting me very much, he is repairing all my teeth without anesthesia and I am a real dental martyr . . . and he gets at all my molars without anesthesia and he is hurting me terribly. . . . [etc.]"[2065]

Autogenic standard exercises have also been helpful in facilitating the adaptation to prosthetic devices.[295] Patients who used to complain about discomfort, irritation, pain, difficulty in chewing properly and who repeatedly had their orthodontic or prosthetic appliances verified and "adjusted," gradually forgot their dental problem as they proceeded through the standard series of autogenic training. Likewise autogenic approaches have been used successfully for the elimination of nausea or gagging due to the wearing of dentures (see Case 76).[101,2065]

Case 76: A 39-year-old sales manager who three years earlier had followed his dentist's advice to have all teeth extracted, had difficulty in wearing his dentures. He was able to keep his lower dentures in place without discomfort but each morning, when he tried to place the upper part, he started gagging and retching. Often he was unable to keep the upper dentures in place, and went to his office without them. On other occasions, particularly during certain business situations, when he got tense and nervous, he started gagging and had to disappear in order to remove his dentures. Such episodes created embarrassing situations for him and his associates. Since his administrative and organizational talents were highly appreciated, he was considered for promotion. However, the board of directors let it be known, that much as they would like to promote him, they could not do so unless he solved his dental problem

During non-specific heaviness training, he started to feel more confident, and noted that he seemed to have less difficulty in placing the upper dentures in the morning, that there was less local irritation and the need for removing the upper dentures during business hours had decreased. As he continued to progress through the standard exercises, his complaints progressively diminished and he felt more confident. After about eight weeks, the partial exercise "My neck and shoulders are heavy" was added. This formula, which he practiced when placing his dentures and whenever he noticed a critical build-up of tension during business hours, helped him to regain relaxation and calmness, thus avoiding any further development towards gagging and urge to remove his dentures. In the twelfth week after beginning autogenic standard training, he felt that no further appointments were needed because he had been able to place and keep his dentures without difficulty for three weeks.[2065]

Other dentally undesirable habits such as bruxism (grinding of teeth during sleep) (see Case 77),[295,1476,1528,1533,2065] bruxomania and nail-biting are known to respond well to autogenic training. However, when the neurotic dynamics are particularly strong and no satisfactory response occurs within about three to four months of regular practice of autogenic training, it is advisable to attempt neutralization of the underlying repressed aggressivity by intensive use of autogenic verbalization (e.g., 30 min. q.d.).

Reports on isolated cases with idiopathic lingua geographica[2065] or bleeding gums[758] for which no other medical reasons were found, indicated that autogenic training may be helpful (see Case 172; Case 86).

Case 77: A 30-year-old female patient who for many years suffered from disturbing onset of teeth grinding. This disorder disappeared while she was progressing through the heaviness formulae of the First Standard Exercise.[1528]

Case 78: A 28-year-old female patient exposed to a series of continuing conflict situations suffered from easy bleeding of her gums while brushing her teeth. Treatment with medication remained without improvement. She started to practice autogenic training and the bleeding subsided progressively and disappeared.[758]

References: 39, 73, 101, 216, 295, 741, 758, 1042, 1217, 1252, 1403, 1433, 1476, 1528, 1533, 1588, 2012, 2051, 2065, 2162, 2252, 2271, 2292.

PART II. APPENDIX

Glossary of Terms Used in Autogenic Therapy

PREFACE

This glossary was composed following recommendations by colleagues who are already familiar with the field of autogenic therapy and suggestions from others who wished to understand autogenic therapy more readily.

Since excellent dictionaries of psychiatric, psychological and psychoanalytical terms are readily available, the scope of this glossary has been limited to terms frequently used in the field of autogenic therapy.

The reader's critical comments and suggestions which would help us to improve the usefulness of this glossary in later editions will always be welcome.*

WOLFGANG LUTHE

Abbreviations

abbr. — abbreviation, -ated

adj. — adjective

anal. — analysis, analytical

contr. w. — contrast (ed) with

dstg. fr. — distinguish (ed) from

e.g. — for example

fr. — from

gen. — general

Germ. — German

i.e. — that is

prefd. — preferred

psychoan. — psychoanalysis

syn. — synonym(s), -ous

vs. — versus

z/ — indicates an inverted phrase

= — means that two terms are virtually equivalent

bold face type — cross references

---

* Letters and reprints will receive prompt attention by mailing a copy simultaneously to both addresses:

(A) W. Luthe, M.D., Scientific Director, Oskar Vogt Institute, Faculty of Medicine, Kyushu University, Fukuoka, Japan.

(B) W. Luthe, M.D., ICAT Information Centre, Medical Centre, 5300 Côte des Neiges, Montreal 249, P.Q., Canada.

AA (or A.A., *not prefd.*) = **autogenic abreaction.**

abstinence formula: intentional **formula** designed to support and facilitate refraining from, for example, an addicting drug, from alcohol or smoking (*e.g.*, "I know that I avoid drinking a single drop of alcohol in any form, at any time, under any circumstances, in any situation; others drink, but for me alcohol does not matter").

active concentration: an ergotropically oriented, stress-related mental process and attitude implying efforts to maintain exclusive and persistent attention focussed on a problem (object, activity) with an active, goal-directed investment of energy and voluntaristic striving toward the desired functional result. *Dstg. fr.* **passive concentration, meditative concentration.**

AD (or A.D. *not prefd.*) = **autogenic discharge.**

ALH = *abbr.* standard formula (**SE I**): *"My arms and legs are heavy."*

ALW = *abbr.* standard formula (**SE II**): *"My arms and legs are warm."*

AM (or A.M. *not prefd.*) = **autogenic modification.**

AN (or A.N.*not prefd.*) = **autogenic neutralization.**

anal autogenic state: psychoanalytically oriented term (*I. Gubel*) which conveys the view that a trainee's therapeutic development appears to pass from an initial stage of regressive gratification (**oral autogenic state**) to a psychodynamically more advanced developmental stage (considered to coincide with the practice of the **Fifth Standard Exercise**) as he proceeds through the six **standard exercises** of **autogenic training.** During the anal autogenic state ("anal facie") *I. Gubel* observed that the trainee's relation towards the therapist becomes more lax and that this change tends to be associated with a shift towards "pleasing somatization" particularly involving the symbolically important region of the abdomen.

antagonizing resistance (*not prefd.*): see **brain-antagonizing resistance** (*prefd.*), *vs.* **brain-facilitating resistance.**

armchair training posture: one of the three standard training postures recommended for the practice of autogenic training.

A.-stage: see **stage of adjustment after termination of autogenic exercises.**

AT (or **A.T.**, *not prefd.*) = autogenic training.

autogenic abreaction, or **AA** (A.A., *not prefd.*): a psychophysiologically oriented method of **autogenic neutralization** (*W. Luthe*) which evolved from studies of **brain-directed** processes (e.g., **autogenic discharges**) as occurring during **autogenic standard exercises.** Essential elements of this psychotherapeutic method: 1. Regular practice of autogenic training. 2. A mental shift to a spectator-like attitude (**passive acceptance,** "carte blanche" attitude) after attaining the **autogenic state** by **passive concentration** on **autogenic standard formulas.** 3. A continuous unrestricted (tape-recorded) verbal description (expression) of phenomena elaborated and programmed by a trainee's brain (*e.g.*, sensory, motor, visual, auditory, olfactory, gustatory, psychical, vestibular) and expression of affective and relevant psychophysiologic components (*e.g.*, crying, laughing, swearing, vomiting). 4. Both the patient and the therapist accept and respect the implications of the **brain-directed** dynamics of multidimensional elaborations of processes of **autogenic neutralization** by observing the **principle of non-interference:** (a) going along with and supporting developments and processes of autogenic neutralization as indicated by the patient's self-regulatory brain mechanisms, (b) limiting technically oriented **therapist-directed** or **trainee-directed** interventions to instances of unavoidable management of **brain-antagonizing forms of resistance** (*i.e.*, only after observing repeatedly that the patient's autogenically working brain mechanisms have unusual difficulties in advancing certain dynamics of neutralization in a direction already indicated by the patient's brain). 5. Active participation of the patient in his treatment by engaging in intensive therapeutic homework: (a) listening to and transcribing his tape-recorded verbal descriptions (self-confrontation, mobilizing feedback during normal state), (b) reading aloud the transcribed material (self-confrontation, re-expression during normal state), (c) elaboration of a commentary focussing on different aspects of the material obtained by autogenic abreaction, (d) notes on dreams (often indicating therapeutic progress and material requiring autogenic neutralization), (e) carrying out unsupervised (tape-recorded) autogenic abreactions as soon as a trainee has acquired a satisfactory level of technical competence with the method and reliable collaboration is assured. Since the brain-directed processes of autogenic neutralization follow dynamics which (except for certain technical implications) are largely uninfluenced by insight-promoting interpretations, and since disturbing dynamics of transferential nature are subject to the normalizing efficiency of brain-directed processes of autogenic neutralization, relatively little time is devoted to relevant areas of psychoanalytically oriented work. Insight and understanding are considered helpful in improving certain adaptational functions, but insight and understanding have a very limited or no appreciable effect as far as the neutralization of the disturbing potency of already accumulated material (*e.g.*, accidents) is concerned. It is in this connection that a distinction is made between forms of psychotherapy which emphasize techniques aimed at multidimensional psychophysiologic neutralization and others which favor therapeutic variables (*e.g.*, learning, understanding, insight, transference, acting out) which do not neutralize the disturbing potency of already accumulated material. *Dstg. fr.* other forms of abreaction which are *not* associated with (a) the practice of autogenic training, (b) the **autogenic state**, (c) a "**carte blanche**" attitude of **passive acceptance** and (d) appropriate verbal description and expression of **brain-directed** multidimensional processes of **autogenic neutralization**. 1. *abreaction (psychoan.)*: (a) a technical term referring to the end-result of *catharsis* considered to be a non-autogenic but closely related method which helps to bring repressed material of a *complex* into consciousness by provoking, mobilizing and promoting a combination of mental processes (*e.g.*, recollection of forgotten memories, reliving of related experiences, adequate expression of usually repressed feelings, accompanying affect, repressed or non-repressed emotionally toned ideas with common affective ties) under a variety of (non-autogenic) therapeutic circumstances (*e.g.*, free association, hypoanalysis, therapist-directed cathartic methods); (b) often used as referring to the cathartic process instead of the end-result brought about by the method of catharsis. 2. *abreaction (gen., loosely)*: (a) efforts to obtain a decrease of emotional tension by merely thinking about the complex-related situation(s). (b) aiming at a relief of emotional tension through (non-autogenic) acting out, which under certain conditions is considered to have a curative value.

autogenic anal facie: see **anal autogenic stage.**

autogenic cinerama: technical term referring to a specific category of **brain-directed** cinerama-like visual elaborations occurring during the **autogenic state** (*e.g.*, **autogenic training, autogenic abreaction**) implying variable degrees of "self-participation." *Dstg. fr.* other categories of visual elaborations, *e.g.*, **filmstrips** during which the trainee remains a describing observer without "self-participation."

autogenic discharge(s) (*abbr.* **AD**): training symptoms of brief duration, the physiologic or psychic nature of which appears to be unrelated to the thematic content of the autogenic formula(s) used. *Dstg. fr.* 1. **Formula-**

related training symptoms; 2. spontaneously occurring discharges, when autogenic training is not practiced; 3. reactive stimulus-related discharges; 4. prolonged, systematized, differentiated and complex processes of **brain-directed autogenic neutralization** as occurring during **autogenic abreaction.**

autogenic discharge activity: see **profile of autogenic discharge activity, modalities of autogenic discharges.**

autogenic discharges/selective release of: see **principle of selective release.**

autogenic discharges/serial repetition of: see **principle of serial repetition.**

autogenic filmstrip(s): technical term referring to a specific category of **brain-directed** film-like visual elaborations occurring during the **autogenic state** (*e.g.,* **autogenic training, autogenic abreaction**). *Dstg. fr.* **autogenic cinerama.**

autogenic formula: a combination of psychophysiologically adapted verbal stimuli used for **passive concentration** during treatment with autogenic approaches designed (a) to facilitate and promote trophotropically oriented **brain-directed** functions, (b) to provide additional case-specific support in the management of a variety of physiologically or psychodynamically oriented disorders. Major categories: 1. **standard formulae,** *abbr.* **SF** (see **standard exercises**); 2. **intentional formulae,** *abbr.* **IF** (see **autogenic modification**); 3. **organ-specific formulae,** *abbr.* **OSF** (see **autogenic modification**); 4. **Meditative formulae,** *abbr.* **MF** (see **meditative exercises**); 5. **Experimental formulae,** *abbr.* **EF.**

autogenic modification (*abbr.* **AM**): 1. techn. term applied to distinguish a group of autogenic approaches (*e.g.,* **intentional formulae, organ-specific formulae**) from other autogenic methods (*e.g.,* **autogenic standard training, autogenic neutralization, autogenic meditation**). Methods of autogenic modification may be applied after a trainee masters the **standard exercises** adequately, and **passive concentration** during the **autogenic state** can be used effectively to obtain desirable functional modifications through **trainee-directed** application of specifically designed, case-adapted intentional formulae or organ-specific formulae which, somewhat similar to post-hypnotic suggestions, are imposed onto the brain, 2. A psychodynamically or physiologically oriented functional change which was brought about by **trainee-directed** application of passive concentration on a specifically designed, case-adopted formula (*e.g.*, intentional formula, organ-specific formula) after the autogenic state had been established by passive concentration on autogenic standard formulae.

autogenic neutralization: (*abbr.* **AN**) 1. technical term designating a category of methods (*W. Luthe*) in **autogenic therapy, (a) autogenic abreaction, (b) autogenic verbalization.** *Dstg. fr.* other categories of approaches used in autogenic therapy: *e.g.,* **autogenic modification, autogenic meditation, autogenic training. 2.** A highly complex, differentiated psychophysiologic, **brain-directed** process following biologically given principles of homeostatic and self-normalizing nature while aiming at a reduction and progressive elimination of the functionally disturbing potency of accumulated neuronal material. Progressive normalization of various types of psychodynamic and psychophysiologic disorders can be observed as a patient's brain mechanisms (*e.g.,* **centrencephalic safety-discharge system**) are given *adequate* opportunity to engage in autogenic neutralization (see **autogenic abreaction**).

autogenic oral facie: see **oral autogenic stage, anal autogenic stage.**

autogenic shift: a multidimensional psychophysiologic shift (*Germ. Umschaltung*) from a normal state to the **autogenic state,** brought about by **passive concentration on autogenic formulae** in combination with other technically and psychophysiologically oriented factors associated with the practice of **autogenic standard training.**

autogenic standard exercises (*abbr.* **SE**): a series of six physiologically oriented autogenic exercises (*J. H. Schultz*) composed of thematically different **autogenic standard formulae: 1. first standard exercise** (*abbr.* **SE I**): heaviness formula(e) *e.g.,* "My right arm is heavy." **2. second standard exercise** (*abbr.* **SE II**): warmth formula(e) *e.g.,* "My right arm is warm." **3. third standard exercise** (*abbr.* **SE III**): cardiac formula, *i.e.,* "Heartbeat calm and regular." **4. fourth standard exercise** (*abbr.* **SE IV**): respiratory formula(e) *i.e.,* "Breathing calm and regular," "It breathes me." **5. fifth standard exercise** (*abbr.* **SE V**): abdominal formula, *i.e.,* "My solar plexus is warm." **6. sixth standard exercise** (*abbr.* **SE VI**): forehead formula, *i.e.,* "My forehead is cool."

autogenic standard therapy: case-adapted application of the series of six autogenic standard exercises. *Syn.* **autogenic standard training.**

autogenic standard training: see **autogenic standard therapy.**

autogenic state: a trophotropically oriented psychophysiologic state characterized by a specific profile of a variety of physiologic changes (see **autogenic shift**). Different stages of reactivity associated with the regular practice of **autogenic training** and the autogenic state are distinguished: *e.g.,* **R.-stage, P.C.-stage, P.A.-stage, N.-stage, A.-stage.**

autogenic therapy: treatment with **autogenic standard training** and other complementary autogenic approaches, *e.g.,* **intentional formulae, organ-specific formulae, autogenic abreaction, autogenic verbalization.**

autogenic training (*abbr.* **AT**): the basic method of **autogenic therapy.** AT is a psychophysiologically oriented therapeutic approach (*J. H. Schultz*) which requires case-specific adaptation and has been applied to a large variety of medical and psychodynamic disorders. The method requires regular practice (training) of brief mental exercises of **passive concentration** upon psychophysiologically adapted combinations of verbal stimuli (**autogenic formulae**) designed to promote a multifunctional shift to a specific psychophysiologic state (**autogenic state**) which is known to be associated with facilitation and promotion of a variety of trophotropically oriented **brain-directed** functions of homeostatic and self-normalizing (**autogenic**) nature. In autogenic therapy four groups of autogenic approaches are distinguished: **1. autogenic standard training** composed of six **standard exercises; 2. autogenic meditative training** consisting of a series of seven **meditative exercises; 3. autogenic modification:** (a) five categories of largely psychologically oriented **intentional formulae;** (b) a variety of physiologically oriented **organ-specific formulae;** and **4.** methods of **autogenic neutralization** (*W. Luthe*): (a) **autogenic abreaction;** (b) **autogenic verbalization.**

autohypnosis: self-induced hypnosis achieved through use of a variety of (non-autogenic) procedures. See **self-hypnosis.**

autosuggestion: 1. Self-applied suggestion (*gen.*); **2.** Goal-directed (non-autogenic), usually ergotropically oriented self-applied suggestions involving an attitude of voluntaristic striving and *active* forms of *concentration, e.g.,* a (non-autogenic) formula recommended by *E. Coué:* "every day in every way I am getting better and better." Such approaches are not related to the psychophysiologically distinctively different elements and techniques of **autogenic therapy.**

AV (or A.V. *not prefd.*) = **autogenic verbalization**

BAH = *abbr.* standard formula (**SE I**): "Both arms are heavy."

BAW = *abbr.* standard formula (**SE II**): "Both arms are warm."

BLH = *abbr.* standard formula (**SE I**): "Both legs are heavy."

BLW = *abbr.* standard formula (**SE II**): "Both legs are warm."

brain-antagonizing forms of resistance: technical term for a group of six categories of negatively oriented forms of resistance which may block or interfere unfavorably with **brain-directed** processes of **autogenic neutralization** and which are frequently associated with onset or amplification of psychodynamic or physiologically oriented functional disorders. Categories: 1. Intentional resistance: (a) direct intentional resistance (b) indirect intentional resistance. 2. Thematic avoidance. 3. Thematic evasion. 4. Abortive engagement. 5. Repetition resistance. 6. Associative resistance: (a) missed association; (b) inadequate response. *Dstg. fr.* **brain-facilitating forms of resistance, indirect psychophysiological resistance, essential forms of resistance.**

brain-directed: *adj.* referring to, *e.g.,* **autogenic discharges** or functions participating in more complex processes of **autogenic neutralization** which are elaborated (*i.e.,* selected, started, coordinated, programmed, modified, adapted, repeated, terminated, verified) by self-regulatory brain mechanisms while the trainee maintains a passively accepting attitude (**passive concentration, passive acceptance, principle of noninterference**). *Contr. w.* (a) **therapist-directed** developments and elaborations (see **principle of noninterference**), (b) a trainee's actively oriented efforts to direct his brain in a manner which usually is either not at all or only partially in agreement with the needs and programming of autogenically working brain mechanisms (see **trainee-directed**).

brain-directed programming: a phenomenon resulting from a combination of unknown brain-directed functions which participate in determining the sequence and pattern in which disturbing neuronal material is permitted to undergo processes of **selective release**, *e.g.,* **autogenic discharges,** processes of **autogenic neutralization** during **autogenic abreaction.** See also "Centrencephalic Safety-Discharge System," **principle of selective release.**

brain-directed thematic adaptation: referring to the work of an unknown combination of brain functions which are participating in adapting the intensity and duration of **autogenic discharges** and processes of **autogenic neutralization** in such a manner that (a) no damaging effects result to its own system and (b) a trainee's level of tolerance is not exceeded and brain-directed elaborations and discharges are allowed to continue in a psychophysiologically desirable manner.

brain-directed thematic analogies: a pattern of brain-directed processes of **autogenic neutralization** which emphasizes thematic repetition by elaborating series of thematic analogies. *Dstg. fr.* **brain-directed thematic antitheses.**

brain-directed thematic anticipation: a usually favorable neutralization-facilitating delay or slowing down of brain-directed elaborations aiming at a thematic confrontation of disagreeable or otherwise surprising nature (*e.g.*, being attacked and devoured by a tiger), thus permitting mental adjustment to a coming situation through preparatory associative functions (*e.g.*, "I have the impression something is going to happen, maybe there is a tiger somewhere"). Occasionally difficult to distinguish from relevant forms of **brain-antagonizing resistance.** See **essential forms of resistance.**

brain-directed thematic antitheses: a pattern of **autogenic neutralization** emphasizing **serial repetition** of thematic antitheses. See **brain-directed thematic analogies, facilitating forms of resistance.**

brain-directed thematic determination: referring to the work of unknown combinations of brain functions which determine the specific nature of the neuronal material to be submitted to processes of **autogenic neutralization.** *Contr. w.* **therapist-directed** (or **trainee-directed**) thematic engagement. See **principle of selective release, principle of noninterference.**

brain-directed thematic direction: in the course of many **autogenic abreactions** it can be observed that thematic neutralization (*e.g.*, aggression) advances by adopting a pattern characterized by brain-directed alternation of thematic direction (*e.g.*, aggression against others—against self—against others—against self, etc.). *Contr. w.* **therapist-directed** (or **trainee-directed**) thematic elaborations.

brain-directed thematic disintegration: usually a favorable neutralization-facilitating phenomenon consisting of a brain-directed "splitting-up for release" of disturbing material (*e.g.*, car accident), thus circumventing existing barriers of resistance by proceeding with a functionally camouflaged presentation of disturbing elements through "piecemeal" neutralization and **serial repetition.** Occasionally difficult to distinguish from phenomena of functional regression as resulting from relevant forms of **brain-antagonizing resistance.** See **essential forms of resistance.**

brain-directed thematic dissociation: usually a favorable, neutralization-facilitating phenomenon characterized by the trainee's impression or attitude that the things produced by his brain have nothing to do with him. Sometimes difficult to distinguish from effects resulting from relevant forms of **brain-antagonizing resistance.** See **essential forms of resistance.**

brain-directed thematic distortion: see **brain-facilitating forms of resistance.**

brain-directed thematic integration: a phenomenon observable during advanced phases of thematic neutralization when previously disintegrated, dissociated and distorted elaborations progressively approach reality features with corresponding dynamics of reintegration.

brain-directed thematic modification: technical term designating a group of neutralization-facilitating dynamics: (a) thematic disintegration; (b) thematic dissociation; (c) thematic distortion.

brain-directed thematic programming: pattern analyses and studies of processes of thematic neutralization as reflected by long series of **autogenic abreactions** indicated that unknown brain mechanisms (*e.g.*, **Centrencephalic Safety-Discharge System**) are responsible for programming the nature and sequence of thematic neutralization in a psychophysio*logic* manner with a high degree of efficiency and precision.

brain-directed thematic progression: referring to a normal phenomenon of **autogenic abreactions,** when dynamics of thematic neutralization advance through various phases to higher degrees of chromatic, dynamic, structural and integrative elaborations. Dynamics of thematic progression may alternate with phases of **brain-directed thematic regression.**

brain-directed thematic regression: referring to a variety of functionally regressive phenomena of thematic neutralization which are *not* due to **brain-antagonizing forms of resistance.** See **brain-directed thematic progression.**

brain-directed thematic repetition: considered as the vehicle of **autogenic neutralization.** See **principle of serial repetition.**

brain-directed thematic resynchronization: a phenomenon of **thematic re-integration** of previously desynchronized, disintegrated and distorted processes of neutralization.

brain-directed thematic termination: an invariably observed phenomenon occurring during **autogenic abreaction**, when self-regulatory brain
mechanisms (a) engage in thematic shift, or, (b) when thematic neutralization has come to an end for the time being. *Dstg. fr.* **therapist-directed**
(or **trainee-directed**) termination.

brain-directed thematic verification: referring to specific dynamics of
autogenic neutralization which strongly suggest that unknown brain
mechanisms periodically engage in verifying the efficiency of their own
self-normalizing work.

brain-facilitating forms of resistance: techn. term designating a group
of **brain-directed** forms of resistance (brain-directed inhibition of continuation of further development of processes of **autogenic neutralization**)
which serve a positively oriented purpose, but which the beginner in
autogenic therapy may erroneously consider as negatively oriented
forms of resistance (*e.g.,* **brain-antagonizing forms of resistance**) and
thus commit technical errors which may result in blocking of brain-
directed dynamics of neutralization and be followed by onset or amplification of various functional disorders (*e.g.,* headache, gastrointestinal
reactions, precordial pain). Categories distinguished: 1. Antithematic
resistance. 2. Recuperative resistance. 3. Integration-promoting resist-
ance. 4. Counter-resistance: (a) promoting counter-resistance; (b) arrest-
ing counter-resistance; (c) terminating counter-resistance. 5. Reality
resistance: (a) thematic distortions; (b) paratransferential distortions;
(c) transferential distortions. See also **brain-antagonizing forms of resistance, essential forms of resistance, indirect psychophysiologic resistance.**

Brodman, Korbinian: *Germ.* psychiatrist and neuropathologist (1868-
1918) who after working with *H. Binswanger (Jena) and H. Berger
(Jena)* became a disciple and close collaborator of **Oskar Vogt** (1896:
Neuro-Psychiatric Hospital, Alexanderbad; 1901-1910 *Oskar Vogt's Neuro-
Biological Institute, Berlin*). In 1918 he was named head of the Dept. of
Topographical Anatomy at the *Deutsche Forschungsanstalt für Psychia-
trie (Munich).* Together with *A. Forel* and *O. Vogt, K. Brodmann* edited
the *Journal für Psychologie und Neurologie,* and is renowned for his
neuro-cytological research from which evolved the distinction of different
cortical areas which are associated with his name. *K. Brodmann* and
O. Vogt shared an interest in trying to understand the psychological
changes associated with different stages of sleep, of heterohypnosis and
with different forms of autosuggestion through neurophysiologically and
neuroanatomically oriented research. It is in this connection that

K. Brodmann's scientific reports on *Oskar Vogt's* "fractioned method" (*Germ. "fractionirte Methode"*) of hypnotherapy (*Zur Methodik der hypnotischen Behandlung. Z. f. Hypnotismus,* 1897, Vol. VI, 1-10; 193-214; 1898, Vol. VII, H.1/2, 1-35; H.4, 228-246; H.5, 266-284) is of particular interest for the understanding of the background which stimulated *J. H. Schultz* in his development of **autogenic training.**

carte blanche attitude: a passively-accepting permissive, non-directive, non-restrictive, non-interfering attitude of a trainee towards all kinds of **brain-directed** elaborations which his self-regulatory brain mechanisms may choose to produce (release, discharge) during certain stages of the **autogenic state** (*e.g.,* **P.A.-stage**) and particularly as associated with processes of **autogenic neutralization** during **autogenic abreaction.** See **passive acceptance, principle of noninterference.** *Dstg. fr.* a noncarte blanche attitude as, for example, associated with **autogenic verbalization** or other approaches during which the patient (therapist, tape-recorder) assumes an actively oriented, directing role (see **therapist-directed, trainee-directed**) or during which brain-restricting emphasis is given to certain modalities of brain elaborations (*e.g.,* visual, intellectual).

centrencephalic safety-discharge system (*abbr.* **CSDS**): hypothetical self-regulatory ganglionic system (*W. Luthe*) assumed to involve parts of the higher brain stem (*W. Penfield: centrencephalic system*), and considered to play a coordinating role in permitting (selecting, adapting, releasing, limiting, repeating, modifying, programming, terminating) **autogenic discharges** and psychophysiologically more complex and systematized processes of **autogenic neutralization** during **autogenic abreaction.**

cinerama: see **autogenic cinerama.**

concentration/active: see **active concentration.**

concentration/meditative: see **meditative concentration.**

concentration/passive: see **passive concentration.**

CSDS (or C.S.D.S. *not prefd.*) = **centrencephalic safety-discharge system.**

discharges/autogenic: see **autogenic discharges.**

discharge profile: see **profile of autogenic discharge activity.**

ecclesiogenic neurosis: descriptive term (*Germ. ekklesiogene Neurose,* f.) introduced by *E. Schaetzing* emphasizing the psychodynamically disturbing (neurosis generating) role of educational and other variables of ecclesiastic nature in bringing about or reinforcing certain neurotic disorders and psychophysiologic reactions. *Dstg. fr.* **ecclesiogenic syndrome** (*prefd.*).

ecclesiogenic syndrome: a pattern of clinically significant symptoms involving psychodynamic and psychophysiologic disturbances which (according to material obtained during autogenic abreaction) are closely related to psychodynamically disturbing variables of religious education and other variables of ecclesiastic nature (*e.g.,* hadephobia, hamartophobia, satanophobia, theophobia, consequences related to affective and sexual deprivation).

EF (or **E.F.**) = **experimental formula.**

ergic: *adj.* implying striving, purpose. *Syn.* purposive, (sometimes) dynamic (**erg:** a unit of energy; **erg(o):** work).

ergotropic: *adj.* techn. term used by *W. R. Hess*, having to do with those mechanisms which physiologically belong to bodily work and relevant dynamics of activation. *Syn.* dynamogenic. See **ergotropic zone.**

ergotropic zone: techn. term used by *W. R. Hess* (*Diencephalon.* Grune & Stratton, New York, 1954) in describing the diencephalic spatial organization of autonomic functions, *e.g.,* (a) "In the middle and posterior part of the diencephalon, ascending to the lower border of the aqueduct, all those effects are grouped which go with a general excitation, and those mechanisms which physiologically belong to bodily work. This zone has been designated the *dynamagenic* or the *ergotropic* zone. It represents a link in the sympathetic nervous system, serving as a mediator between the diencephalon and autonomically innervated organs" (p. 13 *ff.*); (b) ". . . the effects elicited by stimulation of a region between the posterior and medial hypothalamus are transmitted to the effector organs almost exclusively by way of the sympathetic system and that it is adequate to speak of an ergotropic, or dynamogenic zone" (p. 62). *Syn.* dynamogenic zone. *Contr. w.* endophylactic or **trophotropic zone.**

essential forms of resistance: technical terms designating a group of four categories of resistance (inhibition of continuation or further development of processes of **autogenic neutralization**) which are usually **brain-facilitating forms of resistance,** but which occasionally may assume the role of **brain-antagonizing forms of resistance.** Since the flexible role of these forms of resistance does not permit simple classification into "brain-facilitating" or "brain-antagonizing" forms of resistance, the following four categories are distinguished as essential forms of resistance: 1. Program-related resistance. **2.** Protective resistance: (a) thematic disintegration; (b) thematic dissociation. 3. Anticipatory resistance. 4. Presentation resistance.

experimental formula (*abbr.* **EF**): a special, physiologically or psychodynamically oriented formula (constructed in accordance with the pattern of verbal stimuli used for **autogenic formulae**) which is under investigation and not yet recommended for therapeutic purposes (*e.g.*, "My right kidney is heavy").

FAC = *abbr.* "My forehead is agreeably cool" (**modified standard formula**) instead of "My forehead is cool" (see **Fifth Standard Exercise**).

facilitating resistance: see **brain-directed facilitating forms of resistance.**

FC = *abbr.* standard formula (**SE VI**). "My forehead is cool."

Fifth Meditative Exercise: (*abbr.* **ME V**) aiming at the experience of a selected state of feeling.

Fifth Standard Exercise: (*abbr.* **SE V**) passive concentration on the fifth standard formula: "My solar plexus is warm."

filmstrip(s): see **autogenic filmstrip(s).**

First Meditative Exercise: (*abbr.* **ME I**) aiming at a non-selected spontaneous experience of colors.

First Standard Exercise: (*abbr.* **SE I**) implying passive concentration on one or several of the heaviness formulas (*e.g.*, "My right arm is heavy," "My left arm is heavy," "Both arms are heavy," "My right leg is heavy," "My left leg is heavy," "Both legs are heavy," "My arms and legs are heavy") composing SE I.

forehead exercise: *syn.* **Sixth Standard Exeecise** (*abbr.* **SE VI**).
formula/abstinence: see **abstinence formula.**

formula/autogenic: see **autogenic formula.**

formula/experimental: see Experimental Formula (*abbr.* **EF**).

formula/intentional: see Intentional Formula (*abbr.* **IF**).

formula/organ-specific: see Organ-specific Formula (*abbr.* **OSF**).

formula/paradoxical: Intentional Formula with paradoxical thematic content (*abbr.* **IFP**).

formula-related training symptom(s): training symptoms which appear to be related to the thematic content of the **autogenic formula(e)** used (*e.g.,* feeling of heaviness, feeling of warmth, feeling of coolness spreading over the forehead). *Dstg. fr.* **autogenic discharges.**

formula/standard: see **autogenic standard formula(e).**

formula/supportive: see **supportive formula.**

Fourth Meditative Exercise (*abbr.* **ME IV**): aiming at visualization of abstract objects (*e.g.,* justice, happiness).

Fourth Standard Exercise (*abbr.* **SE IV**): passive concentration on the fourth standard formula: "Breathing calm and regular—It breathes me."

generalization phenomenon: the experience of progressive spreading of **formula-related** sensations (*e.g.,* heaviness, warmth) to parts of the body which have not yet been focussed upon (*e.g.,* generalized feeling of heaviness during passive concentration on "My right arm is heavy").

group training: practice of autogenic training in small groups (*e.g.,* 5-8). Since the practice of autogenic exercises must be adapted to the individual and requires experienced guidance and control, the **International Committee for the Coordination of Clinical Application and Teaching of Autogenic Training (ICAT)** recommended in 1961: "When autogenic training is applied to groups of persons, sufficient individual control by a qualified physician is mandatory. Autogenic training should not be applied to groups larger than 20 because sufficient medical control is not possible." (*Ref.* 874, p. 491). ICAT members (1961) agreed "that outpatients do best in groups below ten, while inpatients who are under continuous medical supervision may practice autogenic exercises in larger groups."

group training/organ-specific: see organ-specific group training.

HCR = *abbr.* standard formula (SE III): "Heartbeat calm and regular."

heart exercise: *syn.* Third Standard Exercise (*abbr.* SE III).

heaviness training: practice of passive concentration on formulas composing the First Standard Exercise (*abbr.* SE I).

hetero-verbalization of autogenic formulas: verbalization of autogenic formulas by a therapist, *e.g.*, when a new standard formula is introduced to a trainee (group of trainees). The heterosuggestive elements of this approach are considered unfavorable (non-autogenic) and it is emphasized that trainees should practice autogenic exercises alone, without outside support (*e.g.*, therapist, tape-recorder, record) as soon as the technique is understood and the patient's clinical condition is considered favorable enough for the unaided practice of autogenic training.

horizontal training posture: one of the three standard training postures recommended for the practice of autogenic training. Preferred for group training with children, patients with epilepsy and during advanced phases of pregnancy. Occasionally disliked by schizophrenic trainees.

IBM = *abbr.* standard formula (SE IV): "It breathes me."

ICAT = International Committee for the Coordination of Clinical Application and Teaching of Autogenic Therapy. Honorary members: *J. H. Schultz, M.D. (Berlin, West Germany).* Members: *T. Abe, M.D. (Tokyo, Japan); R. Alnaes, M.D. (Oslo, Norway); G. Crosa, M.D. (Genova, Italy); M. Dongier, M.D. (Liège, Belgium); R. Durand de Bousigen, M.D. (Strasbourg, France); A. Friedemann, M. D. (Biel, Switzerland); P. Geissmann, M.D. (Bordeaux, France); I. Gubel, M.D. (Buenos Aires, Argentina); Y. Ikemi, M.D. (Fukuoka, Japan); A. Jus, M.D. (Warsaw, Poland); Th. Kammerer, M.D. (Strasbourg, France); H. Kleinsorge, M.D. (Wiesbaden, West Germany); G. Klumbies, M.D. (Jena, East Germany); D. Langen, M.D. (Mainz, West Germany); W. Luthe, M.D. (Montreal, Canada); S. Maeda, M.D. (Fukuoka, Japan); D. Müller-Hegemann, M.D. (Bln.-Biesdorf, East Germany), G. Naruse, Ph.D., D.M.Sc. (Fukuoka, Japan); P. Polzien, M.D. (Würzburg, West Germany); M. Sapir, M.D. (Paris, France); J. Seabra-Dinis, M.D. (Lisbon, Portugal); A.M. Sviadosch, D.M.Sc. (Leningrad, U.S.S.R.).* From periodic meetings of ICAT members and participating observers (*Montreal 1961, Paris 1965, Madrid 1966, Kyoto 1967, Mainz 1970*) a number of recommendations concerning exchange of research information, the clinical application, and the teaching of autogenic therapy evolved. The following excerpts from the minutes of various ICAT meetings held in the past may be of general interest:

1961 (*Montreal*): "III. Autogenic training is a psychophysiologic form of medical treatment. The application of this therapy requires a medical evaluation of the prospective trainee, critical adaptation of the method and clinical guidance and regular control of the patient's technique and progress by a qualified physician."–"IV. The non-clinical use of tape-recorded autogenic exercises and 'Relaxation Records' using autogenic training or parts of it should be prohibited because of risk of health-damaging consequences."–"V. Incorrect or insufficient information about autogenic training by non-medical means of publication (*e.g.*, radio, television, films, newspapers, magazines) should not be tolerated because of the possibility of health-damaging consequences for persons who start using autogenic principles without qualified medical supervision. Incorrect or inadequate information given by non-medical means of communication should be corrected immediately."

1966 (*Madrid*): "IV. It was suggested that English be adopted as the official language of communication. Papers and articles not written in English should include a comprehensive summary in English."–"VI. *Psychologists* and *Autogenic Training*. The discussion dealt with various aspects and implications of participation by psychologists in the field of autogenic training. It was agreed that (a) psychologists already have made valuable contributions in AT research and psychologists should be encouraged to participate more actively in relevant areas of experimental and clinical AT research. In view of this it was considered essential that psychologists are given all opportunities to receive adequate training in the field of autogenic training. (b) Psychologists cannot assume medical responsibilities (*e.g.*, psychologists are not qualified to establish a differential diagnosis of various training symptoms, not qualified to perform physical examinations, not qualified to evaluate the implications of various medical disorders, etc.). Therefore, for their own protection, psychologists cannot be given permission to apply autogenic training without the reliable and continuous supervision of a qualified physician who has learned autogenic training himself and who has adequate experience with clinical and non-clinical application of autogenic training."

1967 (*Kyoto*): "V. *Psychologists* and *Autogenic Training*. Based on the resolutions agreed upon by the participants of the Third ICAT meeting, Madrid, 1966 (VI. a-d), our Japanese colleagues engaged in an extensive discussion. Due to growing application of AT in non-clinical areas (*e.g.*, education, schools, sports) it was felt that desirable standards of medical supervision and control were difficult to maintain. In Japan, clinical psychologists are widely engaged in non-clinical application of AT, and very active in related areas of research. However, since AT is a differentiated and profound psychophysiologic 'operation' involving all known physiologic systems, it was felt that medical responsibilities exist in all instances when AT is applied (regardless of designations such as 'non-clinical' or 'experimental'). *D. Langen* and other participants emphasized that the participation of psychologists is extremely valuable, but that adequate medical evaluation of each trainee and competent medical supervision of trainees are basic medical responsibilities which must be respected whenever AT is applied to a person."

IF (or I.F.) = **intentional formula.**

IFP (or I.F.P.) = intentional formula with paradoxical thematic content (*e.g.*, writer's cramp: "I want to write as messily as possible").

indirect psychophysiologic resistance: techn. term for a group of psychophysiologically oriented forms of resistance which may interfere with processes of **autogenic neutralization** during **autogenic abreaction.** 1. Side-effect resistance (*e.g.*, increase of diuresis with increasing need to void); **2.** Circumstantial resistance: (**a**) intrinsic concomitant factors (*e.g.*, sleep deficiency); (**b**) extrinsic concomitant factors (*e.g.*, low room temperature); **3.** Pharmacodynamic resistance (*e.g.*, inadequate application of barbiturates).

International Committee for the Coordination of Clinical Application and Teaching of Autogenic Therapy: see **ICAT.**

LAH = *abbr.* standard formula (**SE I**): "My left arm is heavy."

LAW = *abbr.* standard formula (**SE II**): "My left arm is warm."

LLH = *abbr.* standard formula (**SE I**): "My left leg is heavy."

LLW = *abbr.* standard formula (**SE II**): "My left leg is warm."

long-term trainee: a trainee who has practiced autogenic standard exercises regularly for more than six months. *Dstg. fr.* **short-term trainee.**

LSH = *abbr.* standard formula (**SE I**): "My left side is heavy."

ME (or M.E. *not prefd.*) = **meditative exercise.**

meditative concentration: a mental activity considered to be associated with " a state of meditative concentration" which according to *G. Naruse* is a state of "pure trance" as may occur during "neutral hypnosis" (*Dstg. fr.* "disturbed trance" during "non neutral hypnosis"). "Pure trance" as a "state of meditative concentration" is considered a feature of autogenic training (*G. Naruse*). In a very general sense, it has been hypothesized that "pure trance" or a "state of meditative concentration" is a common feature of neutral hypnosis, Zen-training, Yoga-exercises and autogenic training (*G. Naruse, A. Onda*). See **autogenic state, meditative exercises, stages of the autogenic state.**

meditative exercises: (*abbr.* **ME**) after having practiced all standard exercises satisfactorily for several months and after another training period emphasizing a series of **preparatory exercises,** a trainee may begin with **autogenic meditation** consisting of a sequence of seven meditative exercises (*J. H. Schultz*): 1. Spontaneous experience of colors (*abbr.* **ME I**). 2. Experience of selected colors (*abbr.* **ME II**). 3. Visualization of concrete objects (*abbr.* **ME III**). 4. Visualization of abstract objects (*abbr.* **ME IV**). 5. Experience of a selected state of feeling (*abbr.* **ME V**). 6. Visualization of other persons (*abbr.* **ME VI**). 7. Answers from the unconscious (*abbr.* **ME VII**). Since a spontaneous conversion of meditative exercises into **brain-directed,** complex processes of **autogenic neutralization** may easily occur in trainees who have accumulated clinically significant disturbing neuronal material, the practice of meditative exercises is generally restricted to well-selected healthy trainees. Particular caution and critical supervision is indicated when the application of meditative exercises is attempted in patients suffering from neurotic and psychotic disorders (*e.g.,* relatively sudden deteriorations in certain schizophrenics). Meditative exercises should not be practiced without competent medical guidance and supervision.

meditative series: see **meditative exercises.**

meditative training: see **meditative exercises.**

meditative training/preparatory exercises for: see **preparatory exercises for meditative training.**

modalities of autogenic discharges: a variety of training symptoms, *e.g.,* motor (twitches, jerks, involuntary movements, fibrillation, trembling, tension); visceromotor; sexual; sensory (tingling, numbness, pain, pressure, electrical, burning, swelling, itching); viscerosensory; vestibular (feeling of displacement, spinning, sinking, floating, lopsidedness, falling, flying, vertigo); changes of body image; olfactory; gustatory; visual; auditory; intellectual (intruding thoughts); psychic (anxiety, depressive, euphoric, loneliness, longing for love).

neck and shoulder exercise: implying passive concentration on the special formula: "My neck and shoulders are heavy" (*abbr.* **NShH**). Frequently recommended as "**partial exercise**" to advanced trainees who may obtain a reduction of tension by briefly thinking "My neck and shoulders are heavy" when feeling tense and while being engaged in other activities (*e.g.*, driving in heavy traffic).

neutralization/autogenic: see **autogenic neutralization.**

neutralizing intentional formula: a formula belonging to the category of intentional formulae (**autogenic modification**) with case-adapted thematic content usually including: ". . . does not matter."

nirvana therapy: case-adapted application of autogenic approaches aiming at a reduction of suffering in clinically hopeless cases (J. H. Schultz).

non-interference/principle of: see **principle of non-interference.**

NShH = *abbr.* "My neck and shoulders are heavy." See **neck and shoulder exercise.**

NShW = *abbr.* "My neck and shoulders are warm.

N.-stage: see **stage of functional neutrality.**

OF (or **OSF**) = organ-specific formula.

oral autogenic stage: psychoanalytically oriented term ("oral facies") referring to therapeutic effects considered to occur in the beginning of autogenic training when the practice of standard exercises may be viewed as a source of regressive gratification ("oral autogenic facies"). *Dstg. fr.* **anal autogenic stage.**

oral facie/autogenic: see **oral autogenic stage.**

organ-specific formula: (*abbr.* **OSF** or **OF**) a topographically oriented verbal formula which, in accordance with autogenic principles, emphasizes a specific case-adapted thematic content (*e.g.*, heaviness, warmth, coolness) designed to bring about desirable functional modifications (*e.g.*, "My throat is cool," "My lower abdomen is warm") complementary to those psychophysiologic changes that have been already established by passive concentration on **autogenic standard formulae.** See **autogenic modification.**

organ-specific group training: (*Germ. organspezifisches Gruppentraining*) practice of autogenic training in small groups composed of patients with similar disorders (*e.g.*, heart disorders: heart group; gastrointestinal disorders: abdominal group). *H. Kleinsorge,* who promoted the clinical use of this approach (*Germ. gezieltes Organtraining*), emphasized that therapeutically better resuts are obtained by organ-specific group training than by group training with patients suffering from a variety of disorders.

OSF (or O.F.; O.S.F. *not prefd.*) = **organ-specific formula.**

Oskar Vogt Institute (*abbr.* **O.V.I.**): an *International Research Organization for the Application and Teaching of Autogenic Therapy* established in 1969 by the Medical Faculty of Kyushu University, Fukuoka, Japan. Organization: 1. *Clinical Division:* Dept. of Psychosomatic Medicine (about 250 beds). 2. *Research Division:* (a) Dept. of Psychopharmacology, (b) Dept. of Psychophysiology, (c) Dept. of Neurophysiology, (d) Dept. of Psychology, (e) Dept. of Medical Electronics, (f) Dept. of Non-Clinical Application, (g) Dept. of Oriental Methods, (h) Dept. of Administration and Services. 3. *Affiliated Services for Training and Research:* various Depts. of the Medical Faculty (*e.g.*, obstetrics and gynecology, psychiatry, dentistry). Medical Director: Y. Ikemi, M.D., Ph.D.; Scientific Director: W. Luthe, M.D.

Objective: "(a) to pursue research in the field of autogenic therapy, and to perform those functions in agreement with sound scientific principles. As corollary objectives it is the task of the O.V.I. (b) to advise and assist in areas of clinical and non-clinical application of autogenic therapy, and (c) to provide nationally and internationally acceptable teaching facilities for those who wish to learn and practice methods of autogenic therapy."

Training and teaching (in accordance with ICAT recommendations): (a) in-service training (all year), (b) international training programme (8 wk., 200 hr.).

O.V.I. = **Oskar Vogt Institute.**

paradoxic reaction: a psychologically or physiologically oriented functional change, the direction or quality of which is diametrically opposed to the thematic content of the formula used, or known, habitually occurring physiologic changes (*e.g.*, increase of blood pressure instead of decrease, increase of heart rate instead of decrease, feeling of weight-lessness instead of heaviness). See **autogenic discharges.**

partial exercise: (*Germ. Teilübung*) see **neck and shoulder exercise.**

passive acceptance: a passively accepting ("**carte blanche**") spectator-like attitude that a trainee is recommended to adopt during occurrence of **autogenic discharges** and other **brain-directed** (*distg. fr.* **therapist-directed, trainee-directed**) elaborations as they occur during **autogenic abreaction.** See **brain-antagonizing resistance, brain-facilitating resistance.**

passive concentration: a **trophotropically** oriented mental activity associated with a casual attitude emphasizing almost effortless themati-cally specified goal-oriented thinking without engaging in energetic volun-taristic striving (active interest, apprehension) towards the achievement of the thematically specified goal or result. *Dstg. fr.* **active concentration, meditative concentration.**

P.A.-stage = stage of passive acceptance.

P.C.-stage = stage of passive concentration.

phenomenon of generalization: see **generalization phenomenon.**

preparatory training for meditative exercises: after several months of **autogenic training,** when a trainee masters all **standard exercises** ade-quately, and before he actually engages in the practice of **meditative exercises,** a preparatory training phase is recommended. During this phase the trainee improves his technique by practicing certain prepara-tory exercises *e.g.,* 1. Prolongation of autogenic standard exercises up to 30 or 50 min. 2. Maintaining an undisturbed **autogenic state** in the presence of otherwise disturbing variables (*e.g.,* noise, ringing of an alarm clock, radio, presence of other persons, exposure to illumination). 3. **Time sense training.**

principle of non-interference: since observations and studies of **brain-directed processes** of **autogenic neutralization** led to the conclusion that a trainee's self-regulatory brain-mechanisms tend to engage in highly sophisticated and efficient self-normalizing activities when given adequate opportunity (*i.e.,* not directed by the therapist or the actively oriented efforts of a trainee), it is considered a technical error to interfere with the brain's own program of self-curative activities unless repeated evi-dence of **brain-antagonizing forms of resistance** requires transitory specifically adapted technical support. The principle of noninterference is a guiding maxim for both the therapist and the patient (see **passive acceptance**, **"carte blanche" attitude**) during **autogenic abreaction.**

principle of selective release: based on the observation that **autogenic training** facilitates the activity of brain-directed functions which participate in permitting the selective release of **autogenic discharges** and more complex and more systematized combinations of neuronal material as occurring during **autogenic abreaction** (**autogenic neutralization**) without provoking undue spreading of excitation. Relevant studies indicate that the selective release of impulses related to accumulated brain-disturbing material tends to follow certain sequences and patterns the nature of which is determined by unknown self-regulatory brain functions (e.g., **brain-directed programming**, **"Centrencephalic Safety-Discharge System"**).

principle of serial repetition: the brain-directed selective release of impulses related to accumulated disturbing neuronal material (e.g., **autogenic discharges, autogenic neutralization**) invariably follow various types of relevant modalities of discharges. **brain-directed** dynamics of serial repetition are considered to be the vehicle of **autogenic neutralization.**

profile of autogenic discharge activity: a quantitative representation (e.g., frequency of discharges, discharge scores) of different **modalities of autogenic discharges** (e.g., motor, sensory, vestibular) as observed in a trainee (group of patients) during the practice of **autogenic standard exercises.** Clinically significant differences in profile of autogenic discharge activity have been observed in different groups of trainees (e.g., depression, schizophrenia, ECT vs. no ECT, sexual deprivation vs. no deprivation, severe accidents vs. no accidents).

RAH = abbr. standard formula (**SE I**): "My right arm is heavy."

RAW = abbr. standard formula (**SE II**): "My right arm is warm."

resistance/brain-antagonizing: see **brain-antagonizing forms of resistance.** Dstg. fr. **brain-facilitating forms of resistance, essential forms of resistance, indirect psychophysiologic resistance.**

resistance/brain-facilitating: see **brain-facilitating forms of resistance.**

resistance/essential: essential forms of resistance.

resistance/indirect psychophysiological: see indirect psychophysiological resistance.

resting formulas (*abbr.* RF) see supportive formula.

RF = (*Germ.* Ruheformel) see supportive formula.

RLH = *abbr.* standard formula (SE I): "My right leg is heavy."

RLW = *abbr.* standard formula (SE II): "My right leg is warm."

RSH = *abbr.* standard formula (SE I): "My right side is heavy."

R.-stage: see stage of reflectory reactivity.

SE (or S.E. *not prefd.*) = standard exercises.

Second Meditative Exercise: (*abbr.* ME II) aiming at an experience of trainee-directed colors.

Second Standard Exercise: (*abbr.* SE II) implying passive concentration on one or several of the warmth formulae (*e.g.*, "My right arm is warm." "My left arm is warm," "Both arms are warm," "My right leg is warm," "My left leg is warm," "Both legs are warm," "My arms and legs are warm") composing SE II.

selective release of autogenic discharges: see principle of selective release.

self-hypnosis: general term used in connection with various techniques which a person may learn and apply himself in an attempt to obtain functional changes which are known to occur during (hetero) hypnosis. For many years autogenic training has been considered as a special form of self-hypnosis. More recently the implications of the term self-hypnosis have been considered inadequate for justifying further use of this term in connection with AT. Research has shown that functional changes associated with hypnosis and certain forms of self-hypnosis (*e.g.*, graduated active hypnosis) reduce certain effects or reverse certain changes characteristic for the facilitation of a brain-directed self-regulatory (autogenic) reactivity as associated with the regular practice of autogenic standard exercises or processes of autogenic neutralization.

serial repetition of autogenic discharges: see principle of serial repetition.

Seventh Meditative Exercise: (*abbr.* SE VII) the last exercise of the meditative series aiming at obtaining answers from the unconscious.

SF (or S.F. *not prefd.*) = special formula. *Contr. w.* standard formula.

shift/autogenic: see autogenic shift.

Sixth Meditative Exercise: (*abbr.* ME VI) aiming at a trainee-directed visualization of other persons.

Sixth Standard Exercise: (*abbr.* SE VI) implying passive concentration on the sixth standard formula "My forehead is cool."

short-term trainee: a person who has practiced *autogenic standard exercises* for less than six months.

simple sitting posture: one of the three standard training postures recommended for the practice of autogenic training (*Germ. Droschkenkutscherhaltung*). Frequently used for group training (with adolescent or adult trainees). Preferred by schizophrenic trainees. Not recommended during advanced pregnancy (*prefd.* reclining armchair posture, horizontal training posture).

solar plexus exercise: see Fifth Standard Exercise.

SPW = "My solar plexus is warm" (SE V).

stage of adjustment after termination of autogenic exercises: (*abbr.* A.-stage) a psychophysiologic stage of reactivity following termination of autogenic exercises, when certain physiologic changes associated with the autogenic state are in the process of functional adjustment (*e.g.,* peripheral circulation, blood pressure, muscular reflexes) as associated with a normal state of conscious control. *Dstg. fr.* R.-stage, P.C.-stage, P.A.-stage, N.-stage.

stage of functional neutrality: (*abbr.* N.-stage) which may follow after passive concentration on autogenic formulae has come to an end, and a trainee's mental activity remains comfortably suspended between engagement in brain-directed and trainee-directed mental elaborations.

stage of passive acceptance: (*abbr.* P.A.-stage) a psychophysiologic stage of the autogenic state which may follow after a trainee has stopped passive concentration on autogenic formulas (p.c.-stage). *Dstg. fr.* R.-stage, P.C.-stage, N.-stage, A.-stage.

stage of passive concentration: (*abbr.* **P.C.-stage**) a psychophysiologic stage of the **autogenic state** during which a trainee is engaged in **passive concentration** on **autogenic formulas.**

stage of reflectory reactivity: (*abbr.* **R.-stage**) a psychophysiologic stage of reactivity associated with certain changes (*e.g.*, reflectory increase of finger temperature) characterizing the **autogenic state,** as encountered in persons who practice autogenic standard exercises regularly and who experience a reflectory onset of psychologically or physiologically oriented changes as soon as they assume a **training posture,** before actually beginning **passive concentration** on **autogenic formulas.** *Dstg. fr.* **P.C.-stage, P.A.-stage, N.-stage, A.-stage.**

standard formula: a formula used during the practice of **autogenic standard exercises.**

standard training postures: body postures permitting symmetric relaxation of muscles (reduction of afferent and efferent impulses) as recommended for the practice of autogenic training: **1. horizontal training posture; 2. simple sitting posture; 3. reclining armchair posture.**

supportive formula: (*Germ. Ruheformel: "Ich bin ganz ruhig")* "I am at peace" (*abbr.* **RF**).

thematic adaptation/brain-directed: see **brain-directed thematic adaptation.**

thematic analogies/brain-directed: see **brain-directed thematic analogies.**

thematic anticipation/brain-directed: see **brain-directed thematic anticipation.**

thematic antitheses/brain-directed: see **brain-directed thematic antitheses.**

thematic determination/brain-directed: see **brain-directed thematic determination.**

thematic direction/brain-directed: see **brain-directed thematic direction.**

thematic disintegration/brain-directed: see **brain-directed thematic disintegration.**

thematic dissociation/brain-directed: see **brain-directed thematic dissociation.**

thematic distortion/brain-directed: see **brain-directed thematic distortions.**

thematic integration/brain-directed: see **brain-directed thematic integration.**

thematic modification/brain-directed: see **brain-directed thematic modification.**

thematic programming/brain-directed: see **brain-directed thematic programming.**

thematic progression/brain-directed: see **brain-directed thematic progression.**

thematic regression/brain-directed: see **brain-directed thematic regression.**

thematic repetition/brain-directed: see **principle of serial repetition.**

thematic re-synchronization/brain-directed: see **brain-directed thematic re-synchronization.**

thematic termination/brain-directed: see **brain-directed thematic termination.**

thematic verification/brain-directed; see **brain-directed thematic verification.**

therapist-directed: *adj.* referring to technical procedures or psychophysiologic responses which are related to influences of heterosuggestive nature as resulting from a therapist's (tape-recorder's) directive activity. *Dstg. fr.* **trainee-directed.** *Contr. w.* **brain-directed.**

Third Meditative Exercise: (*abbr.* **ME III**) aiming at (trainee-directed) visualization of concrete objects.

Third Standard Exercise: (*abbr.* **SE III**) implying passive concentration on the third standard formula: "Heartbeat calm and regular."

time sense training: an autogenic exercise usually applied during the **preparatory training** phase preceding the actual practice of **meditative exercises:** at the end of passive concentration on standard formulas the trainee focusses briefly on an intentional formula designed to wake up automatically at a given time (*e.g.,* "I wake up at 3:25").

trainee: a person practicing autogenic training (see **long-term trainee; short-term trainee**).

trainee-directed: *adj.* referring to a trainee's actively oriented efforts to direct or restrict certain brain functions, *e.g.*, during **autogenic abreaction** (see **therapist-directed**). *Contr. w.* **brain-directed**. See **principle of noninterference, brain-antagonizing resistance**.

training posture(s): see **standard training postures**.

training protocol: a record of training symptoms and other observations (*e.g.*, after-effects) associated with the practice of autogenic training.

trophotropic: *adj.* techn. term used by W. R. Hess, having to do with those mechanisms which physiologically belong to recuperation (*Germ. Erholung*), protective mechanisms, unloading, restitution of achievement capacity (*Germ. Leistungsfähigkeit*), normalization and healing. *Syn.* endophylactic. *Contr. w.* **ergotropic**. See **trophotropic zone**.

trophotropic zone: techn. term used by *W. R. Hess* (*Diencephalon.* Grune & Stratton, New York, 1954) in describing the diencephalic spatial organization of autonomic functions, *e.g.*, (a) "The rostral part of the hypothalamus, the area praeoptica and area supraoptica, and the septum, stand in intimate relation to protective mechanisms and unloading. In this sense we speak of a phylactic zone or, more exactly, *endophylactic* or *trophotropic* zone. It becomes clear that, as far as the participation of the autonomic nervous system is concerned, the parasympathetic nervous system represents the corresponding mediator to the peripheral effector of the autonomically innervated organism; and it is noteworthy that the arrangement differs fundamentally in the two zones [*i.e.*, ergotropic and trophotropic zones]. In the first, or ergotropic, zone the various symptoms always appear collectively. There is an organic fusion of ergotropic mechanisms. Within the second, or endophylactic, zone definite mechanisms are evoked by the individual stimuli, either lapping, or vomiting, or defecation, and so on" (p. 16-17); (b) ". . . the anterior and lateral hypothalamus, including the pre-optic and supra-optic areas and the septum, are responsible for the protective mechanisms and for the control of the activity of the digestive apparatus which serves as an organ of restitution" (p. 62). *Syn.* endophylactic zone. *Contr. w.* dynamogenic or **ergotropic zone**.

Umschaltung: f. (*Germ.*) see **autogenic shift**.

visualization of other persons: aim of the sixth meditative exercise (ME VI).

Vogt, Oskar: German psychiatrist, psychophysiologist and neuropathologist (Husum: April 6, 1870-July 31, 1959), who, together (1899-59) with Cécile Vogt (Mugnier; March 27, 1875; Annécy, France), devoted his life to research in the vast area of somato-psychic medicine. An unusually long series of outstanding publications over a period of 65 years of scientific work (1894-1959) reflect different phases of brilliant achievements along dimensions which were regarded as important to advance our understanding of the "Leib-Seele-Problem." For Oskar Vogt, psychologic functions, psychodynamic disorders, neuro-physiology and neuro-histo-anatomy were so closely interrelated that they virtually became one unified field of research. Although Oskar and Cecile Vogt devoted years of intensive and renowned studies to highly specialized areas of brain cytology, topistic, phylogenetic and pathogenetic aspects of brain disease, they never got unilaterally scotomized and from the very beginning (1894) both favored and supported a multidimensional, interdisciplinary somato-psychic approach ("Das Ziel unserer Lebensarbeit ist die empirische Gewinnung von Einblicken in das phylogenetische Geschehen und das Leib-Seele-Problem. . . . Nie haben wir indessen die Absicht gehabt, die Hirnanatomie isoliert zu betreiben. Unser Ziel war von Anfang an, in einer auzustrebenden Gemeinschaftsarbeit möglichst viele derjenigen Forschungsrichtungen zu pflegen, die Einblicke in das somatische Hirn- und in das Seelenleben zu gewähren versprachen" J. F. Hirnfschg. 1956, 2, 6, 404).

Oskar Vogt's interest in psychology was first stimulated by Th. Ziehen (1892) at the University of Jena. His choice to focus his Doctor Thesis on contemporary problems of brain anatomy (1893/94) may be regarded as the actual beginning of an outstanding career in psycho-physio-neuro-anatomical brain research. After spending one year in neuro-psychiatry (O. Binswanger) at the University of Jena, he moved on to Zürich to work at the psychiatric clinic Burghölzli with August Forel (1894), who was particularly interested in morphological brain research and the scientific study of hypnosis. After only a few months, A. Forel delegated the editorial responsibilities of the "Zeitschrift für Hypnotismus, Suggestionstherapie, Suggestionslehre und verwandte psychologische Forschungen" to O. Vogt (1895), who, in a characteristic manner, changed the title to Zeitschrift für Hypnotismus, Psychotherapie sowie andere psychophysiologische und psychopathologische Forschungen. From Burghölzli, O. Vogt moved to Leipzig, where he gave his first conference (5. VII. 95), "Zur Kenntnis des Wesens und der psychologischen Bedeutung des Hypnotismus," before the *Biologische Gesellschaft zu Leipzig* (Z. f. Hypnotismus, 1894/95, III, 277-340). This first paper carries the hallmark of O. Vogt's sober and critical psychophysiologically and neuroanatomically oriented approach; the conciseness and astuteness of observation did not leave any room for contemporary speculative, philosophically or psychoanalytically colored views. He continued to work in Leipzig (1895) and assumed the responsibilities as clinical director of the psychiatric hospital in Alexander-bad (Fichtelgebirge) in 1896. It was here that O. Vogt met his later assist-ant, collaborator and friend, Korbinian Brodmann, for the first time. Noticing Brodmann's talents for critical research, he motivated him to give up his original plan to establish himself as a general practitioner and to move into the field of neuro-psychiatric brain research instead. Both spent their vacation together on the coast of northern Germany, in *Husum*, O. Vogt's hometown. *K. Brodmann* followed O. *Vogt's* suggestion and specialized in psychology (*Berlin* 1896), pathological anatomy (*Leipzig*), and neuro-psychiatry (*Jena, Frankfurt*) until he rejoined O. Vogt in 1901 (-1910) as assistant at the Neuro-Biological Institute in *Berlin*.

Meanwhile, as O. Vogt continued to investigate the psychophysiologic changes of different states of conscious control (*e.g.*, sleep, heterohypnotic and autohypnotic states, effects of different categories of suggestions) he also went to *Paris*, 1897/98, to broaden his experience in the field of neuro-psychiatry and neuro-anatomy. Here he met *Cécile Mugnier*, who studied psychology and medicine. After O. *Vogt's* return to *Berlin*, where he founded his famous Neuro-Biological Institute (1898), they married in 1899.

A long series of psychophysiologically and neuro-anatomically oriented publications by O. Vogt, *Cécile and O. Vogt*, and his collaborators (*e.g.*, *Th. van Straaten, Dr. Isenberg, Dr. Marcinowski, K. Brodmann*) during the period 1895-1904 clearly conveys that O. *Vogt's* experimental and therapeutic use of hypnosis, hypnoanalysis, hypnotic sleep, and various forms of hetero- and autosuggestions were largely conceived as means to gain information about his and *Cécile Vogt's* common field of interest: the "*Leib-Seele-Problem*." In their search for a better understanding of so-mato-psychic interrelations, O. Vogt observed, described phenomena, elaborated hypotheses, developed therapeutic techniques (*e.g.*, "frac-tionirte Methode," "autohypnotic rest periods," experimental establish-ment and subsequent dissolution of neurotic reactivity) which were remarkable advances in a field which much later was called "Psycho-somatic Medicine." O. *Vogt's* work and relevant publications of his disciples and collaborators contain many elements which stimulated J. H. *Schultz* in the development of Autogenic Training. For example, we see the relationship between *O. Vogt's* curative "prophylactic rest auto-hypnosis" and autogenic standard training, between *O. Vogt's* research on the structure, nature and psychophysiologic effects of "Zielvorstellungen," and the thematic structure of autogenic standard formulas, organ-specific formulas and intentional formulas. Likewise it is of interest to note that *O. Vogt* and *K. Brodmann* and other collaborators described and tried to understand brain-directed phenomena which in the field of autogenic therapy are known to occur as autogenic discharges during standard exercises, meditative training or during autogenic neutralization. For example, as recently as 1950, Cécile and O. Vogt described the relieving effect of massive motor discharges in an emotional artist which started during the induction phase of (light) neutral (rest) hypnosis (Nervenarzt, 1950, 21, 8, 338).

Considering the contemporary technical limitations in the area of psychophysiological and neurophysiological research at the turn of the century, it may be considered a logic consequence that *O. Vogt* in his pursuit of the "Leib-Seele-Problem" devoted progressively more time to the development of sophisticated techniques which permitted systematic studies of cortical and subcortical brain structures. It may be assumed that *Cécile Vogt's* personal interest (*e.g., Etude sur la myélisation des hémisphères cerebraux.* G. Steinheil, Paris 1900; La myeloarchitecture du thalamus du cercopithèque. *J. Psychol. u. Neurol.,* 1909, 12, supplément) and *K. Brodmann's* initiative actively supported developments in this direction. Exteriorly, the future emphasis on neuro-anatomic and histologic brain research is reflected by a change of title of the *Zeitschrift für Hypnotismus, Psychotherapie sowie andere psychophysiologische und psychopathologische Forschungen* (Vol. 10, 1902) to *Journal für Psychologie und Neurologie* (Vol. I, 1902-1903), for which *K. Brodmann* assumed editorial responsibilities until his death in 1918. This journal, which continued until 1942 (Vol. 51, H. 1 and 2), reflects reliably the enormous and outstanding brain research by *Oskar Vogt, Cécile Vogt, K. Brodmann* and others.

While limitations of space do not permit a more detailed survey of even the most important contributions (*e.g.,* the importance of thalamus studies as recoginzed in 1905, see *Thalamustudien I-III,* 1940/1941), only a few remarks which are of general interest can be made in this context.

It is generally unknown, that the initial, however decisive, studies which led to the distinction of cortical areas (associated with *K. Brodmann's* name) were carried out by *Oskar Vogt.* It was *Oskar Vogt* who elaborated the basic material and who guided *K. Brodmann's* research in this area. Of particular importance for more recent developments in the area of reticular system functions and relevant interrelations with thalamo-cortical and thalamo-striatum connections are *C.* and *O. Vogt's* discovery (1941) of the existence of special projection systems between the nucleus centralis of the thalamus and the striatum *(i.e., putamen, caudatum).*

Since the beginning (1898) of the Neuro-Biological Institute in Berlin, *Oskar Vogt* had hoped that his work would be appreciated and that funds permitting a more active engagement in coordinated multidimensional psychophysiologically, neuro-physiologically, neuro-anatomically and phylogenetically oriented brain research would come to his help. A publication, *"Ueber die Errichtung neurologischer Centralstationen"* (Z. f. Hypnotismus, 1902, 10, 170-177), in which he proposes a coordinated teamwork of neurologists, anatomists, pathologists, psychologists, physiologists, clinicians, psychotherapists and a particularly close collaboration between psychological and physiologically oriented neuro-anatomical research departments, reflects his wishes. However, his suggestions met deaf ears.

It took about thirty years of frustrating efforts until finally, in 1930, with the decisive help of the Rockefeller Foundation and concerted contributions from the German Government, the city of Berlin and the "Notgemeinschaft" permitted Oskar Vogt to pursue his work under desirable conditions. The Brain-Research Institute in Berlin-Buch (Kaiser-Wilhelm-Institut für Hirnforschung) included a 60 bed research clincic, a staff of 30 scientists and about 70 technicians.

However, after seven years of unusually productive work in the field of somato-psychic research, political intrigues instigated by Nazi (SS) officials (Vahlen, Menzel) led to the dissolution of Vogt's research organization (1937).

Undaunted, together with only a few collaborators, they continued their life work in a small private institute. Under these restricting circumstances, the group decided to limit their research to brain anatomy.

The beginning of World War II finds Cécile and Oskar Vogt at work in the "Institut der Deutschen Hirnforschungsgesellschaft" (later changed to "Institut für Hirnforschung und allgemeine Biologie") in southern Germany (Neustadt/Schwarzwald). Under Oskar Vogt's direction, the relatively small research organization carried on with its work and gradually expanded again during the post-war period. In 1954, Cécile and Oskar Vogt started the new *Journal für Hirnforschung,* which may be regarded as a continuation of the *Journal für Psychologie und Neurologie* (stopped 1942). As Cécile and Oskar Vogt's publications in the *Journal für Hirnforschung* continued with amazing productivity, it was hard for many to believe that Oskar Vogt's long, brilliant and astonishing research carreer had come to an end on July 31, 1959.

warmth training: practice of the **second standard exercise (SE II).**

Author Index

Additional references will be found in the Glossary, directly preceding.

206

Subject Index

G.: *see* Glossary of terms.

Abdominal cramps, 26, 146
Abdominal distension, 26
pain, contraindications, 23, 27
Abortion, autogenic discharges, 12, 17
Accidents, autogenic discharges, 3, 8, 17,
53, 55, 59, 60, 67, 88, 89, 128, 130
bicycle, 128
headaches, 86, 87, 88
history of, autogenic discharges, 36, 61,
105, 109, 110, 111, 128, 146
witnessing of, 36
Achalasia, 4, 13
Achilles tendon reflex, 111
Achlorhydria, 15
Acne, AT, 158
Acrocyanosis, 79
Acroparesthesia, 15
Active concentration, 121
Acute gastritis, AT, 14
Addiction, codeine, 131ff
Adnexitis, chronic, 145
Adolescents, tuberculosis, 102
Adrenal cortical activity, 107, 155
Adrenaline, 38
Adolescents, AT, 1
ophthalmologic disorders, 160ff
Aerophagia, 13
Aerosols, asthma, AT, 93, 94
Age factor, application, AT, 1, 70, 98,
102
Aggression, 69, 103, 125, 130, 143
cardiovascular disorders, 36, 53
Aggressive dynamics, 34
Alcohol, 43
Alcoholics, gastritis, 15
Alcoholism, 108, 112, 141
dyspepsia, 16
Alkalis, ingestion of, 121
Alkalotic tetany, 121
Allergic reactions, 45, 86, 142, 157
Ambisexual dynamics, 143
Amblyopia, 160
American Heart Association, 53
Amenorrhea, 32
secondary, 145
Amputation, pain, 78, 79, 166
Analgesics, 128, 152, 153
Anemia, 41, 53
Anesthesia, AA, 168
inadequate, 12, 17, 166ff, 171, 172
local, AT, 171
Angina pectoris, 51ff, 67ff
Ankylosing spondylitis, 124, 126, 127

Ankylosis, shoulder joints, 126
Anococcygeal region, pain, 147
Anorexia, 4, 17, 103, 136
nervosa, 32
Antidepressive medication, AT, 118
Antihistamine drugs, 142
Antihypertensive drugs, 70, 75
Anxiety, 43, 49, 84, 100, 101, 111, 131,
136
cardiovascular disorders, 36, 37
during AT, 2, 12, 38, 41, 54, 55, 74,
75, 86, 87
ecclesiogenic, 36, 60, 61, 63
reaction, 6, 7, 10, 17, 20, 28, 29, 42,
45, 53, 63, 65, 75, 86, 128, 129,
139, 141, 146, 167, 171
tachycardia, 41
Aortic incompetence, 69
stenosis, 69
Appendectomy, 199
autogenic discharges, 8, 9
Application AT, age factor, 1
Arrhythmia, 57, 131, 136
AT, 46, 47, 53, 58
supraventricular, 44
Arteriosclerosis, 48, 69, 74, 121
Arteriosclerotic heart disease, 43, 118
Arthralgia, infections, 124
Arthritis, infectional, 124
related disorders, 124ff
Arthropathy, hemophilia, 131
neurogenic, 124
Articular cartilage, degeneration of, 126
Asphyxia of the newborn, 155
Asthenopia, 163
Asthma, *see* Bronchial asthma
Atheroma of aorta, 69
Atheromatosis, 53
Atherosclerosis obliterans, 119
Atonic constipation, 27ff
Atrial fibrillation, 44
rhythm, disorders, heart block, 49
Atrioventricular block, AT, 49
Atrophic arthritis, 124
gastritis, 14
Auricular extrasystoles, 40
fibrillation, 44
tachycardia, 67ff
Autogenic abreaction, 2, 18, 34, 39, 60,
61, 75, 85, 86, 88, 110, 130, 135,
143, 162, 167ff, 171ff, G.
spontaneous, 54, 57, 94

210